CHINA IN THE 21ST CENTURY

CHINESE INVESTMENTS IN THE U.S. ECONOMY

SELECT ANALYSES

CHINA IN THE 21ST CENTURY

Additional books in this series can be found on Nova's website under the Series tab.

Additional E-books in this series can be found on Nova's website under the E-book tab.

AMERICA IN THE 21ST CENTURY: POLITICAL AND ECONOMIC ISSUES

Additional books in this series can be found on Nova's website under the Series tab.

Additional E-books in this series can be found on Nova's website under the E-book tab.

CHINA IN THE 21ST CENTURY

CHINESE INVESTMENTS IN THE U.S. ECONOMY

SELECT ANALYSES

ZACKARY A. MICHAUD
EDITOR

New York

For permission to use material from this book please contact us:
Telephone 631-231-7269; Fax 631-231-8175
Web Site: http://www.novapublishers.com

Library of Congress Cataloging-in-Publication Data

ISBN: 978-1-62618-833-4

Published by Nova Science Publishers, Inc. † New York

CONTENTS

PREFACE

Once hardly noticeable, Chinese investments in U.S. companies are now rising sharply. Cumulative Chinese investments in U.S. companies remain modest compared to those of other major countries. However, a combination of "push and pull" factors are moving China's annual investment levels closer to levels consistent with China's current economic stature. The Chinese government has made a conscious decision to diversify its foreign currency assets into hard assets. This had led to the creation of sovereign wealth funds that make portfolio investments in U.S. equities, private firms, and real estate. The Chinese government has also altered is policy toward foreign direct investment (FDI). Whereas it previously encouraged investments almost exclusively toward energy and resource acquisition in developing countries, it now also encourages investments in advanced countries. The government's goals for these investments include securing energy and mineral resources and acquiring advanced technologies in industries where China wishes to leapfrog existing competitors. This book provides an overview of select analyses on Chinese investments in the U.S. economy, with a focus on the economic benefits and policy challenges.

Chapter 1 – Once hardly noticeable, Chinese investments in U.S. companies are now rising sharply. Cumulative Chinese investments in U.S. companies remain modest compared to those of other major countries. However, a combination of "push and pull" factors are moving China's annual investment levels closer to levels consistent with China's current economic stature.

First, the Chinese government has made a conscious decision to diversify its foreign currency assets into hard assets. This has led to the creation of sovereign wealth funds that make portfolio investments in U.S. equities, private firms, and real estate.

Second, the Chinese government has altered its policy guidance toward foreign direct investment (FDI). Whereas it previously encouraged investments almost exclusively toward energy and resource acquisition in developing countries, it now also encourages investments in advanced countries. The government's goals for these investments include securing energy and mineral resources and acquiring advanced technologies in industries where China wishes to leapfrog existing competitors.

Third, U.S. state governments and, to a lesser extent, the federal government are vigorously trying to attract Chinese greenfield investments in the hope of creating jobs and jump-starting local economies.

Fourth, Chinese investments are being drawn to the United States by the availability of financially weak firms, some of which possess potentially useful technologies for China.

Fifth, some firms that are already competitive with U.S. producers are investing to enhance their U.S. market shares or in response to trade remedies proceedings against unfair trade practices, such as Chinese subsidies.

Chapter 2 - Given its relatively low savings rate, the U.S. economy depends heavily on foreign capital inflows from countries with high savings rates (such as China) to meet its domestic investment needs and to fund the federal budget deficit. The willingness of foreigners to invest in the U.S. economy and purchase U.S. public debt has helped keep U.S. real interest rates low. However, many economists contend that U.S. dependency on foreign savings exposes the U.S. economy to certain risks, and some argue that such dependency was a contributing factor to the U.S. housing bubble and subsequent global financial crisis that began in 2008.

China's policy of intervening in currency markets to limit the appreciation of its currency against the dollar (and other currencies) has made it the world's largest and fastest growing holder of foreign exchange reserves, especially U.S. dollars. China has invested a large share of these reserves in U.S. private and public securities, which include long-term (LT) Treasury debt, LT U.S. agency debt, LT U.S. corporate debt, LT U.S. equities, and short-term debt. As of June 2011, China was the largest holder of U.S. securities, which totaled $1.73 trillion. U.S. Treasury securities constitute the largest category of China's holdings of U.S. securities—these totaled $1.16 trillion as of September 2012, but were down from their peak of $1.31 trillion in July 2011.

China's large holdings of U.S. securities have raised a number of concerns in both China and the United States. For example, in 2009, Chinese Premier Wen Jiabao stated that he was "a little worried" about the "safety" of China's holdings of U.S. debt. The sharp debate in Congress over raising the public debt ceiling in the summer of 2011 and the subsequent downgrade of the U.S. long-term sovereign credit from AAA to AA + by Standard and Poor's in August 2011 appears to have intensified Chinese concerns. In addition, Chinese officials have criticized U.S. fiscal monetary policies, such as quantitative easing by the U.S. Federal Reserve, arguing that they could lead to higher U.S. inflation and/or a significant weakening of the dollar, which could reduce the value of China's U.S. debt holdings in the future. Some Chinese analysts have urged the government to diversify its reserves away from U.S. dollar assets, while others have called for more rapid appreciation of China's currency, which could lessen the need to hold U.S. assets.

Many U.S. policymakers have expressed concern over the size of China's holdings of U.S. government debt. For example, some contend that China might decide to sell a large share of its U.S. securities holdings, which could induce other foreign investors to sell off their U.S. holdings as well, which in turn could destabilize the U.S. economy. Others argue that China could use its large holdings of U.S. debt as a bargaining chip in its dealing with the United States on economic and non-economic issues. In the 112th Congress, H.R. 2166 and S. 1028 would seek to increase the transparency of foreign ownership of U.S. debt instruments, especially China's, in order to assess if such holdings posed potential risks for the United States. The conference report accompanying the National Defense Authorization Act of FY2012 (H.R. 1540, P.L. 112-81) included a provision requiring the Secretary of Defense to conduct a national security risk assessment of U.S. federal debt held by China. Many analysts argue that China's holdings of U.S. debt give it little leverage over the United States because as long as China continues to hold down the value of its currency to the U.S. dollar, it will have few options other than to keep investing in U.S. dollar assets. A Chinese attempt to sell a large portion of its dollar holdings could reduce the value of its remaining dollar holdings, and any subsequent negative shocks to the U.S. (and global) economy could dampen U.S. demand for Chinese exports. They contend that the main issue for U.S. policymakers is not China's large holdings of U.S. securities per se, but rather the high U.S. reliance on foreign capital in general, and whether such borrowing is sustainable.

In: Chinese Investments in the U.S. Economy ISBN: 978-1-62618-833-4
Editor: Zackary A. Michaud

Chapter 1

AN ANALYSIS OF CHINESE INVESTMENTS IN THE U.S. ECONOMY*

Andrew Szamosszegi

DISCLAIMER

This research report was prepared at the request of the Commission to support its deliberations. Posting of the Report to the Commission's website is intended to promote greater public understanding of the issues addressed by the Commission in its ongoing assessment of U.S.-China economic relations and their implications for U.S. security, as mandated by Public Law 106-398 and Public Law 108-7. However, it does not necessarily imply an endorsement by the Commission or any individual Commissioner of the views or conclusions expressed in this commissioned research report.

EXECUTIVE SUMMARY

Once hardly noticeable, Chinese investments in U.S. companies are now rising sharply. Cumulative Chinese investments in U.S. companies remain modest compared to those of other major countries. However, a combination

* This is an edited, reformatted and augmented version of U.S.-China Economic and Security Review Commission, dated October 2012.

of "push and pull" factors are moving China's annual investment levels closer to levels consistent with China's current economic stature.

First, the Chinese government has made a conscious decision to diversify its foreign currency assets into hard assets. This has led to the creation of sovereign wealth funds that make portfolio investments in U.S. equities, private firms, and real estate.

Second, the Chinese government has altered its policy guidance toward foreign direct investment (FDI). Whereas it previously encouraged investments almost exclusively toward energy and resource acquisition in developing countries, it now also encourages investments in advanced countries. The government's goals for these investments include securing energy and mineral resources and acquiring advanced technologies in industries where China wishes to leapfrog existing competitors.

Third, U.S. state governments and, to a lesser extent, the federal government are vigorously trying to attract Chinese greenfield investments in the hope of creating jobs and jump-starting local economies.

Fourth, Chinese investments are being drawn to the United States by the availability of financially weak firms, some of which possess potentially useful technologies for China.

Fifth, some firms that are already competitive with U.S. producers are investing to enhance their U.S. market shares or in response to trade remedies proceedings against unfair trade practices, such as Chinese subsidies.

Economic Benefits

On an aggregate basis, the economic benefits of Chinese investments in the United States have been modest. The precise benefit is difficult to measure due to the convoluted ownership structures of many Chinese investments and the time lags in official U.S. data. Still, based on a combination of official and private data, it is reasonable to conclude that jobs in Chinese-owned companies in the United States increased by 10,000 to 20,000 workers during the past five years.

While hardly significant relative to overall U.S. employment and even to jobs in other countries' U.S. affiliates, any job creation is welcome given continued slackness in the U.S. labor market.

Chinese FDI in U.S. companies has helped stabilize some financially troubled firms. Portfolio investments by sovereign wealth funds also have helped the economy by solidifying the financial system and providing liquidity to certain property markets.

Chinese investments have occurred in all U.S. regions and in many sectors. According to one private data source, they have been especially prominent since 2007 in the Southwest, Great Lakes, Southeast, and Far West regions, and in the fossil fuels and chemicals, industrial machinery, and information technology industries. According to another private source, as well as government data, the financial sector is also a major recipient of Chinese FDI.

Policy Challenges

These welcome, though still modest, economic benefits are counterbalanced by policy challenges tied to Chinese FDI. First, U.S. affiliates of Chinese companies are not pure market actors and may be driven by state goals, not market forces. China's outward investments are dominated by state-owned and state-controlled enterprises (SOEs). These entities are potentially disruptive because they frequently respond to policies of the Chinese government, which is the ultimate beneficial owner of U.S affiliates of China's SOEs. Likewise, the government behaves like an owner, providing overall direction to SOE investments, including encouragement on where to invest, in what industries, and to what ends.

Second, SOEs may have unfair advantages relative to private firms when competing to purchase U.S. assets. SOEs benefit from substantial subsidies in China and their investments in developing countries also receive ample financial support from the national and sub-national governments, state-owned financial institutions and local governments. Government pronouncements out of China suggest that investments in the United States and other advanced countries will also receive ample financial support. This raises the possibility that Chinese largesse could determine market outcomes for purchases of U.S. businesses.

Third, an increased SOE presence may be harmful to the U.S. economy. In China, SOEs are a major force but as a group they are less efficient and profitable than private firms. To the extent that SOEs purchase U.S. companies on the basis of artificial advantages and operate inefficiently, they may not be beneficial to long-term U.S. economic performance.

Fourth, Chinese investments will create tensions related to economic security and national security if they behave in accordance with China's industrial policy as articulated in the 12th Five Year Plan, government pronouncements, and official investment guidance. China's current policy guidance directs firms to obtain leapfrog technologies to create national champions in key emerging industries, while investment guidance encourages technology acquisition, energy security, and export facilitation. Based on this juxtaposition, some will conclude that Chinese FDI in the United States is a potential Trojan horse. Indeed, this study describes three investments in new energy products after which production utilizing the desired technology was shifted to China.

Other Findings

U.S. data collection efforts related to FDI are substantial. However, they likely undercount Chinese FDI due to the complicated ownership structures of many Chinese investments. Moreover, although Chinese-owned companies report their data to the U.S. government, many data points are not publically disclosed due to standard U.S. reporting procedures that protect the identities of individual firms. This issue will resolve itself in the coming years if Chinese FDI grows as expected because limits on disclosure will no longer apply.

The United States is relatively open toward FDI, though there are some sectoral restrictions and a national security review undertaken by the Committee on Foreign Investment in the United States (CFIUS). There are a host of laws that subject foreign investors to rules on antitrust, foreign corrupt practices, and trade in arms and sensitive technology products. However, there is no procedure that explicitly considers issues related to economic security, one of the major concerns about Chinese FDI.

Portfolio investments in equities fall under the purview of the Securities and Exchange Commission (SEC). SEC disclosure requirements and practical considerations make it highly unlikely that Chinese SOEs could successfully collude to accumulate significant equity positions in important U.S. firms.

Reverse mergers offer a back door into U.S. capital markets but are not an effective way to acquire important U.S. assets. Indeed, the target of a reverse merger is typically a shell company devoid of meaningful assets. This technique is typically used by private firms that have difficulty accessing capital in China or by provincial SOEs trying to support restructuring efforts in China. There is no indication that any major SOE has used or plans to use this technique to enter the U.S. capital market.

The Chinese legal and regulatory framework for outward FDI requires approvals by three agencies at sub-national and/or national levels. For SOEs, the primary gatekeeper is the State-owned Assets Supervision and Administration Commission (SASAC), though for some investments approval from the State Council is required. The process is widely considered to be cumbersome and is being reformed to facilitate outward FDI.

The level of Chinese FDI in the United States is relatively low compared to investments from other major economies. This may reflect the impact of certain high profile investments which failed to navigate the CFIUS process. However, when compared to other OECD countries, the United States has fared relatively well. Through 2010, it had attracted more Chinese FDI than all OECD countries except Australia and Canada, which have benefitted from China's focus on securing access to energy and raw materials.

There is no unified U.S. government position toward FDI from China. State and local officials seeking to increase economic activity work hard to attract FDI from China, with support at the federal level from SelectUSA, a government-wide initiative to attract investment from foreign and domestic sources. At the same time, other federal officials are extremely concerned about the potential impact of Chinese FDI on national security and economic security. This division of labor makes sense, as the investments being sought tend to be greenfield investments that support jobs, while the investments being analyzed tend to be merger and acquisition transactions aimed at technology and energy.

I. Introduction

As an outward investor, China has come a long way since 1978, the year marking the start of China's historic economic reforms. Foreign direct investment (FDI) by Chinese firms, at least the values presented in official statistics, was zero that year, and every other year back to 1949, when the People's Republic of China was founded. Statistics indicate that in 1984, only a single OECD country, Germany, recorded any FDI from China.[1] Three decades later, outward direct investment (ODI) from China is booming. Chinese ODI during 2008-2010 exceeded its ODI during the previous quarter century by more than 70 percent. According to UN statistics, China was the largest developing country investor and the fifth largest investor in the world in 2010.[2]

Initially concentrated in resource rich and mostly developing countries, China's investments have begun increasing in advanced countries, such as the United States. For years, inward FDI from China was a rounding error in the official U.S. statistics. Through 2010, the latest available statistics at the time this report was written, the Chinese footprint remained relatively modest. But contemporaneous reporting from non-government sources indicates the Chinese investments have been increasing rapidly. Based on a number of economic and policy considerations, FDI from China to the United States is expected to grow in the coming years.

Although foreign investment is considered, on balance, to be economically beneficial for both the recipient and the investing economies, there are certain aspects about inward FDI from China that concern many individuals in U.S. business and policy circles. These concerns, to some degree, are reminiscent of the U.S. reaction to FDI from Japan, which expanded dramatically during the 1980s in concert with that country's rising economic clout. Although the parallel with Japan is instructive, it also misses two distinguishing features about the increase in FDI from China. First, by value FDI from China is dominated by state-owned enterprises that actively follow the industrial policies of the Chinese government. Second, whereas Japan and the United States were largely on the same page with regard to geopolitics, China and the United States frequently are not.

Together, these two factors raise U.S. concerns regarding FDI from China to a different level.

This study, prepared for the United States-China Economic and Security Review Commission (the China Commission), seeks to answer a number of questions about Chinese investments in the United States. The China Commission's request for proposals included 14 topics, each of which are addressed sequentially by this report. These questions can be broadly grouped as follows:

1. FDI by the numbers: What are the sectoral and regional patterns of FDI from China? Is FDI from China likely to increase? What can be expected in the future?
2. FDI from the state sector: How much investment can be attributed to SOEs, state — owned structured investment vehicles, and private firms? What role do state-controlled financial services entities play?
3. U.S. regulations and oversight: How does the United States regulate FDI from China? What kinds of data does the U.S. government

collect? Do U.S. disclosure requirements provide sufficient protection for key U.S. assets and U.S. investors?

4. Investment motives: Why do Chinese enterprises invest in the United States? Does Beijing try to influence investment decisions? To what extent do national and state-level governments seek to attract Chinese investments?
5. Economic benefits of FDI: Has Chinese FDI been beneficial? How do the benefits compare to FDI from other countries?

The sources consulted for this study include recent books and articles by Chinese and western authors that describe and analyze China's outward investment and its causes; official U.S., Chinese, and third country data on FDI and other balance of payments aggregates; documents related to China published by multilateral organizations such as the World Bank, the United Nations Conference on Trade and Development (UNCTAD), and the Organization for Economic Cooperation and Development (OECD); and various laws, regulations, and official presentations on Chinese investments. Most of the official Chinese FDI data were drawn from the *Statistical Bulletin of China's Outward Direct Investment*, published by China's Ministry of Commerce, while U.S. data were sourced from the Bureau of Economic Analysis (BEA) of the U.S. Department of Commerce. OECD data and other macroeconomic aggregates were obtained from Haver Analytics. Unofficial data on China's FDI activities were an important source for this study. These were obtained from *The China Global Investment Tracker*, maintained by Derek Scissors of The Heritage Foundation, and the *China Investment Monitor*, maintained by Daniel H. Rosen and Thilo Hannemann of the Rhodium Group. This study also benefitted from prior and recent informal communication with individuals having specialized knowledge in certain areas covered in this report.

The predictions made in this study are based on past economic and policy trends. As anyone who follows China knows, the pace and direction of ongoing economic reforms in that country are subject to change. The underlying assumption of this report is that China will remain a "multi-ownership-oriented basic market economic system, with the public ownership in the dominance."[3] However, there are preliminary indications that China's next leadership may be inclined to dilute state control over SOEs in particular and the Chinese economy overall. If the Chinese government does significantly loosen its grips on SOEs, many of the concerns expressed in this report will become less relevant.

II. Overview of China's Investment Capabilities and Investment Patterns

This section identifies patterns in China's outward investments over the past ten years and assesses the existing resources and capabilities of China's investors to invest in foreign markets.

A. China's Capacity to Invest Overseas

China currently has significant capacity to invest abroad. Overseas investments, whether in the form of direct investments or portfolio investments, have both macroeconomic and microeconomic causes.[4] Current account surpluses are an important macroeconomic enabler of outward FDI.[5] According to the well known macroeconomic identity linking savings, investment and trade balances, countries with current account surpluses, by definition, have excess savings.[6] This excess saving provides the basis for foreign direct and/or portfolio investments.[7] China has run large current account surpluses driven by large surpluses in merchandise trade over the past fifteen years. These surpluses, shown in the table below, indicate that China has sufficient capacity to invest in overseas markets.

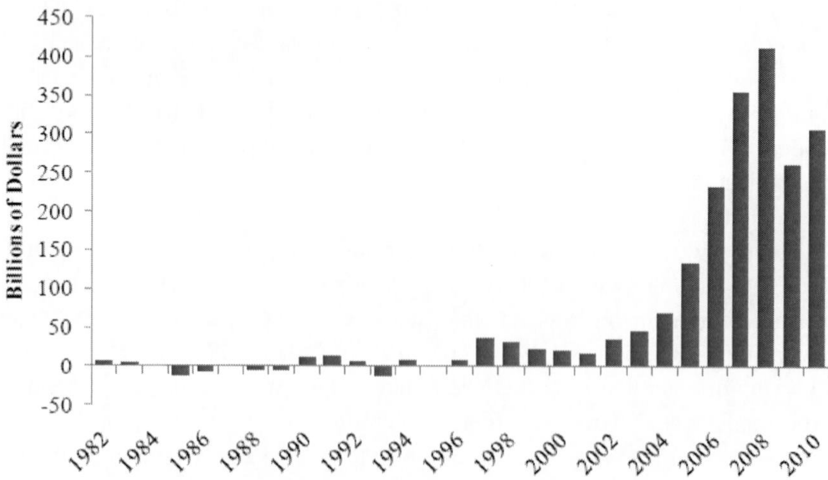

Source: China's National Bureau of Statistics, via Haver Analytics.

Figure 1. China's Current Account Balances, 1982-2010.

To achieve balance in China's international accounts, this current account surplus must be invested outside China. Thus a country with a current account surplus typically runs a deficit in the capital account.[8] The two accounts offset each other and their sum is equivalent to zero.[9] In China's case, investment inflows (credits) exceed investment outflows (debits) and it runs a capital account surplus, shown in Figure 2. This means that China has even more to invest than implied by its current account surplus alone.[10] Hence, from a macroeconomic perspective, China in recent years has generated *hundreds of billions of dollars* that it could have deployed as direct investment in overseas markets.

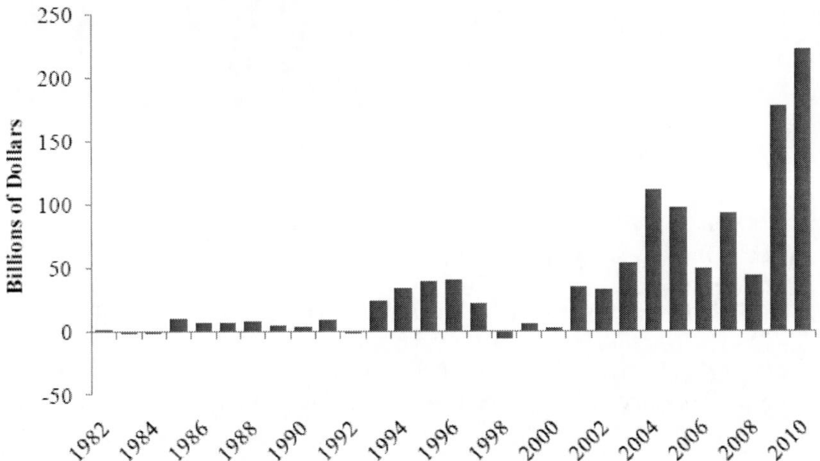

Source: China's State Administration of Foreign Exchange, via Haver Analytics.

Figure 2. China's Capital Account Balances, 1982-2010.

But the macro perspective does not tell the whole story. Direct investment is undertaken by companies, and companies generally have a difficult time making large investments unless they are profitable. Thus, profitable companies, or at least companies considered healthy enough to borrow money, are necessary for foreign direct investment to occur.

By this measure, China also has generated sufficient capacity to engage in overseas investments. Figure 3 below illustrates profits at state-controlled and private industrial enterprises through 2010. During the period, profits expanded from $7 billion to $441 billion. By 2007, industrial profits in all enterprises had reached $562 billion. Profits are growing in the financial sector as well. From 2007 to 2010, after-tax profits in the banking sector expanded from $59 billion to $133 billion.

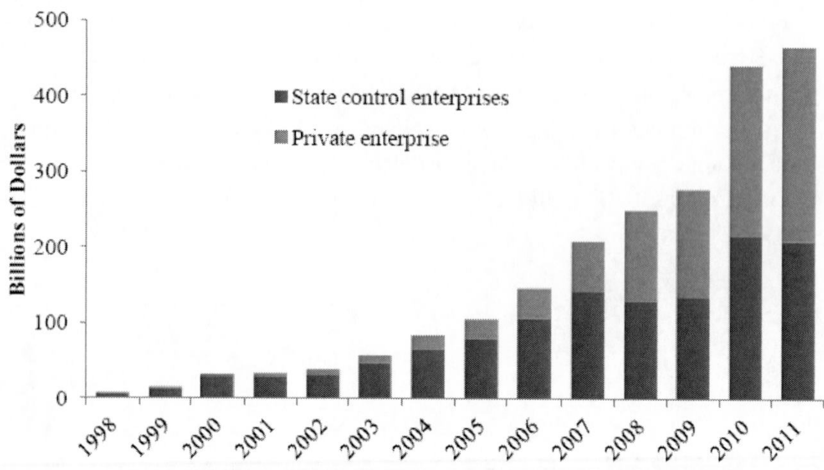

* Estimated based on data through November 2010.

Source: China's National Bureau of Statistics, via Haver Analytics; and Federal Reserve Bank of St. Louis.

Figure 3. Total Profits at State-Controlled and Private Enterprises, 1998-2010.

Moreover, Chinese financial authorities also have massive existing holdings of Treasury bills and other official assets that have been accumulated as a result of China's exchange rate policy. These reserves provide backstop capacity to invest via FDI and portfolio equity investments even if China's current account surplus recedes.

In short, China's international accounts and enterprise profitability indicate that the country has a large and growing capacity to invest in foreign markets. Put in this light, the large increases in China's outward FDI, shown in Figure 4, make perfect sense.

B. Patterns in China's FDI

There are several sources of data on Chinese outward FDI. China's Ministry of Commerce annually publishes the *Statistical Bulletin of China's Outward Direct Investment*, which contains country and industry breakdowns. The People's Bank of China and State Administration of Foreign Exchange publish highly aggregated balance of payments and investment position data. The official Chinese data are believed to be deficient for a number of reasons.[11]

The United Nations Conference on Trade and Development annually publishes the World Investment Report, but the data for China are based on official Chinese statistics. There are several other entities that track foreign investments or subsets of foreign investments, such as mergers and acquisitions (M&A), and provide information on individual transactions for a fee.

The Heritage Foundation compiles data on China's worldwide outward FDI by country, industry, investor, and foreign partner and makes the raw data available on its web site.[12]

The Rhodium Group provides summaries of Chinese FDI in the United States segmented by industry, type of investment (greenfield versus acquisition), ownership (private or state-owned), and the state in which the investment occurred.[13] These data are also available on its web site, but not in a database format.

The U.S. Bureau of Economic Analysis, as discussed in greater detail below, presents a variety of inward FDI data, though its offerings do not identify the foreign investors or provide state-specific information.[14]

China's outward FDI flows are shown in Figure 4 below. Initial outward investments during the 1980s were minor.[15] From 1982 to 1990, China's outward FDI (ODI) amounted to only $4.5 billion, approximately $500 million per year.

From 1991 to 2004, the level of China's ODI increased, with annual outflows averaging $2.9 billion per year. Since then, China's ODI has exploded. China's cumulative ODI from 2005 to 2007 totaled $55.9 billion, which exceeded China's ODI from the prior 23 years ($45.5 billion) by more than $10 billion.

The 23-year total was then surpassed annually from 2008 to 2010. In 2010, FDI outflows from China even surpassed those of Japan, making China the fifth largest source of FDI in the world.[16] Three of China's 50 SOEs engaged in FDI are among the world's largest state-owned transnational corporations.[17]

Despite the large increase in ODI from China in recent years, outward investments are likely to continue rising. China's ODI as a percentage of GDP in 2010 remained well below the worldwide average and the average for developing countries.

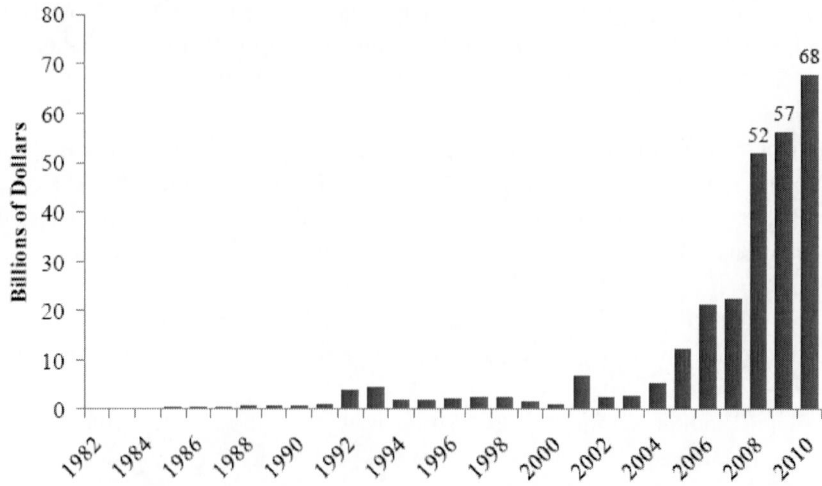

Source: UNCTADSTAT http://unctadstat.unctad.org/TableViewer/tableView.aspx.

Figure 4. China's Foreign Direct Investments, 1982-2010.

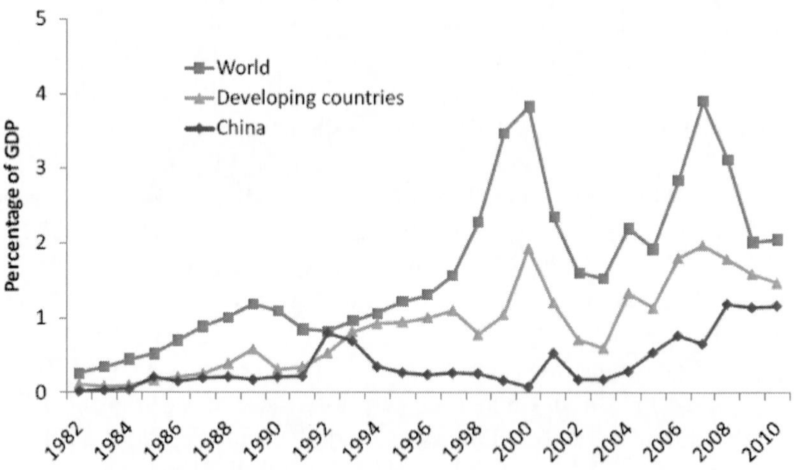

Source: UNCTADSTAT http://unctadstat.unctad.org/TableViewer/tableView.aspx.

Figure 5. ODI as a percentage of GDP for China, the World, and Developing Countries, 1982-2010.

1. Analysis of Regions

The expansion in China's ODI to the United States has drawn much attention, but China's official data indicate that the United States has been a minor destination for Chinese ODI. China's U.S.-bound ODI has increased, but it has significantly lagged China's ODI to other destinations, as shown in Figure 6 below. In 2010, ODI to countries other than the United States exceeded U.S.-bound ODI by a factor of 50.

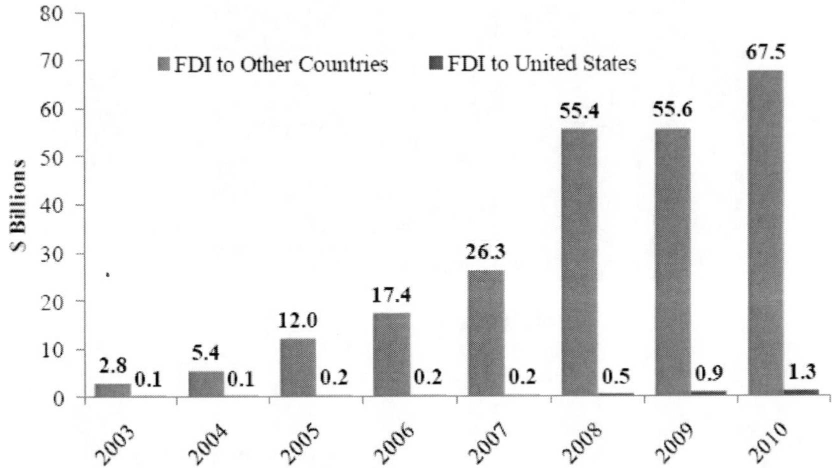

Source: Statistical Bulletin of China's Outward Foreign Direct Investment, various issues.

Figure 6. China's Outward FDI Flows to the United States and Rest of World.

The Chinese data indicate that 63 percent of China's FDI stock is in Hong Kong. The proclivity for Hong Kong exists primarily for two reasons. First, foreign-invested firms in China received favorable tax treatment until recent reforms unified the tax code.[18] Second, Hong Kong's laissez faire economy was a far superior base for conducting business than China's economy.[19] Chinese firms also have substantial investments in the Cayman Islands and the British Virgin Islands. It is reasonable to conclude that the vast majority of Chinese investments in these three relatively small economies are undertaken by Chinese firms that wish to invest in other markets, including China. Figure 7 below shows the distribution of China's ODI stock as of 2010. It indicates that three quarters of China's FDI stock resides in the three haven economies and that Chinese investors have favored non-OECD countries over OECD countries.[20] Time series data indicate that since 2004, the non-haven, non-

OECD countries have gained 5.8 percentage points in share while OECD countries have gained 3.8 percentage points, both at the expense of the haven economies.

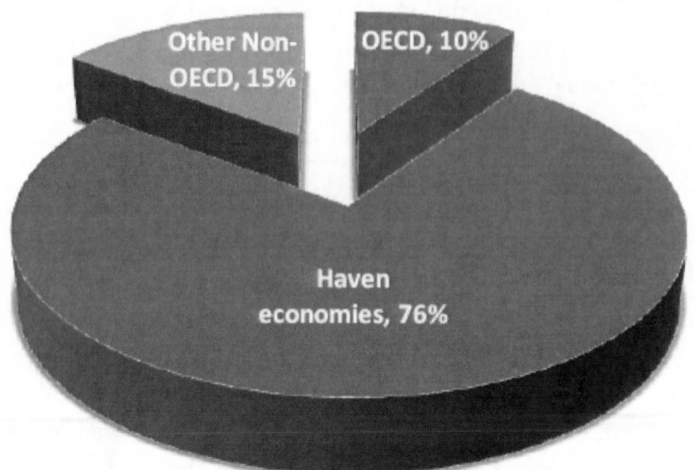

Source: 2010 Statistical Bulletin of China's Outward Foreign Direct Investment.

Figure 7. Distribution of China's ODI Stock, 2010.

According to official Chinese data shown in Table 1, Australia is the most popular destination for Chinese ODI to OECD countries followed by Luxembourg. The United States was the top OECD destination in 2004, but was ranked third by 2010, giving credence to the argument that the United States is losing ground in attracting FDI from China, a failure some attribute to the high profile failure of CNOOC's attempt to acquire Unocal and Huawei's failure to conclude its acquisition of 3-Com.[21]

However, the U.S. performance is better when viewed in a broader perspective. Australia's prominence as a target for Chinese FDI is not surprising given the initial focus of Chinese investments on securing needed resources. Luxembourg resembles a haven economy like the Cayman Islands and the Virgin Islands. Even taking into account the large increases in Chinese FDI to Australia, Luxembourg, and Canada, the United States still accounted for 15 percent of the increase in the stock of Chinese ODI in OECD countries between 2004 and 2010. Thus, when viewed in the context of other OECD countries, the United States has remained an important target for Chinese investors.

Table 1. China's ODI Stock in OECD Countries, 2004 and 2010 (Chinese statistics)

	2004	2010	Change	Share of change
		Millions of Dollars		
Total OECD	2,824	31,687	28,863	100%
Australia	495	7,868	7,373	26%
Luxembourg	0	5,787	5,787	21%
United States	665	4,874	4,209	15%
Canada	59	2,603	2,544	9%
Germany	129	1,502	1,373	5%
Sweden	6	1,479	1,473	5%
United Kingdom	108	1,358	1,250	4%
Japan	139	1,102	962	3%
Korea	562	637	75	0%
Netherlands	9	487	478	2%
Hungary	5	466	460	2%
Turkey	3	404	401	1%
Spain	128	248	120	0%
France	22	244	222	1%
Italy	21	224	203	1%
19 others	236	1,203	967	3%

Source: 2010 Statistical Bulletin of China's Outward Foreign Direct Investment.

OECD data, shown in Table 2 below, differ significantly from Chinese data. For example, according Chinese statistics, China's FDI stock in Australia was $7.8 billion in 2004, compared to OECD statistics showing $13.0 billion in FDI from China. Similarly, Chinese data show only $2.6 billion of Chinese FDI in Canada by 2010, compared to the OECD figure of $14.0 billion. The OECD partner data illustrate the Chinese preference for investing in resource rich economies.

China's FDI stock is concentrated in resource rich OECD economies of Canada and Australia, and the stock of Chinese FDI in these two economies has risen significantly since 2004.[22] Indeed, by 2010, China had become the leading foreign investor in Australia.[23]

The United States ranks third and also has experienced a significant increase in inflows compared to the other countries ranked below it. Seen in this light, the relatively low level of Chinese FDI in the United States says just as much about China's preference for investing in developing countries and resource-rich countries as it does about the attractiveness of the U.S. economy to Chinese investors.

Table 2. China's ODI Stock in OECD Countries, 2004 and 2010 (Partner statistics)[24]

	2004	2010	Change
		Millions of Dollars	
Total OECD	3,171	35,047	31,876
Canada	119	14,043	13,925
Australia	n/a	13,026	n/a
United States	435	3,150	2,715
Norway	n/a	1,865	n/a
Korea	1,100	1,078	-21
United Kingdom	230	977	747
Germany 1/	260	883	623
France 1/	221	540	320
Denmark	148	506	358
Japan	89	399	310
Poland	23	331	308
Austria	0	186	186
Mexico	n/a	167	n/a
Hungary	26	139	114
Chile	n/a	100	n/a
Others with data	521	-764	-1,285

1/ FDI stock is reported for 2009 because data for 2010 were not available.
Source: OECD, via Haver Analytics.

2. Analysis of Sectors

The resource orientation of China's ODI is demonstrated in Figure 8, which is based on the Heritage Foundation's China Global Investment Tracker (CIT). Investments, especially after 2007, have been focused on primary industries.[25]

Finance and real estate transactions have also been prominent. Investments in manufacturing industries have been modest, though the profile of manufacturing began to rise in 2010.

Chinese data yield a dramatically different conclusion, as investments in the leasing and business services sector are more prominent than those in primary industry. The reasons for this outcome are hard to discern, but probably reflect investment in the haven countries, especially given the large resource-related investments known to have been made by Chinese investors.

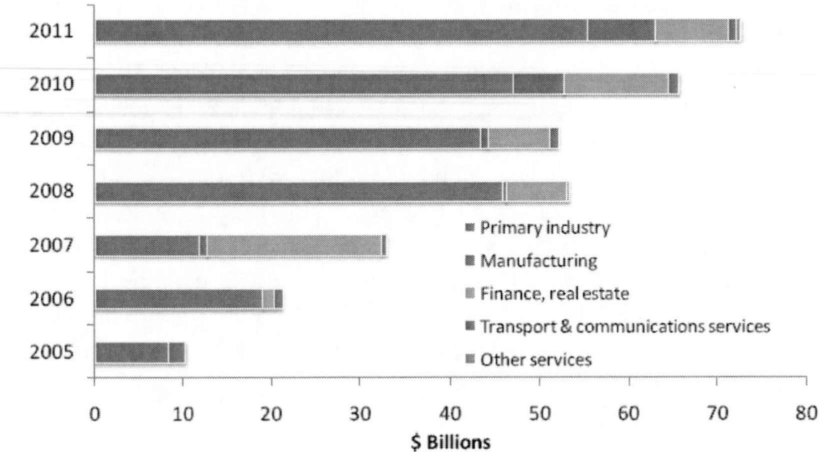

Source: The Heritage Foundation, China Global Investment Tracker 2012.

Figure 8. China's FDI Outflows by Industry (Per Heritage Database).

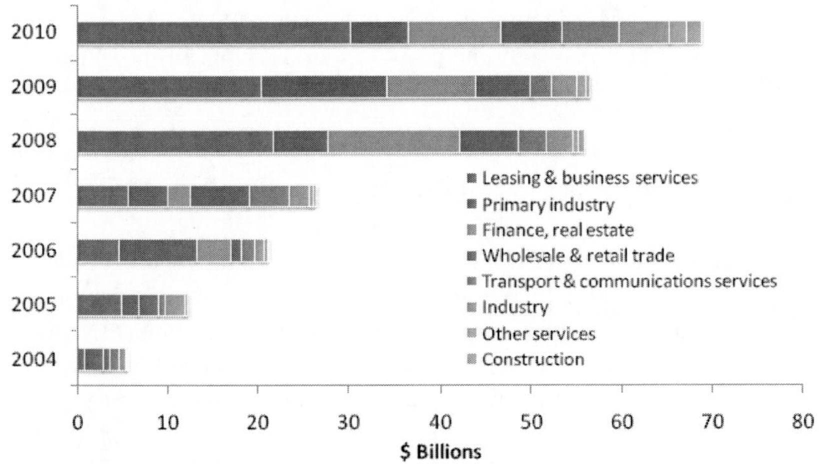

Source: 2010 Statistical Bulletin of China's Outward Foreign Direct Investment.

Figure 9. China's FDI Outflows by Industry (Per Ministry of Commerce).

As a general matter, official statistics do not capture the phenomenon of Chinese ODI very well because most of China's ODI flows to Hong Kong, the British Virgin Islands, and the Cayman Islands. Subsidiaries in those countries subsequently make investments in other countries (including China) and the ultimate source of the investment is not always identified in the official statistics of the host countries. Still, some common themes are evident from this survey of China's ODI, despite the sometimes contradictory information. China's outward investments have been growing rapidly in recent years, especially after 2007. This investment has favored developing countries over advanced countries, though advanced countries that are resource-rich also have seen significant inflows over the past several years. Despite indications that the United States has not been a major target of Chinese direct investments, it is one of the top recipients of Chinese ODI to OECD countries. Though investments have likely been slowed by CNOOC's public failure to acquire UNOCAL, and other failed investments involving Huawei, Chinese investors have continued to invest in the U.S. market.

III. Likely Patterns of Chinese Foreign Investments over the Next 5 Years

This section estimates the amount of available capital from China that might be available for foreign investment in the United States, the sectors and regions where such investment might occur, and the types of investment that might be used.

A. Available Investor Capital for Future Investments

Official and non-government data sources, as well as reports of Chinese investment activities in the press, indicate that Chinese FDI is rising, both to the world and to the United States. While it is impossible to predict the precise value of U.S. FDI from China five years from now, it should be possible to make a rough ball park estimate based on the relationship between China's capacity to invest, reflected in its current account surplus and the profitability of its companies, and its proclivity to invest, reflected in its FDI-to-GDP ratio.

An analysis of recent forecasts of China's current account balance, GDP, and corporate profits suggests China's investment capacity will expand over the next five years. Based on IMF forecasts from September 2011, China's current account is expected to remain in surplus over the next five years, rising to 7.2 percent of GDP by 2016. Using the exchange rate of 2011, this implies a current account surplus of approximately $912 billion.[26] Oxford Economic

Forecasting ("Oxford") predicts China's current account surplus will reach $450 billion by 2016.[27] Both estimates exceed China's prior peak surplus of $411 billion, which occurred in 2008, prior to the collapse in trade resulting from the global financial crisis.

Predictions of corporate profits in China over the next five years are not readily available. Though corporate profits vary from year to year as a percentage of GDP, one can infer that the growth in China's GDP over the next five years will also be reflected in rising corporate profits. Based on IMF estimates, China's nominal GDP is anticipated to expand by 12.3 percent, on average.[28] Even if the share of corporate profits in GDP declines, China's corporate profits probably will be much higher five years from now than they are today, especially if the Yuan appreciates from current levels.[29]

Both the Economist Intelligence Unit ("EIU") and Oxford publish estimates for China's outward FDI. The two forecasts are based on different assumptions regarding China's preference for recycling through FDI. EIU assumes that the share of ODI to GDP will remain roughly constant in the range of 1-to-1.2 percent. On the other hand, Oxford's estimates imply that the ODI will rise to nearly 3 percent of GDP. Thus, there is a wide disparity between the two estimates: $140 billion by EIU and $370 million by Oxford. Both estimates far exceed China's actual outward FDI of nearly $70 billion in 2010, illustrated in Figure 6.[30] Thus, even the more conservative of the two estimates has China's ODI doubling over the next five years. This prediction is consistent with those of other observers of China's ODI.[31]

With China's GDP, current account surplus, corporate profits, and ODI likely to grow over the next five years, what are the likely U.S. inflows of Chinese FDI? The figure below presents three estimates compared to average capital inflows from Japan from 2003 to 2010. The "business as usual" scenario assumes that China's ODI remains at approximately 1.1 percent of GDP (the EIU assumption) through 2016 and that China's outflows to the United States as a share of total ODI are similar to 2009-2010. The "preference for ODI grows" scenario is based on the Oxford assumption that China's ODI is 2.9 percent of GDP by 2016.[32] The "preference for ODI and U.S. grows" scenario adopts the Oxford assumption along with an assumption that the share of China's ODI devoted to the United States rises by 50 percent over 2009-2010. The implied growth rates for China's ODI to the United States are then applied to U.S. capital inflows from China in 2010. These scenarios suggest that China's ODI five years from now will be approximately 1.9 to 7.5 times higher than in 2010. Though such levels of inward FDI from China are higher relative to prior years, they remain well below average capital inflows from Japan, as shown in the figure below. If these growth rates are applied to estimated flows on a UBO basis, then Chinese investments are likely to surpass the Japanese average by 2016.

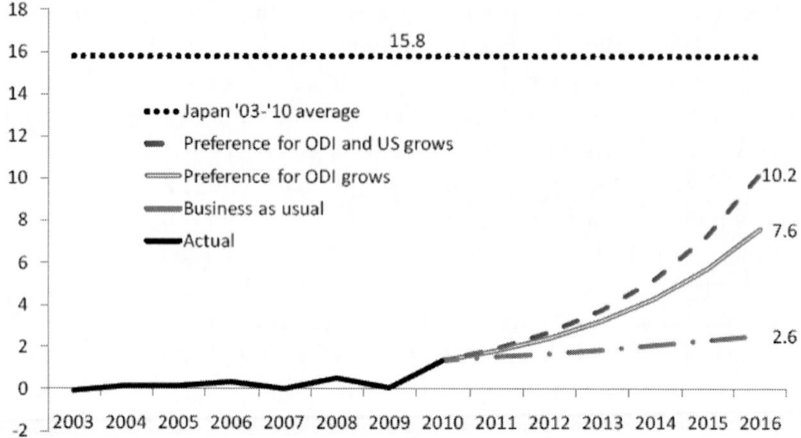

Sources: China's Ministry of Commerce; Bureau of Economic Analysis; Economist Intelligence Unit; Oxford Economics; author's estimates.

Figure 10. Actual Capital Inflows from China through 2010 and Three Potential Scenarios through 2016.

Of course, inward FDI from China will look nothing like the profile shown in Figure 10. There are likely to be mega-investments that yield capital inflows that exceed the maximum of $10.2 billion shown above. Similarly, capital inflows in a given year may decline.[33] Still this exercise is useful because it demonstrates that under vey plausible assumptions, inward FDI from China is likely to increase significantly over the next five years, potentially reaching levels consistent with those achieved by countries that are long-time investors.

Conversely, only a reversal of current trends could prevent a significant increase in FDI from China. Either the trend toward rising Chinese ODI would have to be reversed or the U.S. economy would have to become much less attractive relative to other countries' economies. Given that China's government remains committed to the "Go Out" strategy and the U.S. economy appears, as of this writing, to be recovering, FDI from China is unlikely to stagnate or decline from levels achieved in 2010.[34] Absent a dramatic change in the global economy, an increase in inward FDI from China consistent with or exceeding the levels shown in Figure 10 seems more plausible.

B. Outlook for Sectors and Regions over the Next Five Years

1. The Current Picture

The CIM data, which are focused on the United States, also show that investments have been geared toward fossil fuels in recent years. Prior to 2007, the primary focus of Chinese investments in the United States was the information technology sector, as shown in the figure below. Since then, there has been a noticeable shift in the composition of Chinese FDI, as well as increases in the value invested in each sector. The fossil fuel and chemical sector was the largest recipient of FDI since 2007. The industrial machinery sector also experienced a substantial increase. In contrast, the level of annual investment in the information technology industry has shrunk.

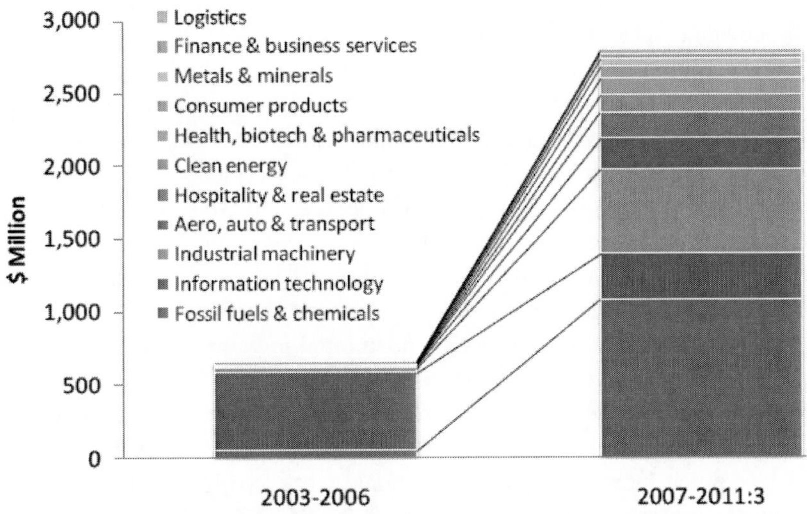

Source: China Investment Monitor through 2011:Q3.

Figure 11. Average Annual Value of Chinese Direct Investment Deals in the United States, by Industry.

Official U.S. data on capital inflows from China by industry are available but industry detail is limited because the direct Chinese presence in many industries was not significant enough, through 2009 anyway, to avoid suppression. The table below provides two industry-specific measures of Chinese FDI in the United States published by BEA: total capital inflows from China in 2010 and total assets in 2009 of companies in which Chinese firms are majority owners on a UBO basis.[35] The data indicate direct investment capital inflows from China of $1.4 billion in 2010. This compares to $228.2 billion in total direct investment capital inflows, so on an aggregate basis, capital flows from China are a rounding error. The industry-specific detail indicates a significant capital outflow of $-711 million in manufacturing. Underlying data suggest that Chinese manufacturers paid off or otherwise reduced their debts to parent companies, which is considered to be a reduction of inward FDI. Data on assets, shown in the second column, are more comparable to the information on deals collected by non-government sources of FDI data. According to official data, Chinese FDI assets in manufacturing were less than $1 billion in 2009, compared to $1.6 trillion in U.S. manufacturing assets held by all majority-owned foreign affiliates. Through 2009, at least, official data indicate that Chinese FDI played an extremely minor role in the U.S. manufacturing sector. Instead, the official data through 2009 indicate that nearly 90 percent of assets owned by majority-owned Chinese affiliates were in the financial sector.

Since the CIM presents its FDI estimates by state and industry, it offers a useful vehicle for examining the regional composition of FDI from China. Figure 13 illustrates the number of deals by BEA region.[36] By this measure, the Far West hosted 97 separate investment deals from 2003 to 2011:Q3, making it the most attractive region for Chinese investors. The Mideast hosted 62 deals, while the Southeast has hosted 40. Together, these three regions hosted 68 percent of the deals covered by the CIM.

Figure 14 illustrates how regions have fared in value terms by comparing investment over two period, 2003-to-2006 and 2007-to-2011:Q3. In the first period, the Mideast received $494 million per year on average, significantly more than all other regions combined. However, in the second period, Chinese FDI was much more evenly disbursed. The largest recipient of FDI was the Southwest, which received an average of $568 million per year. The Great Lakes region was the second most attractive region, receiving $525 million per year.

The Far West received $407 million per year. The Mideast was the only sector to experience a decline, but it has continued to attract more than $300 million in Chinese FDI annually, according to CIM.

	Capital flows from China. 2010	Assets owned by Chinese investors, 2009 1/
All industries	1,364	18,708
Manufacturing	-711	708
Food	2	0
Chemicals	(D)	(*)
Primary and fabricated metals	-3	(D)
Machinery	14	(D)
Computers and electronic products	2	(D)
Electrical equipment, appliances, and components	(D)	(D)
Transportation equipment	-73	88
Other manufacturing	-14	N/A
Wholesale trade	214	607
Retail trade	0	3
Information	38	(D)
Depository institutions	21	16,712
Finance (except depository institutions) and insurance	(D)	
Real estate and rental and leasing	0	(D)
Professional, scientific, and technical services	3	(D)
Other industries	(D)	366

1/ Presented on a UBO basis for majority-owned foreign affiliates. Data for 2010 were not available at the time this report was prepared.

*Indicates assets of less than $500,000.

(D)Indicates information is being withheld to avoid disclosing the data of individual companies.

Source: (Bureau of Economic Analysis).

Figure 12. FDI Capital Inflows from China and Assets of Majority-Owned Affiliates of Chinese firms.

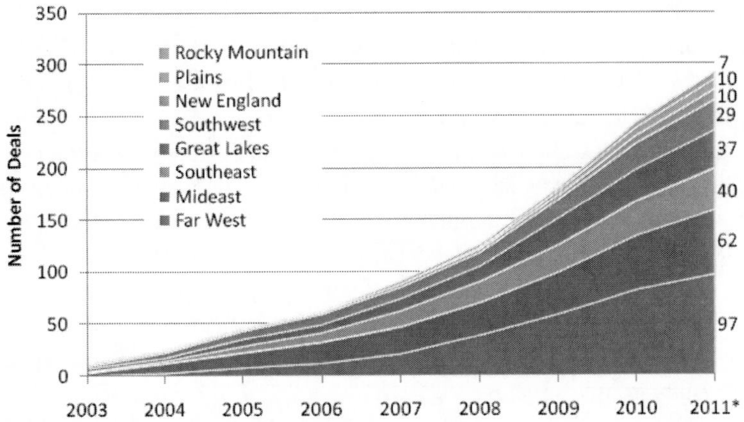

*Contains data through 2011:Q3.

Source: China Investment Monitor, 2012.

Figure 13. Cumulative Number of Chinese FDI Deals, by U.S. Region.

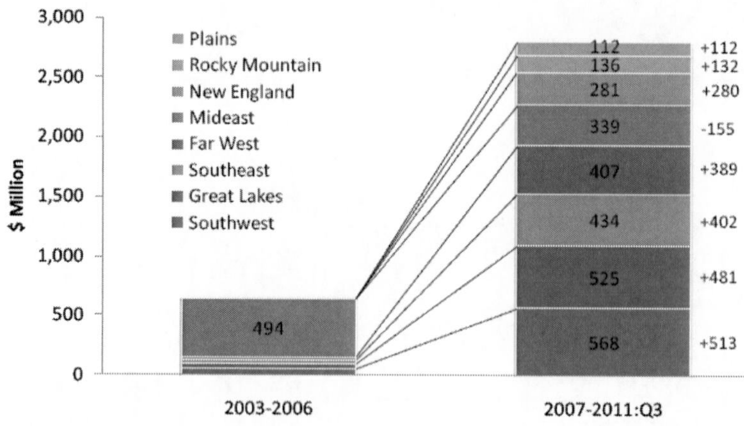

*Contains data through 2011:Q3.
Source: China Investment Monitor, 2012.

Figure 14. Annual Averages of Inward FDI from China.[37]

2. Projections

As will be discussed in greater detail below, the majority of Chinese foreign direct investments in terms of value are controlled by SOEs or their subsidiaries. SOEs – and even private sector firms in China – tend to be very sensitive to the goals articulated in the government's five-year plans. The 12th Five-Year Plan is thus a good point of departure when considering the direction of FDI from China over the next five years.

The plan contains a modest, yet comprehensive, section on speeding up China's "Go Out" strategy. The plan indicates that China will continue to favor FDI targeted at energy resources and technology R&D; FDI that creates marketing and sales channels and "famous brands;"[38] and FDI in agricultural and construction projects in developing countries. The plan also states that the government intends to take a number of measures that will facilitate FDI:

- assisting with research and evaluation of investment projects;
- improving interagency coordination and project assessment;
- accelerating changes to the legal/administrative framework governing outward investments;
- securing agreements that protect Chinese investment and avoid double taxation;
- improving the investment promotion system to facilitate investments, protect the rights of Chinese investors, and minimize risks;

The plan also encourages Chinese investors "to bear corporate social responsibility in mind in order to bring benefits to the local people."[39]

Although it is too early in the plan cycle to make any firm conclusions, the Chinese press is reporting that investments are shifting away from energy resources and toward "the technology, brand name, and distribution sectors" and increasingly involve private equity.[40]

Moreover, the World Bank recently released a study conducted in cooperation with the Development and Research Center of the State Council.[41] There are indications that the report will be influential among China's incoming leadership.[42] Regarding FDI, the study argues that China should continue to promote outward investment, particularly by private enterprises.[43] However, with regard to China's efforts to secure energy resources and technology, the report dovetails with the 12th Five-Year Plan in promoting such investments.[44]

As such, the sectors most likely to receive investments from China are energy, particularly oil and gas from shale; clean energy technologies making use of resources that are abundant in China, such as coal; industrial machinery, which can help Chinese producers increase productivity levels across multiple industries; and, to the extent that China is unable to extract technology from foreign companies investing in China, transport equipment industries where China is known to lack technology, such as aerospace and auto parts. Other potential magnets for Chinese investment include the construction, steel, and high speed train industries, where Chinese producers are already competitive and seek greater access to U.S. consumers and businesses, and the financial sector. Again, the latest five year plan is instructive, particularly Part I, Chapter 10, which lists the fields where China's government hopes to leapfrog its competitors:

> Develop new strategic industries energetically, such as energy-saving and environment-friendly new-generation IT, biology, high-end equipment manufacturing, new energy sources, new materials and new energy automobile. In the energy conservation and environmental protection industry, focus on the development of key technological equipment for efficient energy conservation, advanced environmental protection and resource recycling, products and services. In the new-generation IT industry, focus on the development of new-generation mobile communication, new-generation Internet, three-network convergence, Internet of things, cloud computing, IC, new displays, high-end software, high-end servers and information services. In the biological industry, focus on the development of biopharmaceuticals, biomedical

> engineering products, bioagriculture and bio-manufacturing. In the high-end equipment manufacturing industry, focus on the development of aviation equipment, satellites and application, rail traffic equipment and intelligent manufacturing equipment. In the new energy industry, focus on the development of new-generation nuclear energy and solar energy utilization, photovoltaic and photo-thermal power generation, and wind power technological equipment, intelligent power grids and biomass energy. In the new material industry, focus on the development of new functional materials, advanced structural materials, high-performance fibers and compound materials, and common basic materials. In the new energy automobile industry, focus on the development of plug-in hybrid electric vehicles, pure electric vehicles and fuel cell automobile technologies.[45]

It is difficult to predict with precision which regions of the United States will be attractive to the Chinese. Clearly regions of the country where novel technologies are being used to extract energy will be attractive to Chinese investors. The Great Lakes region, which contains significant manufacturing expertise in industrial machinery and auto parts, should experience inward investments as well. The Far West and other areas with strength in information technology, should also anticipate increased investments from China.

Not all of these investments will technically be considered FDI from China. Many will be conducted by firms whose proximate ownership is in Hong Kong, the BVI, or the Cayman islands. Others will be conducted using arrangements that are not considered FDI under official definitions. Examples of such approaches will be discussed below in Section V.

C. Outlook for Investments by Type

In the United States, data on foreign direct investment are collected by the BEA, while data on portfolio investments are collected by the Treasury. International portfolio inflows from China had been dominated by corporate bonds.[46]

The volume of such purchases had been expanding markedly prior to the financial crisis, but purchases have moderated substantially since then, as shown in Table 3. Net purchases of equities and FDI also declined, but these purchases have exceeded bond purchases in both 2009 and 2010. Still, the volume of direct investment and indirect equity purchases by China remains modest relative to bond purchases prior to the Great Recession.

Table 3. Average Net Quarterly Purchases of Bonds and Equities by Chinese Investors, 1999-2011

	Corporate Bond	Equities and FDI
	Millions of dollars	
1999	130	61
2000	202	-28
2001	1,672	62
2002	1,491	10
2003	1,188	-36
2004	3,084	-39
2005	6,533	-96
2006	7,813	195
2007	10,375	1,001
2008: H1	14,115	-61
2008:H2	685	-43
2009	-1,013	1,025
2010	-89	1,035
2011 1/	766	135

1/ Excludes FDI inflows in the fourth quarter.
Sources: Bureau of Economic Analysis and the U.S. Treasury via Haver Analytics.

Important voices in China have urged policy changes that would enable the country to obtain better returns on its foreign investment. In response, China has substantially funded sovereign wealth funds to invest in foreign assets. As discussed below, these vehicles have been active in U.S. equities markets, and they are likely to continue purchasing (and selling) equities. Given capital controls in China, these state-controlled investment vehicles (SIVs) are likely to remain the dominant vehicles for investing in U.S. equities. According to press reports, the government is planning to increase funding in its two main SIVs, State Administration of Foreign Exchange (SAFE) and Chinese Investment Corporation (CIC).[47]

The increases, speculated to be $50 billion for CIC and $300 billion for a SAFE affiliated SIV, offer a strong indication that the Government remains committed to recycling its foreign exchange cache into assets other than government debt.[48] As such, investments in U.S. equities from China are likely to increase as long as returns on U.S. equities remain competitive. Further, if China decides to liberalize capital controls, a recommendation contained in the recent World Bank study, then equity purchases from China are likely to increase even more.[49] Inward FDI from China is also likely to expand from current levels.

Such expansion can take two forms: "greenfield" investments in which Chinese firms enter the market by building new facilities and hiring new workers or M&A in which the Chinese firms merge with or take over an existing corporate entity. Neither U.S. nor Chinese official statistics currently track the breakdown between greenfield and M&A, but some databases do. A recent analysis by the U.S. International Trade Commission (USITC) based on private information found that the majority (about 60 percent) of China's global ODI has been greenfield, with the energy (33 percent) and metals (29) percent, accounting for the majority of investments.[50] However, UNCTAD found that Chinese companies have had a preference for M&A in certain years (e.g., 2003 and 2008).[51]

The CIM does not publish information on individual transactions, but it does provide fairly detailed breakdowns of greenfield and M&A activity by quarter, state and industry. From 2003 to 2011:Q3, the sample was split almost evenly between greenfield investments and M&A. However, in terms of value, it is clear that Chinese investors have favored acquisitions: $12.6 billion was spent on acquisitions (79 percent), while $3.3 billion (21 percent) was spend on greenfield investments. This breakdown is what one would expect to see from investment oriented toward technology acquisition, but is in contrast to China's global investments, which tend to be greenfield. Table 4 below provides a breakdown by BEA region. The data indicate that acquisitions constitute the majority of investments in all eight regions, with all but Far West and Southwest having acquisition shares in excess of 84 percent.

Table 4. Acquisition and Greenfield FDI from China by BEA Region, 2003-2011:Q3

	Acquisition	Greenfield	Acquisition	Greenfield
	Millions of Dollars		*Percent*	
Far West	1,186	818	59.2%	40.8%
Great Lakes	2,265	402	84.9%	15.1%
Mideast	3,288	300	91.6%	8.4%
New England	1,247	96	92.9%	7.1%
Plains	519	12	97.7%	2.3%
Rocky Mountain	645	20	97.0%	3.0%
Southeast	1,858	333	84.8%	15.2%
Southwest	1,616	1,298	55.5%	44.5%

Despite the dominance of acquisitions in terms of value, the value greenfield FDI has expanded in all BEA regions. The largest increases have occurred in the Southwest, Far West, and Great Lakes regions, as shown in the figure below. On the other hand, greenfield activity remains scant in New England, the Rocky Mountains, and the Plains.

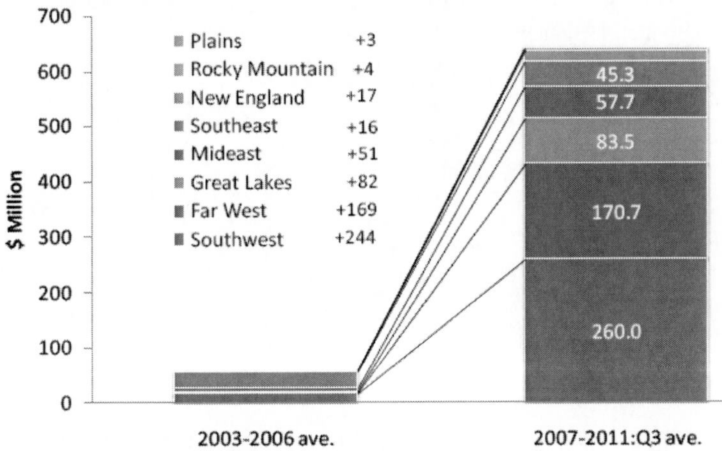

Source: China Investment Monitor, 2012.

Figure 15. Annual Greenfield FDI from China by BEA Region, 2003-2011:Q3.

The CIM's breakdown between M&A and greenfield FDI by industry is shown in Figure 16. The FDI in fossil fuels and chemicals, the industry that has received the most investment dollars, is dominated by acquisitions, as is information technology; aero, auto, & transport; and hospitality and real estate. Greenfield investments are more prominent in industrial machinery, clean energy, consumer products, and metals and minerals.

These patterns underscore the important role played by China's government, not only in determining where investments occur, but in determining the character of those investments. The "Go Out" policy initially was aimed at enhancing China's energy security (and access to raw materials) and this focus is likely to continue. But technology acquisition to advance the goals of China's five-year plans and the promotion of China's famous brands are increasingly important goals. China intends to acquire leapfrog technologies in a number of sectors. These sectors, primarily new energy and information technology, will likely continue receiving FDI in the form of M&A as long as China sees promising U.S. technologies in these areas. Given

U.S. sensitivities, China may also try acquiring technologies through non-equity relationships.

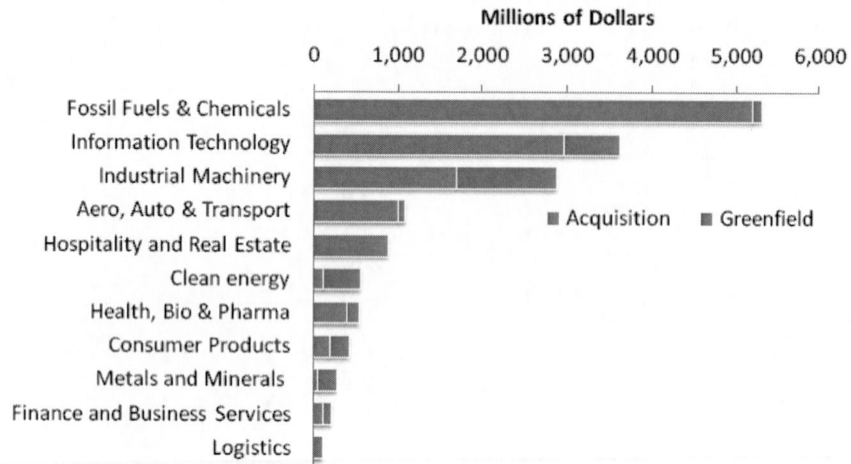

Source: China Investment Monitor, 2012.

Figure 16. China's FDI—U.S. M&A versus Greenfield by Industry, 2003-2011:Q3.

Metals, auto parts, chemicals, and solar panels may remain attractive as well in order to preserve market access. U.S. producers in these industries have been prone to import surges from China because Chinese policies frequently lead to capacity expansions far beyond what China can absorb domestically. The U.S. steel, tire, citric acid, and solar panel industries have employed trade laws to limit the flow of imports from China. Some Chinese producers, Anshan and TIPCO, for example, appear to be using FDI as a way to bypass trade remedies and this type of investment is likely to continue. Chinese firms from the solar panel industry appear to have invested to oppose the application of trade laws preemptively.[52] These investments are likely to be a mix of M&A and greenfield investments.

SOEs have remained the dominant source of FDI from China according to both official and private sources. SOEs are likely to remain important investors, though it appears that China understands that many in the United States view SOEs with suspicion.[53] This may result in an increased role for investments from private firms. According to CIM, private firms investing in the United States are nine percent more likely to engage in greenfield investments than SOEs.

IV. Identification of U.S. Data Collection and Oversight Activities

Although significant inward direct investments from China are a relatively recent phenomenon, foreign-owned companies are important participants in the U.S. market and have been for decades. This section describes U.S. data collection and oversight activities toward FDI.

A. Data Collection

A variety of U.S. data on inward and outward foreign direct investment are collected and published by the BEA.[54] Broadly speaking, the BEA has collected three types of data on inward investment:

- Balance of payments and direct investment position data, which track the transactions and positions of new and existing U.S. affiliates;
- Financial and operating data of U.S. affiliates of foreign companies, which include income statement, balance sheet, and other business related data; and
- Data on establishments and acquisitions, which track new direct investments irrespective of whether the investing funds were raised in the United States or abroad.

The agency collects these data by means of mandatory surveys of the U.S. affiliates of foreign companies.[55] Annual expository articles with extensive data summaries are published in the *Survey of Current Business* and available online from the BEA web site. A selection of the data collected is presented in Table 5.

Several data series are presented by country and by industry (e.g., sales by U.S. affiliates of Chinese firms in manufacturing).

Information on the source country of the foreign investment is available on two bases: by country of the foreign parent company and by country of ultimate beneficial owner ("UBO").

The UBO is the ultimate beneficiary of the income generated by the U.S. affiliate. In many instances, the foreign parent company and the UBO are the same.

Table 5. Selected U.S. data collected from U.S. affiliates of foreign multinational corporations by BEA

Balance of payments & direct investment position data	Financial and Operating Data	Acquisition and Establishment Data*
Investment position Capital inflows -Equity capital -Reinvested earnings -Intercompany debt Income -Earnings -Interest Royalty and license fees Other service charges	Employment Total assets -Net property plant and equipment Sales -Goods -Services -Investment income Net income Merchandise exports by affiliates Merchandise imports by affiliates	Investment outlays -Acquisitions -Establishments -By foreign direct investors -By U.S. affiliates of foreign companies

*The acquisition and establishment data survey was discontinued with the 2008 report. A new survey is currently being developed.

Source: Quijano, 1990.

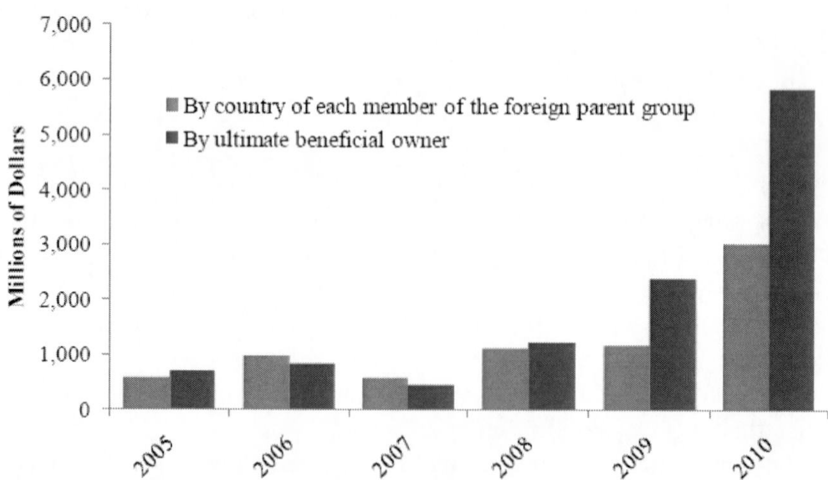

Source: Survey of Current Business, various issues.

Figure 17. China's Historical-cost Foreign Direct Investment Position in the United States, by Foreign Parent Group and Ultimate Beneficial Owner.

However, in instances when the investor is an affiliate of the foreign investor and is located in different country than the parent, the country of the foreign parent and the country of the UBO are different. This distinction is relevant for investments from China because many Chinese firms have established companies outside the mainland (e.g., in Hong Kong, Macau, and the British Virgin Islands) and use those beachheads to finance foreign investments and investments in China as well. As shown in Figure 1, there has been a significant increase in Chinese capital inflows from destinations outside of China in recent years.

Although these data offer a useful window into FDI by Chinese firms and their activities in the United States, there are important limitations on how these data can be used. First, confidentiality issues prevent the BEA from presenting data for all countries and for all industries. According to the law under which data collection occurs, information cannot be disseminated in a manner that would allow the company providing the data to be identified. Thus, for Chinese FDI, which is still relatively minor compared to FDI from traditional advanced country sources, specific industry data points are frequently suppressed in order to prevent the disclosure of data from a single firm. As a result, industry-specific detail on Chinese FDI is frequently lacking. Second, there are limitations on how the data can be used, even by the U.S. government. The law governing data collection specifies that the company-specific information collected through the surveys can only be used for statistical and analytical purposes and cannot be used for tax, investigative, or regulatory purposes.[56] Third, the BEA typically publishes country data on FDI eighteen months or more after the investment occurs. As such, it is less timely than other non-government sources of FDI data.[57] On the other hand, these unofficial sources do not have access to the mandated survey data and are frequently based on corporate announcements (or articles and commercial databases reporting those announcements) that may not accurately represent the amount of capital investment flows (or other information) for a given year.[58] This, as well as timing differences, may explain why deals reported by non-government sources indicate different values for Chinese FDI in the United States than BEA. The BEA data, even those presented on a UBO basis, have also been criticized for not capturing all Chinese FDI, which can emerge from complicated deal structures.[59]

B. Regulatory and Institutional Framework

The U.S. system is set up to provide disclosure, not to screen foreign investments by SOEs that could potentially erode economic security.

However, the disclosure requirements applied by the Securities and Exchange Commission do provide information that can be used to assess the activities of Chinese investors. Other U.S. laws and regulations apply to both foreign affiliates and domestic firms, ensuring that both types of firms face the same constraints.

1. Securities and Exchange Commission

The U.S. market is generally open to FDI and inward investment is generally promoted and praised by government officials.[60] Nevertheless, several U.S. government agencies are responsible for regulating foreign direct and there are important regulations that apply to foreign investments, including FDI from China. Even the Dodd-Frank Wall Street Reform and Consumer Protection Act, signed into law on July 21, 2010, influenced the regulation of foreign investment.[61]

The U.S. Securities and Exchange Commission (SEC) oversees securities exchanges, securities brokers and dealers, investment advisors, mutual funds, and other key participants. The SEC is relevant to Chinese investors purchasing shares in U.S. corporations or listing on U.S. exchanges.

Securities registered in the United States are governed by the Securities Act of 1933 (Securities Act) and the Securities Act of 1934 (Exchange Act). The Securities Act of 1933 has two basic objectives: it 1) requires that investors receive financial and other significant information concerning securities being offered for public sale; and 2) prohibits deceit, misrepresentations, and other fraud in the sale of securities.[62] The SEC also has enforcement authority and can thus bring civil enforcement actions against individuals and firms who violate securities laws.

Foreign and domestic investors are subject to a number of disclosure requirements. A foreign investor, or the ultimate beneficial owner, who accumulates 10 percent of voting securities is considered a corporate insider and must file certain ownership documents. Form 3 is the initial filing of a merger or exchange, Form 4 identifies changes in ownership and Form 5 is an annual summary of Form 4. Foreign firms must file form 20-F, analogous to the form 10-K filed by domestic corporations, within six months of the end of their fiscal year.[63]

Investments by sovereign wealth funds are subject to additional disclosure. The SEC requires Form 13D for beneficial owners of more than 5 percent of an issuer's equity securities, which requires the beneficial owner of the securities to disclose the source and amount of funds being used to purchase the shares, and announce whether the purpose of the purchase is to acquire control as well as any plans or proposals with regard to future actions by the purchaser.[64] Form 13F requires institutional investment managers to disclose if they exercise investment discretion over $100 million or more of U.S. exchange-traded equity securities.

There are some exceptions to the liberal treatment of FDI in the U.S. economy. For example, the Communication Act of 1934 restricts foreign ownership of broadcast, common carrier, and aeronautical radio station licensees.[65] Specifically, it prohibits foreign entities from owning more than 20 percent of the stock of companies in these industries.[66] FDI in the banking sector is also subject to review by the Federal Reserve, as well other federal and state banking authorities.[67]

Reverse mergers involving Chinese firms have been of particular concern to the SEC. These will be discussed in greater detail in section IX. A reverse merger is an alternative to an initial public offering in which a private company obtains a listing by purchasing a public shell company.[68] As a result of numerous instances of poor financial reporting and outright fraud involving Chinese reverse mergers, the SEC approved new rules in November 2011.[69] The Public Company Accounting Oversight Board (PCAOB), a nonprofit corporation established by Congress to oversee the audits of public companies has been in negotiations with China's Ministry of Finance (MOF) to allow more oversight of Chinese accounting firms but these have foundered.[70] In the meantime, fraudulent reverse mergers involving Chinese firms continue to make news.[71]

2. Committee on Foreign Investment in the United States (CFIUS)

CFIUS is an inter-agency committee that reviews the national security implications of foreign investments in U.S. companies or operations. Established by executive order, CFIUS is chaired by the Secretary of the Treasury and includes representatives from 16 agencies and departments, including the Defense, State and Commerce departments, as well as (most recently) the Department of Homeland Security.[72]

CFIUS reviews begin with a 30-day decision to authorize a transaction or begin a statutory investigation. If the latter is chosen, the committee has another 45 days to decide whether to permit the acquisition or order divestment.[73] Most transactions submitted to CFIUS are approved without the statutory investigation.[74]

In 1988 the U.S. Congress broadened CFIUS when it enacted the Exon-Florio Amendment,[75] which gave the President powers to block a foreign investment deemed to pose a threat to national security. Congress approved the law, but directed that that the President must believe that other U.S. laws are inadequate or inappropriate to protect the national security, and that he must have "credible evidence that the foreign investment will impair the national security.[76] Under the Exon-Florio provision, the President has 15 days to act on any recommendations made by CFIUS.[77]

CFIUS was later strengthened again by Foreign Investment and National Security Act of 2007 (FINSA). Congress passed FINSA in the wake of controversies over foreign investment in the United States, such as the China National Offshore Oil Corporation's (CNOOC) bid for the oil company UNOCAL,[78] and the forced unwinding of the Dubai Ports World deal to operate U.S. maritime facilities. Although CFIUS remains focused on national security, the rise of China and the expansion of its SOEs into core areas have blurred the line between national and economic security.

Thus, FINSA expands the scope of CFIUS by adding to the list of national security factors for the committee's consideration, thereby expanding the number of investment transactions subject to review. These include:

- National security effects of critical infrastructure, including major energy assets;
- Potential national security effects on critical technologies;
- Whether the covered transaction is a foreign government-controlled transaction;
- Whether the government in a foreign government controlled transaction adheres to non-proliferation regimes, presents a risk of transshipment of controlled exports, and is compliant with U.S. counterterrorism efforts; and
- U.S. long-term energy and resource requirements.[79]

Importantly, CFIUS in recent years has adopted procedures for post transaction monitoring of reviewed transactions that require mitigation measures.[80] The Secretary of the Treasury designates a lead member agency to monitor the mitigation and report back to CFIUS.[81]

Agency monitoring efforts include meetings with the companies, on-site reviews, third-party audits, and investigations if non-compliance is suspected.[82]

Other potential changes to CFIUS include the addition of reporting requirements and net benefits testing. The CFIUS review process currently operates on a voluntary basis. Transactions that are not reported are not reviewed unless one of the CFIUS member agencies self-initiates a review.[83]

Absent the third party research that uncovered Huawei's transaction involving 3Leaf Systems, that transaction might have gone under the radar.[84]

Second, CFIUS is not explicitly required to review all economic security dimensions of individual transactions. One possible change to the CFIUS process, suggested in testimony before the Commission, is a net benefits test, similar to that employed by Canada, which would ensure that the investment would be a net benefit to the United States.[85]

3. Other Relevant Laws and Regulations

There are several laws on the books relevant to FDI. Although these laws do not explicitly target foreign investments, they can apply to foreign owned firms under certain circumstances.

FDI through large mergers are subject to provisions of the Hart Scott-Rodino Antitrust Improvements Act of 1976. Title II of the Act, as amended, requires parties to submit a premerger notification for most significant acquisitions.[86]

The Program is designed to provide the Federal Trade Commission and the Department of Justice with information about large mergers and acquisitions before they occur.[87]

The Foreign Corrupt Practices Act of 1977 (FCPA) is a broad anti-corruption statute that addresses bribery.[88] It was enacted for the purpose of making it unlawful for certain classes of persons and entities to make payments to foreign government officials to assist in obtaining or retaining business.

The FCPA also requires companies whose securities are listed in the United States to meet its accounting provisions.[89] These accounting provisions, which were designed to operate in tandem with the anti-bribery provisions of the FCPA, require covered corporations to (a) make and keep books and records that accurately and fairly reflect the transactions of the corporation and (b) devise and maintain an adequate system of internal accounting controls.[90]

The majority of FCPA cases have been against U.S. firms operating in China, but the law has some important implications for Chinese FDI as well. At a basic level, the provisions apply to Chinese nationals in the United States. Moreover, the provisions can apply to SOEs as well as quasi-private entities that are performing state functions.[91]

Thus, private investment funds that seek investments from foreign owned entities, or sovereign wealth funds, or state-owned pensions could face scrutiny under FCPA.[92]

The Export Administration Regulations (EAR) govern exports and re-exports from the United States.[93] While the products subject to EAR tend to have military applications, many products are "dual use".[94] Embargoed countries are also regulated by EAR.

The Department of Commerce amended its licensing policy of dual-use exports to China in June 2007, by removing individual license requirements for certain authorized customers in China while imposing new licensing requirements on a targeted list of items that could contribute to China's military modernization. The rule created a Validated End-User (VEU) program to facilitate exports to trusted customers.[95] The updated regulations also impose new controls on a focused list of items if they are destined for military end uses in China.

Table 6. Key Aspects of the U.S. Legal Framework for FDI

Order, law, or regulations	Key Impact
Executive Order 11858 (1975)	Creates CFIUS to monitor the impact of direct and portfolio investment.
Exon-Florio Amendment (1988)	Adds Section 721 to Defense Production Act of 1950, which conferred upon the President the authority to suspend or prohibit certain transactions.
Foreign Investment and National Security Act of 2007	Requires heightened scrutiny of foreign government-controlled investments and subjects more foreign investment transactions to review.
Hart Scott-Rodino Antitrust Improvements Act of 1976	Requires premerger notification
Foreign Corrupt Practices Act of 1977	Addresses bribery of foreign officials, potentially including employees of SOEs
Export Administration Regulations	Governs exports and re-exports of products with military and dual use applications
International Traffic in Arms Regulations	Controls the trade defense-related articles and services on the United States Munitions List. Prohibits exports of certain items to China.

International Traffic in Arms Regulations (ITAR) control the export and import of defense-related articles and services on the United States Munitions List (USML).[96] U.S. manufacturers, exporters, and brokers of defense articles, defense services, or related technical data, as defined on the USML, are required to register with State Department. Export or re-export to China of USML products, software or technical information subject to the ITAR is prohibited.

The Office of Foreign Assets Control (OFAC) of the U.S. Department of the Treasury administers and enforces economic and trade sanctions based on US foreign policy and national security goals against targeted foreign countries and regimes, terrorists, international narcotics traffickers, those engaged in activities related to the proliferation of weapons of mass destruction, and other threats to the national security, foreign policy or economy of the United States.[97]

The legal and regulatory framework for FDI is summarized in the table below. Of note, there is no explicit law or regulation that requires a review of the economic security implications of FDI. As noted above, other countries, including Canada, do have this type of mechanism in place.[98]

V. FDI BY CHINA'S STATE-OWNED ENTERPRISES AND STATE-INVESTED ENTERPRISES

This section describes activities by U.S. affiliates of Chinese SOEs, state-invested enterprises, and public companies that may be acting with delegated state authority.[99] The analysis is based on data from the Rhodium Group's *China Investment Monitor* (CIM) through the third quarter of 2011; The Heritage Foundation's *China Global Investment Tracker* (GIT) maintained by Derek Scissors;[100] and data on value added published by BEA. This section concludes with case studies to illustrate the nature of these deals.

Figure 18, based on data from the China Investment Monitor (CIM), indicates that the number of FDI deals made by Chinese investors is rising and that deals involving nonSOEs account for a solid majority of transactions. Deals by SOEs averaged 3.5 per year from 2003 to 2006, and then increased to 11.6 per year from 2007 to 2011:Q3, but accounted for less than one quarter of all instances of Chinese FDI.

In value terms, data from CIM indicate that SOEs have become the dominant source of investment dollars from China in recent years. From 2003 to 2006, deals by SOEs averaged $51.3 million per year, only 8 percent of total Chinese FDI.[101]

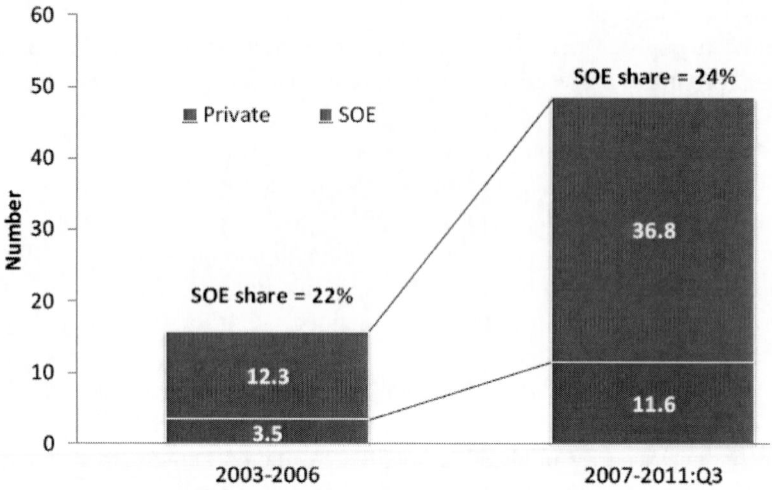

Source: China Investment Monitor through 2011:Q3.

Figure 18. Average Annual Number of FDI Deals by SOEs and Non-SOEs.

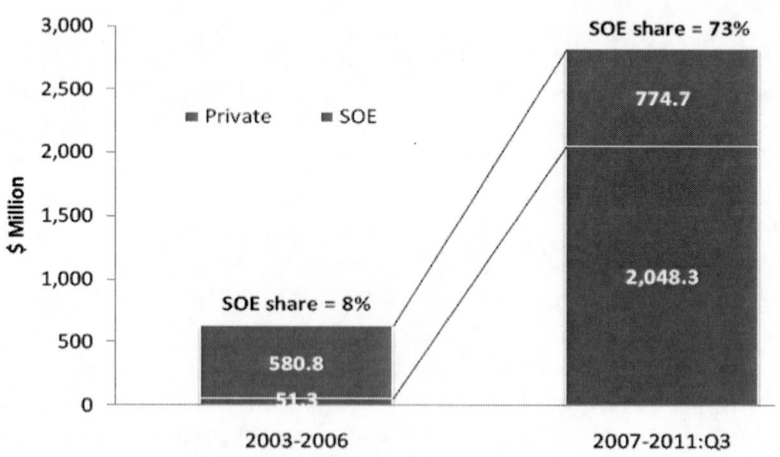

Source: China Investment Monitor through 2011:Q3.

Figure 19. Average Annual Value of FDI Deals by SOEs and Non-SOEs.

From 2007 to 2011:Q3, the deals averaged $2 billion per year and accounted for 73 percent of Chinese FDI. The amount of FDI from private investors also rose, but "only" by $194 million annually. Table 7 and Table 8 provide a SOE-private breakdown over the entire period covered by the CIM database and illustrate the composition of Chinese FDI. Table 7 indicates that the majority of Chinese FDI from 2003 to 2011:Q3 took place in the *fossil fuels and chemicals* industry and that SOEs were the dominant investors in both periods. Private investors were dominant in all other industries tracked by the CIM from 2003 to 2006. From 2007 to 2011:Q3, SOEs accounted for more than 90 percent of investment value in the *industrial machinery; aero, auto, and transport*; and *logistics* industries. They also accounted for the majority of investment in the clean energy industry. SOEs remained less active relative to the private sector in the *information technology*; *hospitality and real estate*; *finance and business services*; and other industries with relatively minor investment levels.

Table 7. Value and Shares of FDI in U.S. by Chinese SOEs, 2003-2011:Q3

	2003-11:Q3 *$ million*	2003-2006 *SOE share of total Chinese FDI*	2007-11:Q3
Fossil Fuels & Chemicals	5,227	92%	97%
Industrial Machinery	2,630	2%	96%
Aero, Auto, & Transport	979	0%	96%
Information Technology	441	2%	27%
Clean Energy	287	0%	52%
Hospitality & Real Estate	158	0%	18%
Logistics	106	N/A	99%
Finance and Business Service	83	28%	40%
Consumer Products	15	0%	4%
Health, Bio, & Pharma	7	0%	1%
Metals & Minerals	2	N/A	1%
Total	9,935	8%	73%

Table 8 provides the SOE-private breakdown over the entire period covered by the CIM. Industries with investments exceeding one billion dollars tend to be dominated by SOEs, with the exception of information technology. Private-sector investments tend to dominate the other industries, with the exception of clean energy, where SOEs maintain a slight majority, and logistics.

Unlike CIM, the Heritage Foundation's GIT provides information on specific transactions, which can be used to break down investments into those made by SOEs and those made by state-invested entities (SIEs). SIE investments are centered in computer manufacturing and in transport equipment, as shown in Table 9.

Table 8. Cumulative Value and Shares of Chinese FDI in U.S., SOE and Private, 2003-2011:Q3

	$ million	SOEs	Private
Fossil Fuels & Chemicals	5,406	97%	3%
Information Technology	3,542	12%	88%
Industrial Machinery	2,877	91%	9%
Aero, Auto, & Transport	1,096	89%	11%
Hospitality & Real Estate	887	18%	82%
Clean Energy	560	51%	49%
Health, Bio, & Pharma	544	1%	99%
Consumer Products	427	3%	97%
Metals & Minerals	272	1%	99%
Finance and Business Service	219	38%	62%
Logistics	107	99%	1%

Source: China Investment Monitor through 2011:Q3.

Table 9. Cumulative Value and Shares of Chinese Investment in U.S., SOE and SIE 2005- 2011

	$ million	SOE	SIE
Finance	18,560	2%	0%
Energy	5,890	69%	0%
Real Estate	4,300	3%	9%
Computer manufacturing	1,700	0%	100%
Transport equipment	1,630	67%	33%
Metals/metal mining	1,170	86%	0%
Software	400	0%	0%
Medical services	360	0%	0%
Agriculture	140	100%	0%
Manufacturing, other	120	0%	0%

Source: The Heritage Foundation, Copy of China-Global-Investment-Tracker 2012 (1/5/2012).

The best known SIE in the computer manufacturing is Lenovo. Though Lenovo is a listed company, its controlling shareholder is Legend Holdings Limited, which owns 42 percent of Lenovo's beneficial shares.[102] Lenovo's chairman, Mr. Liu Chuanzhi, is also the chairman and president of Legend, which is controlled by the Chinese Academy of Sciences (CAS), an SOE.[103] China's SIEs have also made investments in the U.S. automotive sector.

During the summer of 2010, GM sold its Nexteer Automotive steering business, formerly part of Delphi, to Pacific Century Motors, a Chinese firm owned by Aviation Industry Corporation of China and an investment arm of the Beijing municipal government.[104] Beijing West Industries, which is 51 percent owned by SOE Shougang Steel and 25 percent owned by Beijing's municipal government, purchased Delphi's global brake and suspension business, including U.S. facilities, in November 2009.[105] Another SIE investing in the United States is HNA Property Holdings, the real estate arm of the Hainan Group, which is believed to be owned in part by the Hainan Provincial Government.[106]

According to the Heritage database, HNA Property has made two large investments in Manhattan, a $130 million purchase of the Cassa Hotel and a $265 million purchase of a 23 story office tower.[107]

Official data from BEA also suggest that the majority of Chinese FDI in the United States is conducted by the state sector. The BEA presents value added and other data by industry of affiliate and by industry of the ultimate beneficial owner (UBO). If the UBO is an SOE (or government pension) the industry is classified as "Government and government related entities." Figure 20 presents BEA data on value added by industry of UBO for 2009.

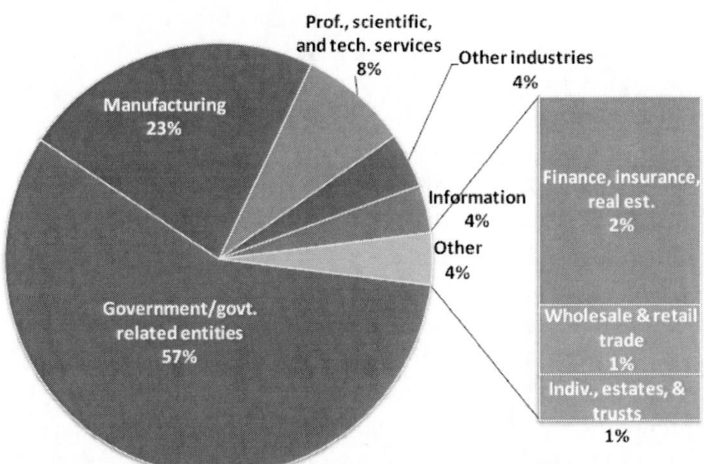

1/ The ultimate beneficial owner (UBO) refers to the entity, following up the chain of the affiliate's ownership, that is not owned 50 percent or more by another entity.
Source: Bureau of Economic Analysis.

Figure 20. Value Added by Government and Government Related Entities, by Industry of UBO, 2009 1/.

Chinese government-owned entities accounted for more than half of value added generated by Chinese-owned affiliates in the United States.[108]

Investments by public companies that may be acting with delegated state authority are difficult to assess. The firm that immediately comes to mind is Huawei, yet no Huawei U.S. investments appear on the GIT's list of completed investments. However, Huawei has invested in at least two U.S. R&D centers that are located in Dallas, Texas and Silicon Valley, but the value of those investments could not be determined.[109] According to its web site, Huawei's North American headquarters is located in Plano, Texas, and it has eight regional offices and nine R&D centers in North America that employ more than 1,000 workers.

B. Case studies of SOE Investments

Lenovo: Lenovo's purchase of IBM's PC business in 2005 was more like a cross investment. Lenovo paid $650 million in cash and $600 million in Lenovo shares for the business and assumed $500 million in debt. IBM received the cash and became a minority shareholder of Lenovo. Lenovo also received a cash infusion of $350 million from three private equity firms to assist with the deal. The BEA likely did not count the Lenovo investment as direct investment from China. A review of BEA's capital inflow and operations data for China from 2004 to 2006 indicates no significant changes in values that could signal that the investment was counted as Chinese. On the other hand, data for Hong Kong suggest that the transaction was treated as an investment by a Hong Kong business, which would seem to be consistent with BEA's rules.[110]

When the acquisition took place, the combined firm had a strong IBM presence. Lenovo assumed some facilities in Armonk, New York, which became Lenovo's global headquarters, as well as facilities in Raleigh, North Carolina. Former IBM workers accounted for 10,000 of the combined firm's 19,000 workers.

Over time, IBM's influence has faded. Executives left the company, some returning to IBM, and Lenovo moved its headquarters away from Armonk. North Carolina's state and local governments offered $14 million in incentives and succeeded in keeping R&D activities in the state. Lenovo also promised to create an additional 400 jobs in the state. Lenovo's headquarters and R&D facilities are now located in North Carolina. Still, it took a while for the new firm to hit stride. There were a number of disappointments, including job cuts in Raleigh and the decision to open new production facilities in other countries, including Mexico, where 1,000 jobs were planned. However, Lenovo did eventually open a new logistical facility in Greensboro, North Carolina, in February 2008 and announced plans to add additional workers in 2011. The firm's financial fortunes also turned around, primarily due to its top position in the Chinese market, where most of its computers are made. By the third quarter of 2008, Lenovo's global market share had reached 14 percent – nearly double the level of the market shares of Lenovo and IBM prior to the acquisition.

Goldwind USA: After pursuing a vigorous industrial policy, China is currently the world's largest producer of wind turbines and state-owned Xinjiang Goldwind Science & Technology Co. (Goldwind) is one of China's largest producers. Goldwind's largest shareholders include four SOEs that are owned by the Xinjiang SASAC. The firm is making an aggressive push into foreign markets, funded by a $6 billion low interest rate loan from the government-owned China Development Bank and $1 billion raised in its Hong Kong IPO in August 2010. According to its listing documents, 24.1 percent of the cash raised in its IPO would be earmarked for expanding into attractive international markets, including the United States. Clearly, this investment is driven by the desire to capture market share.

Goldwind's activities in the United States began in 2009, when it invested in a $10.2 million pilot wind farm project in Minnesota.[111] In May of 2010, Goldwind announced that it would locate its North American headquarters, Goldwind USA, in Chicago, Illinois. By the end of 2010, it had a dozen employees. Its major U.S. sales include large projects in Illinois and Montana. By the end of 2011, Goldwind had completed turbines with nine megawatts of capacity and 117 megawatts under construction. According to the China Daily, Goldwind had concluded 18 deals in the United States by early 2012.

Though its turbines sold in the United States are made in China, Goldwind USA has locally sourced certain goods and services. According to Goldwind USA's CEO, 62 percent of the pilot project's total cost, including the blades (North Dakota), towers (Minnesota), engineering, procurement, transportation, construction, and ancillary services, were sourced in the United States. Moreover, the facility is being operated by a local company. The $200 million Shady Oaks farm in Illinois is expected to create more than 100 construction jobs and 12 permanent maintenance positions. Broadwind Energy, Inc. is manufacturing most of the farm's wind towers in Manitowac, Wisconsin. Goldwind USA's mains supplier of blades for its U.S. projects is the LM Wind Power Group plant in North Dakota.

Although Goldwind has gone from nothing to being one of the world's top firms in terms of market share, the firm's profitability has lagged. Figure 21 indicates that its stock price declined from $2.50 per share to $0.65 per share during the past sixteen months. Its finances have suffered due to the imbalance of supply and demand in China's market for turbines. China's domestic market is saturated with 80 firms and Goldwind is facing increased competition. Moreover, China has been creating wind farms faster than they can be connected to the grid. According to an analysis by Jeffries Equity Research, 30 percent of China's wind power capacity is not even connected. Until existing farms are connected to the grid, domestic demand for new turbines is likely to be muted, making Goldwind's push into the U.S. and other international markets more urgent.

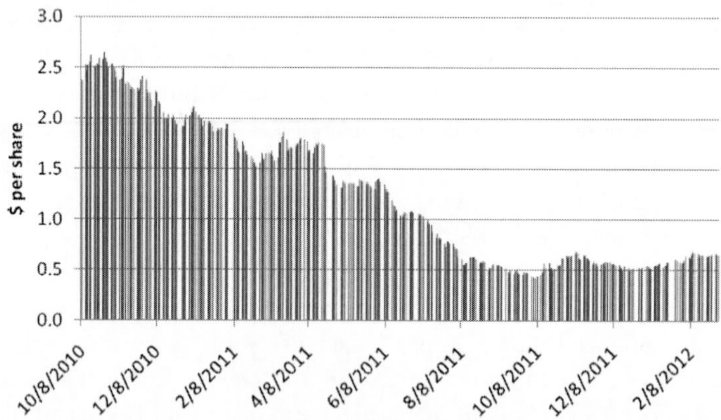

Source: http://finance.yahoo.com, downloaded March 1, 2012.

1/ Converted from Hong Kong dollars to U.S. dollars using an average of daily exchange rates from October 8, 2010 to February 24, 2012.

Figure 21. Goldwind's Stock Price from Aug. 2010 to Feb. 2012 1/.

China National Offshore Oil Corporation (CNOOC):[112] CNOOC is one of China's SOEs devoted to the energy sector. It was created in 1982 and charged with administering and developing China's offshore petroleum operations with foreign companies.[113] Currently, CNOOC is directly under the control of the central SASAC.[114] In 1999, CNOOC transferred its operational and commercial interests in its offshore petroleum business to CNOOC Limited, a Hong Kong limited liability company. However, CNOOC remains the controlling shareholder of CNOOC Limited, which is listed on the Hong Kong and New York Stock Exchanges.[115] In terms of reserves and production,

CNOOC Limited is one of the world's largest companies engaged in the exploration and production of oil and natural gas.

CNOOC International Limited (CIL) is a wholly owned subsidiary of CNOOC Limited and owns all of its overseas interests in oil exploration and production.[116] CIL is thus the primary legal entity through which the Chinese government achieves its goal of securing energy resources for China in foreign markets. Currently, one of those goals, articulated in the 12th Five year Plan, is technological breakthroughs for shale gas.[117] The United States, which is undergoing a boom in shale gas development, has been an important source of shale gas technology for China.

In November 2009, just prior to global talks on climate change, the United States and China agreed to cooperate on shale gas development. This agreement seemed to pave the way for SOE investments in the U.S. energy sector.[118] Whereas CIL's attempt to invest in UNOCAL had floundered, in November 2010 CIL succeeded in obtaining a 33.3 percent equity interest in the Chesapeake Energy Corporation's Eagle Ford Shale project in south Texas, for $2.2 billion.[119] Then, during the first quarter of 2011, CIL purchased a 33.3 percent undivided interest in Chesapeake's 800,000 net oil and natural gas leasehold acres in northeast Colorado and Wyoming for $570 million, with the goal of tapping oil from the shale formation.[120] CNOOC leaves no doubt that technology acquisition was the goal of these investments. Responding to a question posed by Reuters, the firm stated, "Chesapeake has accumulated abundant experience in drilling and completion in various U.S. shale plays. The techniques and experiences we learn from the U.S. shale projects will benefit our potential participation in other areas in the future."[121] This sentiment was shared by the SOE PetroChina, which arguably overpaid for its purchase of shale gas assets in Canada: "We don't care much about whether the market believes it's a good or bad price. The top priority is gaining access to a resource and mature technology. Price is only a secondary consideration."[122]

While these deals are providing China with the technology and experience it desires, they are also providing much needed capital to Chesapeake, enabling the firm to accelerate its drilling for the two projects. The accelerated activity is also creating additional employment opportunities as well.

Although these transactions are investments in U.S. assets, they technically may not constitute direct investments because CNOOC did not receive any ownership or control over Chesapeake Corporation's voting securities. Instead, they may be considered portfolio investments and would appear in statistics maintained by the U.S. Treasury.[123]

VI. INVESTMENTS BY CHINA'S STATE CONTROLLED INVESTMENT VEHICLES (SIVS)

This section describes U.S. investments by China's state investment vehicles (SIVs), special purpose investment funds better known as sovereign wealth funds. It reviews their U.S. holdings using the GIT as a guide and provides brief case studies.

A. U.S. Holdings of SIVs

China currently has four major sovereign wealth funds: SAFE Investment Company (SAFE), China Investment Corporation (CIC), the National Social Security Fund (NSSF), and the China-Africa Development Fund (CAD). The first four Chinese SWFs are among the 11 most endowed SWFs in the world. SAFE is the oldest among China's SIVs. It is the Hong Kong subsidiary of the State Administration of Foreign Exchange and it has been managing a portion of China's accumulated foreign exchange reserves since 1997.[124] The CIC and CADF were created in 2007. The CIC is controlled largely by MOF and holds assets in overseas markets as well as in China's financial system.[125] The CAD is by far China's smallest SIV. It was established by the China Development Bank and is focused on investing in Africa.[126]

SAFE has grown to hold approximately $570 billion in assets. Most of its investments are private holdings but SAFE is known to have large holdings in the UK equity market. The fund's wealth increased substantially over the past five years with a particularly strong growth in its foreign direct investments, which have increased from $645 million in 2005 to $3.1 billion in 2010. SAFE appears to have fairly limited U.S. exposure, with the Heritage Investment Tracker showing only one transaction, a $2.5 billion investment for a 20 percent share of TPG, a U.S. private equity firm.

Table 10. Assets in China's Sovereign Wealth Funds

Name	Assets *$ billions*	Operating Since
SAFE Investment Company	$567.9*	1997
China Investment Corporation	$409.6	2007
National Social Security Fund	$134.5	2000
China-Africa Development Fund	$5.0	2007

*Best estimate of their wealth.

Source: SWF Institute.

CIC's holdings in public and private companies are valued at just over $400 billion and include several holdings in the U.S. firms and funds. In December 2007, CIC purchased $5.6 billion worth of Morgan Stanley "equity units" convertible into common stock.[127] Other U.S. holdings include public stakes in iShares S&P Global Materials, General Growth Properties, AES, iShares S&P Global Energy, Consumer Discretionary Select Sector SPDR, Visa, and private holdings in Diamond S Shipping Group and JC Flowers PE Fund. According to the Heritage Investment Tracker, the book value of CIC's U.S. investments total $20.1 billion. The ownership shares of CIC's U.S. holdings are shown in Table 11. There are several holdings which surpass the 10 percent threshold and therefore constitute FDI. However, CIC claims to be a passive investor, and may not exert any direct influence on management.

The NSSF has been funded through the sale of state-owned shares, fiscal allocations from the government, and other investments. Though focused on China, approximately 20 percent of its investments are outside China, mostly in developing countries and Europe. Most of these foreign investments are undertaken indirectly through money managers. NSSF domestic holdings are primarily in bank deposits, bonds, investment trusts, asset-backed securities, stocks, securities investment funds, equity investment and equity investment funds. Its foreign holdings are in bank deposits, bank bills, negotiable certificates of deposit and other money market products, bonds, stocks, securities investment funds, and swaps for risk management, forward and other derivative financial instruments.[128]

Table 11. U.S. Holdings of CIC

Company	Industry	% Ownership
iShares S&P Global Materials	ETF	30.30%
General Growth Properties	Real Estate	29.90%
AES	Energy	16.10%
Morgan Stanley	Financials	9.95%
iShares S&P Global Energy	ETFs	9.70%
Consumer Discretionary Select Sector SPDR	ETFs	5.60%
Blackrock	Financials	4.80%
Morgan Stanley	Financials	4.30%
Visa	Financials	0.80%
Diamond S Shipping Group	Transport	
JC Flowers PE Fund	PE Fund	~80.00%

Source: SWF Institute.

In addition to these four SIV, China is considering the creation of a yet another SIV, under SAFE, funded with $300 billion as another avenue for diversifying China's foreign exchange holdings. This new SWF would be focused on investing in the United States and Europe.[129] Up until now, SAFE has accumulated only limited holdings in the United States, so this new vehicle could potentially result in a significant increase in China's investments in corporate America. The potential $50 billion increase in investible funds for CIC, which does hold U.S. investments. In terms of value, investments from this new SIV and CIC could potentially be significantly larger than direct investment flows made by SOEs and private Chinese firms.

B. Brief Description of Investments

CIC investment of $5.6 billion in Morgan Stanley in December of 2007 is one of the more prominent SWF investments by China in a U.S. company. Given the central importance of the financial industry to the U.S. economy and the high stakes of the financial crisis at the time, the move was carefully scrutinized and eventually approved by the Federal Reserve. To alleviate any U.S. discomfort in the transactions, CIC *"stated that it does not propose to control or exercise a controlling influence over Morgan Stanley and that its indirect investment will be a passive investment."*[130] This gave the CIC a voting stake just below 10 percent in Morgan Stanley putting it behind only State Street Corp in common shares.[131]

Chinese SWFs and other Chinese private and state-owned enterprises have always had a strong interest in energy and natural resources. This is exemplified by CIC's $1.58 billion investment in AES Corporation. AES Corporation is a U.S. based international energy company that is looking to expand into Asia. As a part of the deal CIC gains a 15percent share in AES and an agreement for the future purchase of a 35 percent stake in one of AES's wind energy subsidiaries, whereas AES receives an injection of capital to help it expand its operations.[132] Chinese investment in natural resources and energy is motivated both by the strategic nature of the industry and by a desire to protect fund returns from future inflationary pressures.

The real estate industry is another investment focus of Chinese SWFs. Among CIC's transactions is its $1.02 billion dollar investment in General Growth Properties (GGP), the second largest U.S. commercial real estate company specializing in shopping malls. CIC's investment came in November of 2010 as GGP was going through bankruptcy and the real estate market remained relatively depressed. The move gave CIC a 7.6 percent stake in GGP, while providing capital to support the firm's restructuring.[133]

Table 12 provides a sectoral breakdown of SIV activities based on the Heritage Investment Tracker. SIVs account for the lion's share of Chinese government-controlled investments in the financial and real estate industries and hold a 29 percent share in the energy industry. However, SIVs appear in none of the other sectors covered by the Heritage Investment Tracker.

Table 12. Cumulative Value and Shares of Investment in U.S. by China's State Sector, 2005-2011

	Million	SIV	SOE+SIE
Finance	18,560	97%	2%
Energy	5,890	29%	69%
Real Estate	4,300	70%	13%
Computer manufacturing	1,700	0%	100%
Transport equipment	1,630	0%	100%
Metals/metal mining	1,170	0%	86%
Software	400	0%	0%
Medical services	360	0%	0%
Agriculture	140	0%	100%
Manufacturing, other	120	0%	0%

Source: The Heritage Foundation, Copy of China-Global-Investment-Tracker2012 (1/5/2012).

VII. Role of State-Controlled Financial Services Companies and Preferential Support

As with other promoted aspects of its economy, the Chinese government subsidizes ODI that is consistent with the government's industrial policies. Preferential loans that carry below market interest rates or provide other forms of preferential access to credit are a common tool for supporting China's ODI. These loans are provided by China's state-owned policy banks, the Export-Import Bank of China (CEXIM) and the China Development Bank (CDB), state-owned insurance provider Sinosure, and to a lesser extent state-owned commercial banks. This section examines the roles played by these state-controlled financial services companies, assesses China's practices in light of international norms, and assesses their activities with regard to China's investments in the United States.

A. Protocols for Trade Finance and FDI

Government support for international trade and investment transactions is not uncommon. Broadly speaking, foreign trade and investments are considered to be desirable economic activities. While the private sector institutions that facilitate trade and investment are present in advanced countries, adequate "buy-side" institutions in many developing countries are deficient. Official credit agencies in advanced countries exist primarily to overcome such problems. The "concessional" element of such loans is limited under the auspices of the OECD's Arrangement on Export Credits.[134] The arrangement sets forth limitations on minimum interest rates, risk fees, maximum repayment terms, and other terms and conditions of officially supported export credits and tied aid. The arrangement also provides a mechanism for member countries to review offers and aid that go beyond prescribed limits.[135] The governments of Australia, Canada, the European Community, Japan, South Korea, New Zealand, Norway, Switzerland and the United States are participants to this arrangement. China is not.

The OECD is also the forum for the Declaration and Decisions on International Investment and Multinational Enterprises, which, among other things, suggests voluntary standards for Multinational Enterprises (MNEs). All 34 OECD members and nine non-members have subscribed to this declaration but China has not.[136]

B. China's State-Controlled Services Firms

The CDB and the CEXIM actively support China's ODI, though the state-owned commercial banks have also supported ODI since the beginning of the "Go Out" initiative.[137]

The importance of supporting ODI to the CDB is articulated in its mission statement, *"In response to the call of the state to encourage domestic enterprises to "Go Global" the Bank engages in a wide range of activities focused on international cooperation."*[138] The bank offers a wide array of loans to help target strategic international investment. Like much of Chinese OFDI, a large amount of the funding and incentives direct funds to developing countries, with some of the banks larger projects taking place in Venezuela, Argentina, Tanzania, Indonesia, and Ethiopia.[139]

The bank's total outstanding loans for international investments and collaboration projects have more than doubled from $64.5 billion in 2008 to $134.6 billion in 2010.[140] CDB's activities include support for PetroChina, Sinopec, CITIC Pacific, and Xi'an Electric Engineering Co. in Venezuela, and a $10 billion commitment to support the overseas expansion of equipment manufacturer with Xinjiang TBEA.[141]

CEXIM is now the largest export credit agency (ECA) in the world.[142] Though CEXIM is an export credit agency, it plays a critical role in supporting Chinese ODI. Indeed, one of its goals, articulated in its mission statement, is to *"assist Chinese companies with comparative advantages in their offshore contract projects and outbound investments.*" The bank promotes FDI with concessionary loans, which are 2 percent below market rates,[143] made to enterprises engaging in international investment projects. These loans support investment in infrastructure or other large projects, with the implicit understanding that follow-on purchases of needed goods and services will come from China.

The bank's total loan commitment to "Go Out" projects over the last five years tripled from approximately $15 billion in 2006 to just under $45 billion in 2010.[144]

CEXIM also operates in tandem with Sinosure, another Chinese government credit agency that offers various insurance products to facilitate exports and China's "Go Out" policy.[145] Sinosure's activities are less well-known than CEXIM's, but it is known to have provided assistance to Huawei and ZTE in support of telecom equipment projects abroad and to LDK Solar in support of photovoltaic exports and investments.[146]

The bulk of China's official support for FDI is likely aimed at investments in developing countries, but there has been some support for FDI in the United States. CNOOC's purchase of UNOCAL,[147] the China's Younger Group's purchase of U.S. textile assets,[148] and a private equity purchase of Boston Power[149] all appear to have benefitted from government-supported financial services firms.

C. Assessment

The official support provided by China's state-controlled financial services firms in support of foreign investment is geared not only to facilitate the expansion of China's companies, but also to expand China's exports. China is, in effect, promoting its ODI through concessional export finance, and promoting exports through ODI.

Though limited amounts of official concessional finance are common among the world's major exporters, there is a general consensus that China's support is excessive. As part of its FDI program, the OECD provides periodic reviews of national investment policies. In its most recent review of China, the OECD noted that China utilizes both financial and non-financial incentives to provide competitive advantages for Chinese firms.

The U.S. Export-Import Bank has characterized CEXIM's activities as consistently operating "with a financial edge over standard OECD financing."[150] European businesses and the EU Commission have also been critical of low Chinese insurance premiums, long repayment terms with long grace periods and subsidized interest rates resulting from official support.[151]

The full extent to which China's state-sponsored ODI support has influenced Chinese FDI in the United States is unknown. However, other U.S. government proceedings indicate that state-owned financial services firms have been providing support to Chinese firms exporting to the United States. As such, it is reasonable to conclude they are supporting China's ODI in the United States as well. One should also be suspicious when, as with CNOOC's attempt to purchase Unocal, a loan with a below-market interest rate is characterized as coming from a state-owned parent. In some cases, that parent has few assets independent of the listed firm and the loan is potentially a pass-through from one of China's policy banks.

VIII. Assessment of Capital Supports by State-Controlled Entities to State-Owned and State-Influenced Entities Investing Abroad

Subsidies have different economic effects, depending on the type of subsidy. Chinese firms investing in foreign markets receive a variety of subsidies in China, including grants, lower tax rates, subsidized loans, export credits, debt forgiveness, equity infusions, and preferential access to key production inputs. [152] In addition, as discussed in Section VII, Chinese financial institutions provide financial contributions to both the investing firms and their customers to support China's FDI and related projects. These subsidies have both direct and indirect effects on China's FDI.

The most direct effect comes from subsidies that reduce the cost of capital to the investing firm. This can happen at two levels. First, favorable lending for an international transaction in a favored industry relative to domestic projects would increase the expected rate of return of the foreign investment relative to a domestic investment. In this scenario, the favorable financial arrangement would motivate the firm to invest overseas rather than in China. Second, this same capital support would make the foreign investor a more formidable bidder for the foreign asset (or project). In a competitive bidding situation with all other things equal, the firm with lower capital costs would be able to outbid firms whose investments were based supported by market-based finance. This dynamic also tends to bid up the price of the asset, which is advantageous to the seller.[153]

A second form of assistance provided to SOEs, SIEs and private firms believed to be acting with delegated authority from the state is favorable project finance arrangements for large scale infrastructure projects sold to foreign governments.[154] As discussed above, these loans are not provided to the investor, but to the buyer. For example, suppose the project costs of the Chinese bid to a government using market-based finance are too high given the government's demand profile for the Chinese bundle of goods and services. However, the favorable financial arrangement lowers the total cost of the Chinese bid relative to the other bids, leading the government to choose the Chinese bundle.[155] Absent the favorable finance, the government would have chosen a different bidder. This type of financial support is increasingly common in developing markets and causing increasing frustration among firms based in the United States and other countries who find they are losing sales and investment opportunities to Chinese firms.

Although other subsidies provided to Chinese enterprises do not influence FDI directly, they too enhance the ability of SOEs to invest abroad. As noted in section II, corporate profits are an important source of FDI capacity. The panoply of subsidies and other preferences offered in China significantly enhances the profitability of Chinese SOEs. According to the Chinese Think Tank Unirule, these subsidies and preferences account for the entire profits of the state-owned sector from 2001 to 2009. Absent subsidies the real return on equity of SOEs would have been minus 1.5 percent.[156] Similarly, a study by the Hong Kong Institute for Monetary Research, cited in *The Economist*, found that SOE profits would disappear if they had to pay a market interest rate.[157] Thus, to the extent that FDI by Chinese SOEs is dependent on their profitability, China's non-FDIrelated subsidies have also played an important role in supporting China's FDI.

In addition to these explicit forms of support, Chinese investors also benefit from the implicit support of the Chinese government. SOEs, especially those owned by the central government, tend to be viewed as a better credit risk than warranted by their financial performance. While understandable in China, there is also evidence that government ownership is important to Chinese firms operating in the United States.[158]

The extent to which capital supports and other subsidies provide a competitive advantage in the U.S. market is difficult to determine. Though Chinese investments in the United States have been increasing, they remain well below investment levels from other countries that presumably finance their investments with market based funds. The impacts of China's official support are evident in certain industries, including wind turbines, when investments and market success came with the help of low interest loans at a time when the domestic industry was in the doldrums due to lack of demand.[159] While the competitive advantages provided by capital supports are not inconsequential, the availability of cheap finance is unlikely to be the deciding factor when the investors are deep-pocketed SOEs following explicit government plans to acquire technology and energy resources.

China's aggressive ODI-promotion and domestic subsidies can influence the U.S. economy in two ways. First, it provides advantages to potentially inefficient Chinese investors over domestic investors. While this advantage may financially benefit the seller, the overall economic effect may be less sanguine. The U.S. economy would be harmed if state largesse allowed less efficient SOEs operating in the United States to muscle out more efficient domestic producers. Second, the U.S. economy would be harmed if the Chinese investors promote exports from China at the expense of U.S. production or if the investors with government support shift production to China. Transactions involving Boston Power, Suntech, Syntroleum, and Altair Nano clearly resulted in displacement, though other investments have seemed to expand U.S. output.

IX. Stealth Investments by Chinese Firms

A. Reverse Mergers

Reverse mergers have been a common tool used by Chinese firms to raise capital in the United States. Normally, raising capital in the United States via an initial public offering (IPO) requires time consuming and expensive financial disclosure to the Securities and Exchange Commission (SEC).[160] Foreign as well as domestic firms can short-circuit this process by purchasing a U.S. company that is already listed. This initial maneuver allows entry into U.S. capital markets through an investment in a U.S. entity and should count as inward FDI because the Chinese entity is purchasing a U.S. firm. This entire process, as opposed to a traditional IPO filing, can be completed in under a couple of months and without close financial scrutiny.[161] In theory, a reverse merger could enable an SOE to invest in the United States without any of the scrutiny that would occur if an SOE decided to issue American Depositary Shares on the New York Stock Exchange.

Reverse mergers have been popular with Chinese firms. According to Morningstar data cited in *Barron's*, 350 Chinese firms used reverse mergers to list in the United States between 2003 and June 2010.[162] Until recently, reverse mergers were little known outside the financial community. This changed in recent years due to a series of de-listings and huge drops in share prices that afflicted more than two dozen Chinese firms that initially listed in the United States via reverse mergers.[163] These de-listings began after a series of investigations turned up numerous irregularities in the financial reporting.[164] According to a speech by SEC Commissioner Luis A. Aguilar, reverse mergers involving Chinese firms raised some unique issues:

- Systemic concerns with the quality of the auditing and financial reporting;
- Limitations on the ability to enforce U.S. securities laws and for investors to recover losses after subsequent disclosure claims are found to be untrue or fraudulent, even though the post-merger entity is registered in the United States.[165]

Although reverse mergers do enable Chinese enterprises to "fly under the radar" of U.S. disclosure requirements, they are unlikely to serve as a venue for large SOEs seeking to purchase valuable U.S. assets. First, the main point of a reverse merger in most cases is to access U.S. capital, not to conduct business in the United States. The target companies in a reverse merger would be of little value to a large SOE because they typically have few if any assets of value to offer.[166] Second, reverse mergers have been much more popular among small and medium sized private Chinese companies. This is because while many SOEs and larger private companies in China have access to large supplies of capital through the Chinese state, small and medium sized private firms often cannot access these funds as easily and thus look for alternative avenues to obtain capital such as reverse mergers.[167] While smaller SOEs owned by local governments have used reverse mergers, the large centrally owned SOEs are likely to enter using traditional means.[168] Third, although the purchase of the shell company takes place under the radar, once the investment occurs, the firm must obey SEC reporting requirements. In fact, it has been misstatements in financial reporting – false claims regarding revenues, facilities, and customers that were investigated by private entities in the United States and elsewhere, that unearthed the questionable activities that culminated in the de-listings. Fourth, due to the recent spate of reverse merger fiascos involving Chinese firms, the SEC in November approved tougher rules on reverse mergers at the NASDAQ Stock Market, New York Stock Exchange, and NYSE Amex. Among other things, the rules require that firms pursuing the reverse merger route file all important reports, including audited financial statements, with the SEC.[169]

Still, a review of 83 firms on Bloomberg's "Table of Chinese Reverse Mergers on U.S. Exchanges" did turn up three listed entities whose chain of subsidiaries includes SOEs. American Lorain Corporation, listed on NYSE AMEX, owns a holding company in the Cayman Islands. The holding company owns a chain of manufacturing facilities in China, one of which is owned with the state-owned Shandong Economic Development Investment Corporation, Ltd. American Loraine is headquartered in Junan County Shandong. In 2010, the firm had $2.9 million in U.S. revenues, accounting for 1.6 percent of its revenues.[170] China Cablecom Holdings ("CCH"), a BVI-registered firm listed on NASDAQ, owns broadcasting networks in China. Officially, CCH a joint-venture provider of cable television services in the PRC, operating in partnership with local SOEs in Hubei and Shandong provinces.[171] Kingold Jewelry, Inc., incorporated in Delaware and listed on NASDAQ, is an indirect holding company for Wuhan Vogue-Show Jewelry Co., Limited through Dragon Lead Group Limited. The entity has 47 shareholders, including the state-owned Beijing Shouchuang Investment Co. Ltd.[172] Zoom Technology, Inc. ("ZTI") is a Delaware holding company that engages in the manufacturing, research and development ("R&D"), and sale of mobile phones, wireless telecommunication modules, digital cameras, cable TV set-top boxes and GPS equipment. ZTI's main operating subsidiary, TCB Digital, is 20 percent owned by the SOE Tianjin Communication and Broadcasting Group Co., Ltd.[173]

For the most part, the U.S. entity resulting from the original Chinese investment does not substantially add to U.S. economic activity, but instead provides a way for Chinese entities to gain access to the U.S. capital market to support and expand operations in China. Investors, especially favored investors such as hedge funds, do obtain an opportunity to participate in China's economic growth. However, many investors instead have been battered by huge losses as the combination of accounting irregularities and illiquid shares led to sharp declines. According to an analysis by Reuters, the market capitalization of 122 reverse mergers stocks had shrunk by more than $18 billion by July 2010 from their peak valuations.[174]

In sum, reverse mergers have offered a back door into the United States for Chinese firms that seek to avoid the cost and full disclosures associated with IPOs. However, in practice, Chinese firms use reverse mergers to purchase U.S. corporate entities of little value. The shell companies are transformed into holding companies whose main revenue-generating assets are in China. Capital raised by selling shares on U.S. exchanges is then used to fund business and investment activities in China. Based on a preliminary analysis of a subset of Chinese reverse merger firms, there appears to be little direct SOE involvement with the process, and the SOEs found to be involved do not appear to pose any competitive threats. Indeed, the reverse merger phenomenon appears to be a symptom of shallow capital markets in China, not a threat to U.S. economic security.

B. Other Potential Back Doors to the U.S. Market

The Commission has expressed an interest in the possibility that SOEs could use other methods to purchase valuable U.S. firms "under the radar." The Commission's RFP specifically mentioned hedge funds, pools of largely unregulated capital that are used to invest in financial assets; and multiple SOEs acting in collusion to accumulate equity positions in publically traded U.S. firms.

Hedge funds typically contain investments from institutions and high wealth individuals. They are generally not required to divulge the identities of their investors. Thus, in theory, a hedge fund with investments from one or more SOEs could take significant positions in a listed U.S. company without regulators' knowledge. Based on data from HedgeStat.com, assets under management among the top 20 hedge funds at the beginning of 2012 ranged from $15.6 billion to $61.5 billion.[175] At full value, these funds would be able to accumulate significant shares of major listed companies.[176]

Though a theoretical possibility, this scenario seems unlikely. First, existing hedge funds have other large investors, existing investment themes, and existing fund managers, making it difficult for an SOE or group of SOEs to join an existing fund and become sufficiently dominant to override firm management and direct fund investments to a given target.

But hypothesize that a relatively small hedge fund with flexible management agrees to accept a large pool of funds from several SOEs and suddenly becomes large enough to take a 20 percent stake in Northrop Grumman Corporation (market cap of $15 billion). Could something like this occur in the real world? The answer is that it could, but it would not fly under the radar for long. The Securities Exchange Act requires beneficial owners of more than 5 percent of an issuer's equity securities to file Form 13D under Section 13(d) with the SEC. This form also requires the beneficial owner to disclose the source and amount of funds used in the purchase, announce whether the purpose of the purchase is to acquire control, and reveal any plans or proposals regarding any future actions. The hedge fund could instead file Form 13G if it does not intend to control or influence the acquired firm. Once ten percent ownership is achieved, additional disclosure is necessary, the new owners are required to disclose their interests via Form 3. Subsequent purchases or sales must be disclosed using Form 4 within two business days.[177]

From both practical and regulatory standpoints, this hypothetical takeover could not fly under the radar. An academic familiar with SEC regulations put it this way:

> If the {hedge fund} or "cabal" of SOEs were to acquire even a 5 percent stake in Northrop Grumman, they would have to disclose who they are, where the funds come from and what they are planning. The disclosure that they are Chinese of course would be reported far and wide and likely trigger a CFIUS review and significant scrutiny from the press, Congress and the administration.

Even if the proper filings were not made in a timely manner, it would be difficult for the Chinese investors to hide their attention from regulators:

> {T}he markets will soon get wind that there's a big player or players buying up the firm's shares and that there appears to be an attempted stealth grab for a controlling interest. Besides causing the share price to rise significantly, possibly to the extent that a takeover would be impractical, it would turn the market's and the regulators' attention toward wanting to know who is buying the shares and whether they're violating the reporting requirements. As it is such an important company,

it would also draw the attention of the media, the Congress and the administration.

In other words, there is scant possibility that the effort to acquire this important company would fly under the radar. However, even if such a takeover occurred, there would be other practical hurdles to technology theft or other acts that could harm U.S. security interests.

> {T}o make this work, they would have to have a significant enough equity stake in the company to name enough board members so they could influence who would be hired as management and then place individuals in the management that would be willing and able to somehow act against U.S. interests. Of course so as not to arouse suspicion, the Chinese would have to find this set of treacherous senior executives among the limited group of business people that the markets, media, corporate world, etc. would consider as viable candidates to run a large defense contractor such as Northrop. Then we would have to assume that treacherous senior executives could somehow be able to direct the company's employees to do things against the interest of the U.S. (such as transfer its technology to China) without anyone the wiser (unless we assume that an entire company's board, management and workforce immediately bows to the whims of their shareholders, even to the point of being traitors).

In short, this academic makes a persuasive case that it would be virtually impossible for state controlled entities to collusively acquire shares of large, strategically important firms. The bottom line is that such a purchase would trigger regulatory filings by the small hedge fund and those filings would have to identify the hypothetical cabal of SOEs. In addition, there would be a price response in the intended target that would alert the market that something was afoot. Even if a takeover occurred, it is inconceivable that the cabal would be able to force the company's employees to suddenly act against their country's interest.

Hedge funds are also part of the reverse merger story. As with reverse mergers in general, their involvement is not so much to generate Chinese FDI in the United States, but to tap U.S. capital markets for Chinese entities operating in China.

As part of the reverse merger process, shares of the merged entity are placed with a hedge fund, usually at a special price, before they are publicly traded. As part of the deal, the hedge funds also gain influence over the entities' choice of auditor, investor-relations firm, and chief financial officer.[178] Although hedge funds are well placed to profit from the arrangement, this type of arrangement is unlikely to result in important U.S. assets ending up with SOEs.

Although purchases of any large U.S. firm by a large SOE would be difficult to hide, it is certainly plausible that purchases of smaller firms by SOEs could go unnoticed, at least initially.

The most well known example of this type of purchase involves Huawei, an ostensibly private firm in China believed to have close ties to China's military.

Huawei appeared to have pulled off a transaction "under the radar" when it purchased assets of 3Leaf Systems (3Leaf) in mid-2010. Huawei purchased $2 million in technology assets from the California cloud computing specialist and employed 15 3Leaf employees without notifying CFIUS as required by law. CFIUS became aware of the deal only after a 3Leaf executive identified himself as a Huawei consultant on the career networking site LinkedIn.[179]

CFIUS subsequently requested that Huawei submit the transaction for CFIUS review.[180] CFIUS decided against the deal and Huawei ultimately decided to withdraw its application and unwind the transaction.[181] This type of approach, which focuses on smaller firms and uses non-equity transactions, perhaps offers the most promising way for Chinese SOEs to acquire U.S. assets without triggering publicity and reviews by CFIUS. However, even this technique is potentially discoverable because CFIUS agencies now have "non-notified transactions procedures" that they use to identify potentially problematic transactions that have not been notified.[182]

X. CHINA'S REGULATORY FRAMEWORK FOR OUTWARD FDI

This section explores how the government of China regulates outward FDI and assesses proposed changes to the current regulatory system.

China does not have a laissez faire attitude toward outward FDI. Most outward investments involve reviews and approvals from officials from the central and sub-central government agencies. In some instances, the review extends all the way to the State Council.

China's regulatory system for outward FDI is cumbersome, requiring approvals from various government agencies. The need to streamline the system is acknowledged by government officials and there is some movement toward reforming the system to facilitate outward FDI.

As with other aspects of China's economic reforms, it would be a mistake to conclude from recent efforts to facilitate outward investments that China's government intends to move toward an approach in which outward investment decisions are made by company management alone. Current reforms are aimed at making the existing system more efficient, not making it more company centric. As one Chinese government researcher explained,

> In most countries, the control over foreign investment has moved historically from strict control to a complete liberalization through gradual loosening of the procedures. However, the principal objective of China's internationalization strategy is not to give up management control, but to improve the efficiency of outward foreign investment.[183]

A. Agencies and Procedures Involved in Outbound Foreign Direct Investment

Due to the existence of capital controls, Chinese businesses that desire to engage in FDI are required to have their investments approved by the government. However, the regulation of outward investment is somewhat of a hodgepodge, involving different departments and levels of government, and is generally perceived to be unnecessarily complicated.[184]

Generally speaking, Chinese investors are required to at least get approval or register with three governmental departments for outbound direct investment: the National Development and Reform Commission ("NDRC") and its provincial equivalents ("DRC"), which examine and approve the proposed investment; the Ministry of Commerce, which issues an overseas investment certificate and handles other details regarding the investment; and the State Administration of Foreign Exchange (SAFE), which provides foreign currency needed for the investment.[185]

First, Chinese enterprises need to obtain approval of the Development and Reform Commissions. The procedure depends on the magnitude of the investment, the type of enterprise making the investment, and the industry and country targeted by the Chinese enterprise. For relatively small outward investments, (i.e., less than $300 million for resource development projects and less than $100 million for other projects) the enterprises require the approval of relevant sub-national DRCs. Investments above these thresholds require approval from the NDRC. State-owned enterprises under the central SASAC are only required to report their investment plans to the NDRC, but their investments must be approved by the central SASAC. Non-central SASACs must also have their investments approved by their appropriate SASAC owner.

Certain investments are considered sensitive go through a somewhat different process that involves provincial DRCs, the NDRC, and potentially the State Council. Projects subject to greater scrutiny include investments in countries with whom China has not established diplomatic relations, countries subject to international sanctions, countries in a state of war or general turmoil, and sensitive industries such as telecommunications, water resource development, large-scale land development, power grids and media.[186]

Once approved by the relevant development commission, the investing enterprise must obtain an overseas investment certificate from the Ministry of Commerce (MOFCOM) or its sub-national equivalents. There are three categories of investments. First, approval from MOFCOM is required when the target country is controversial (e.g., North Korea) or lacks diplomatic relations with China; when the outbound investment is at least $100 million or involves the interest of more than one country; or when the investment is in an offshore special purpose vehicle ("SPV") to be directly or indirectly controlled by a Chinese company or owners. Second, provincial commercial bureaus review lower-value investments (i.e., valued at between $10 million and $100 million); investments in the resource and minerals industries, and investments that seek to raise capital from other Chinese investors. Third, central SOEs and sub-national SOEs that are setting up an overseas non-financial enterprise or acquiring one through M&A must obtain approval from either MOFCOM (central SOEs) or its provincial bureaus (sub-national SOEs).[187] After obtaining approval from commercial authorities, Chinese investors register in embassies and consulates in the investment countries/regions.

The final step in the process is to register with SAFE. Investors register with municipal foreign exchange bureaus when the planned Chinese investment is less than $10 million.[188]

Chinese entities that seek to establish or acquire financial institutions go through a different review process that requires the approval of China's central bank, the People's Bank of China. Financial institutions must have foreign exchange equity of at least RMB 80 million ($12.4 million at the average exchange rate of 2011). The equity threshold for non-financial firms is RMB 100 million ($15.5 million). Chinese entities already operating overseas must also obtain approval from the central bank as well as from the relevant commercial bureaus. Under special circumstances, supervisory agencies such as China Bank Regulatory Commission must also approve of the investment.[189]

B. Government's Role

1. Does the Government Encourage FDI?

The Chinese government encourages outbound FDI activities by Chinese firms through overall guidance, financial support, and through efforts to streamline the current approval process.

Although Chinese outward FDI has only recently been attracting attention, outward investment by Chinese firms began very early in the economic reform process. Initially, this investment was undertaken by sub-national government-owned economic and technical collaboration companies and was geared toward establishing joint ventures in developing countries.[190] The top echelons of China's central government encouraged outward FDI during the 1980s as a tool for structural adjustment and by the 1990s private-sector firms began expanding overseas. The "Go Out" strategy was initially conceived in the mid 1990s, promulgated in 2000,[191] and was emphasized in the official report of the 17th Party Congress in 2007.[192]

Today, the Chinese government makes no secret of its desire to expand the overseas presence of Chinese firms. In a recent essay Li Zhaoxi described China's "Go Out" policy as a combination of national goals and company objectives.[193] Li is the senior research fellow and deputy director of the Enterprise Research Institute of the State Council's Development Research Center, so his opinion is likely authoritative.

According to Li, government encouragement of outward investment has three primary goals:

- securing natural resources, especially energy and raw materials;
- contributing to China's economic adjustment by eliminating excess supply, promoting capital accumulation, and accelerating technological innovation; and
- improving international competitiveness by establishing overseas distribution networks, developing managerial talent, and promoting Chinese brands.[194]

Thus, official support for overseas investments by Chinese firms is not simply an expression of pride in China's successful economic development over the past three decades or a natural outgrowth of China's globalization. For Beijing, the expansion of China's businesses is a means to achieve certain policy goals for China's economy. Because of China's size and its large economy, its efforts to achieve these goals are likely to have, and are already having, noticeable impacts in international markets.

As discussed in Section V, SOEs account for the lion's share of China's FDI by value. The ability of SOEs to invest abroad is supported not only by the government's "Go Out" policy, but also by financial support afforded to the countries SOEs. This support includes not only subsidies in the parlance of international trade law, which must be financial contributions that are specific and confer a benefit, but also through informal preferences that provide China's SOE with preferred access to capital and market power.[195]

China employs a number of programs to facilitate foreign investments. What follows is a sampling of such programs, most of which are aimed at facilitating resource-oriented investments.

- In order to support Chinese enterprises in making industrial investments in Africa, the Chinese government has signed an inter-governmental discount preferential loans agreement framework with 26 African countries, including Sudan, Kenya, Zambia, Tanzania, Gabon, Cameroon, Ghana and Mozambique.
- The Bank of China, working at the direction of the Ministry of Finance and Ministry of Foreign Trade and Economic Cooperation, administers a special fund to provide guarantees required for tendering and meet other needs of projects that are consistent with the economic and trading policies of China.[196]
- The government provides export tax rebates/exemptions to enterprises making capital investments to develop African resources.
- The Central Foreign Trade Developing Fund is a RMB 400 million Fund to support interest rate subsidies for domestic loans that support Sino-Russian cooperation projects.
- The Ministry of Finance and MOFCOM jointly manage a market Development Fund for small-and-medium sized enterprises. The fund can be used for a number of different purposes, including the overseas acquisition of technologies and brands.

Government efforts to promote outward investments are not limited to the central government. Whereas local governments in the United States are putting together missions to attract FDI from China (see section XV), some local governments in China are putting together "trade" missions oriented towards investments and providing financial support as well. For example, the government of Fujian province has an annual budget that compensates local companies for feasibility studies and other costs related to the establishment of overseas processing projects.[197] Local governments also provide funds to support FDI that leads the recipient firm to shift jobs to China.[198]

2. Does the Government Influence Which Sectors Receive Foreign Investments?

The Chinese government lays out the overarching objectives for foreign investments, but also provides specific details. The NDRC and Ministry of Commerce periodically issue the Overseas Investment Industrial Guidance Policy, which sets forth the broad parameters, and the Overseas Investment Industrial Guidance Catalogue, which provides specific details on the sectors where investments are encouraged. Aside from these documents, the "Go Out" policy itself is focused partly on securing energy and other resources for China.[199]

Investments are classified into three groups: banned, allowed, and encouraged. Investments are banned if they could impair national security or harm society or require use of unique arts or technologies.[200] Overseas investments are encouraged if they:

- are used to obtain resources that are in short supply in China;
- boost exports of certain equipment and labor; and
- augment China's capacity for R&D and make use of internationally available advanced technologies and management expertise.

The current FDI Catalogue contains industries from all four major economic sectors. There are five encouraged investments involving agriculture, forestry, and fisheries; nine encouraged investments in mining; nineteen in manufacturing; and seven in services. The table below contains selected examples of investments encouraged by the catalogue.

Table 13. A Sampling of Encouraged Overseas Investments

Major Sector	Specific Types of Promoted Investments
Agriculture, forestry, and fisheries	-Certain kinds of rubber plantations; -Forest harvesting, cultivation, and transport; -Plantations of oil bearing crops, cotton, and vegetables
Mining	-Exploration and production of petroleum, natural gas, and related services -Exploration, production, and use of iron ores, manganese ores, and chrome ores -Exploration, production, and use of copper, bauxite, lead, zinc, nickel, cobalt, titanium, vanadium, niobium and tin -Exploration and production of nonconventional petroleum
	-Wood processing -Paper and pulp processing -Assembly of various machinery, including agricultural machinery and R&D of construction machinery -Manufacturing of chemical products with technologies that are not available in China
Manufacturing	-Manufacturing of civil communication and mobile satellite -Assembly and manufacturing of bearing instruments -Assembly manufacturing of consumer electronics, electrical equipment, batteries, and lighting equipment -Passenger car products, special purpose vehicle products, automatic transmission products, and automotive electronics
Services/other	-International distribution networks -Construction and operation of communications networks -Software development and application -High tech product research -Media to promote Chinese culture

Source: Overseas Investment Industrial Guidance Catalogue.

The selected industries demonstrate that the Chinese government has a very good idea of the types of investments it views as desirable and Chinese companies appear to follow the government's guidance. Given the above, it is perhaps no accident that China has been a major investor in Africa, Australia, and certain resource-rich Latin American countries. Chinese oil companies alone spent $25 billion on overseas assets in 2010, accounting for one-fifth of global deals in extractive industries.[201] Some investments are clearly oriented toward technology acquisition, while others seem aimed at acquiring know-how that would enable China to produce products that it currently imports. Investments in U.S. auto parts companies seem less like the natural outcome of China's comparative advantage and more like the next logical step for Chinese firms in need of technology. CNOOC's investments in U.S. shale oil ventures, Huawei's investments in cloud computing, and Yintong's investment in a lithium-titanate battery producer all seem to be according to plan. However, some other products mentioned in this report, such as solar panels, though encouraged in other planning documents, are not listed in the guidance catalogue.

3. Does the Government Influence Which Countries Receive FDI?

Although Chinese policies do not explicitly direct companies to invest in specific countries, the overall direction provided in the five year plans and in official pronouncements, the specific projects identified in the investment catalogues, and financial programs provided by the government strongly influence the investment activities of Chinese firms, including what countries receive investments. This has been the case since the "Go Out" policy was first articulated at the highest levels of the Chinese government and it continues to be the case today.

When the "Go Out" policy was formalized with the 10th Five Year Plan, President Jiang Zemin left no doubt as to where China's investments should go:

> At this time of energetically expanding export, we shall, with proper steps and leadership, organize and support a group of enterprises with advantages and strengths to go abroad to make investments and set up factories there, particularly in Africa, Central Asia, the Middle East, Eastern Europe, and South America.[202]

Given these explicit government instructions, it is not surprising that such a large share of Chinese investments have been directed toward these developing economies. In recent years, there has been a dramatic increase in investment to OECD countries. These investments are clearly related to the growing importance of technology acquisition, new energy, and famous brands to China's national economic goals. After all, to be really famous, a brand has to be well known in high-income countries. The focus on Europe and the United States can also be inferred from the recently announced plans to create a new SWF focused on the United States and Europe. As discussed in section VI, the planned size of the fund is large, $400 billion, and has potential to dramatically increase the value of China's investments in the United States.

4. Current Policy Direction with Regards to ODI

Oddly, given that the Chinese government is promoting outward investment, China's regulatory framework for FDI is considered to be cumbersome and in need of reform.[203] One would expect that the impetus for reform would come from the firms that currently invest or plan to, but the momentum for reform is also coming from the government itself. Several reforms have already take place, and it appears that more are planned.

In reporting on the "Go Out" strategy in March 2011 before the Eleventh National People's Congress, Premier Wen Jiaobao stated that it is important to "improve relevant support policies, simplify examination, and approval procedures, and provide assistance for qualified enterprises and individuals to invest overseas."[204] Also in 2011, the NDRC's *Suggestions on 2011 Priorities for Reforming the Economic System* indicated it was necessary to improve the laws, regulation, and administration for overseas investments.

Other non-governmental organizations in China are also calling for reforms of China's ODI framework, but these voices are not likely to have a significant voice in the reform process.[205] Suggestions include improving access to capital for smaller firms that want to invest in Africa, simplifying approval procedures through further decentralization, and greater cooperation between Chinese enterprises and local governments and civil organizations in host countries. The joint World Bank-DRC study also advocates continued promotion of ODI, especially by private companies.[206]

The recent expansion of FDI, as well as the experience acquired by Chinese investors, suggests that at some point the urge for government control articulated by Li Zhaoxi will fade. Some studies suggest that this change is already beginning to take place. For example, although the NDRC and MOFCOM are still involved in the investment approval process, their role is increasingly to offer advice, information, and support to foreign investors.[207] Still, the fact that Chinese firms must clear their investments with the bodies instrumental with developing China's general and more specific industrial plans suggests that government guidance remains an important determinant of the industries, countries, and goals of many Chinese companies investing abroad. At the same time, other steps taken by the central government suggest that the impulse to control the investment activities of SOEs remains.

Concerned with some of the poor investment decisions made by SOEs, central SASAC in 2011 announced interim measures requiring SOEs and their foreign subsidiaries to base their FDI transactions prices on formal appraisals. In 2012, additional measures were put in place to prevent SOEs from investing in non-core areas without SASAC approval.[208]

XI. Economic Benefits of Chinese Foreign Investment in the United States

This section considers the economic benefit of Chinese FDI in two ways. First, it presents and analyzes official data on the operations of Chinese-owned firms in the United States. As part of this analysis, it considers how potential undercounting of Chinese investments, as well as recent increases in China's investment activities, affect the overall conclusions drawn from the official data. Second, it presents research on specific investments and attempts to determine whether there were any identifiable changes that can be attributed to Chinese ownership.

A. Benefits on the Basis of Official Data

There are two types of overarching benefits arising from FDI: input-related and efficiency-related. Input-related benefits arise due to enhancements of factors of production: labor and physical capital. The foreign ownership may add workers and increase investment in property plant and equipment. Although such augmentations are most prominent with so-called "greenfield" investments, they can also arise when the foreign invested firm is the product of a merger. Think, for example, of Fiat's announcement in late 2011 that it plans to invest $500 million to expand and retool one of its Chrysler factories in Toledo, Ohio and create 1,100 new jobs.[209] Efficiency-related benefits can arise from several factors, including improved management, the introduction of better manufacturing techniques, the improvements in the use of overhead, and economies of scale that may result from entering new markets.

Table 14 contains different measures of capital inputs for the last five years for which data are available. There are two "flow" measures, capital inflows and expenditures on property, plant, and equipment ("PPE"); and one "stock" measure, total assets. Capital inflows reflect actual FDI flows from

China, while PPE expenditures reflect annual output-enhancing spending by foreign investors.[210] Assets reflect both tangible and intangible assets owned by foreign investors. Data on assets and PPE expenditures are presented for majority-owned affiliates ("MOAs").[211] From 2006 to 2010, capital inflows from China averaged $444 million per year, only 0.2 percent of total capital inflows. Chinese-owned MOAs spent less than $40 million on average from 2005 to 2009, accounting for only 0.2 percent of total PPE expenditures by MOAs. Assets owned by Chinese MOAs were also a small fraction of the assets held by all MOAs. Thus by all three capital input measures, China's share is extremely small.

Table 14. U.S. Capital Inflows, Expenditures on PPE, and Assets, 2005-09 Averages

	China $bil.	Total $bil.	China's Share
Capital inflows 1/	0.44	228.12	0.20%
Expenditures for property, plant, and equipment (MOA)	0.04	165.19	0.02%
Assets (MOA) 2/	7.73	9,663.47	0.08%

1/ Data cover 2006-2010.

2/ The entry for assets in 2008 was suppressed. It has been estimated as the average of the values in 2007 and 2009.

Source: Bureau of Economic Analysis; author's calculations.

Comparative data on employment and compensation by Chinese owned affiliates in the United States are presented in Table 15. The data are consistent with that of capital inputs: Chinese-invested firms have played a minor role in the U.S. economy both in absolute terms and relative to the universe of foreign owned firms.

Table 15. U.S. Employment and Compensation at Affiliates, 2005-09 Averages

	China	Total	China's Share
Employment (thou.) 1/	4.2	5,970.4	0.07%
Employment (MOA) (thou.)	2.4	5,408.0	0.05%
Compensation (MOA) ($bil.)	0.28	386.33	0.04%

1/ Data for Chinese-owned MOAs in 2008 and 2009 were ranged. The average was computed by assuming the range maxima.

Source: Bureau of Economic Analysis; author's calculations.

The employment and compensation at Chinese-owned affiliates are growing; they were at extremely modest levels through 2009.

How much employment have Chinese firms created in the last five years? The answer to this question is hampered by three factors. Official data at the time of this writing only runs through 2009. Moreover, official data are presented on a net basis, so the actual jobs created may be offset by job losses at other firms. Finally, data on actual jobs created by individual firms in the United States are confidential and can only be known if publicized by individual firms. It is possible to provide a ballpark estimate of the increase in jobs at firms since 2007. Official data indicate that in 2007, there were 2,000 employees at firms ultimately owned by Chinese investors. Data for 2009 are confidential, but the range maxima provided by BEA is 9,999. An unofficial tally of data by InvestUSA (now known as SelectUSA) suggests that 13,000 jobs will be created by Chinese investments announced in 2010 and early 2011. Together, this information implies, at best, the creation of 21,000 jobs over the past five years.[212]

Efficiency of investments can be measured by combining a variety of indicators (e.g., value added per employee, sales per employee, return on assets ("ROA"), and return on sales ("ROS"). Because China's footprint in the United States was so modest through 2009, the measurement of efficiency-related indicators, shown in Table 16, has been conducted at a highly aggregated level and should be interpreted with care. Sales per employee at China's MOAs are higher than for all MOAs, though this may reflect the prominence of Chinese affiliates in the wholesale sector. A better measure of labor productivity is value added per employee. By this measure, productivity of Chinese-owned affiliates is 23 percent lower than at all MOAs. Chinese affiliates are significantly lower in ROS and ROA indicators as well.

Based on the discussion above, it is clear that through 2009 Chinese-owned affiliates in the United States were barely even a rounding error in the official FDI statistics. Although it may be true that Chinese firms are underrepresented in the official statistics, it is unlikely that this conclusion would be any different if the full universe of Chinese firms were included in the BEA's data set. Based on nongovernment sources, that situation is now changing and Chinese firms are beginning to play a more pronounced role in the U.S. economy that is likely to be borne out by official data in the coming years. Every five years, the BEA conducts a more thorough benchmark survey of foreign direct investment in the United States. The next survey is scheduled to take place in 2012, with results available in 2014. At that time, the role played by Chinese-owned affiliates will be much clearer.

Table 16. Indicators of Efficiency for MOAs, 2005-09 Averages

	China	Total	China/Total
Sales per employee ($thou./worker)	908.7	558.7	163%
Value added per employee ($thou./worker)	87.4	113.9	77%
Return on sales (%) 1/	0.5%	2.1%	24%
Return on assets (%) 1/	0.2%	0.7%	24%

1/ Income for Chinese-owned MOAs in 2008 was not disclosed. Thus, the Chinese ratios are computed based on only four years of data in both the numerator and denominator.

Source: Bureau of Economic Analysis; author's calculations.

B. Case Studies

Though trivial on a national basis, Chinese FDI can play a more pronounced and noticeable role in the states and localities where investments take place. This section of the report examined three investments that illustrate how Chinese investments have played out, Nexteer Automotive is what remains in Michigan of GM's Saginaw Steering division, which was spun out of General Motors (GM) in 1998 as part of Delphi.[213] In 2010, a joint venture, partly owned by a subsidiary of a major state-owned producer of aviation equipment, purchased the GM's Nexteer facilities in the United States. GM would have closed these facilities if it had not found a buyer, so this investment had a significant effect on the local community.[214] The company has seen its revenues grow since the ownership change, has pursued much needed equipment upgrades, and has added 600 jobs while honoring a preexisting labor agreement. Although Nexteer is considering opening up a factory in Beijing, the chairman of AVIC Auto has pledged not to gut the Nexteer's U.S. facilities.[215]

Another company with substantial U.S. investments is Wanxiang America, the U.S. subsidiary of China's Wanxiang Group (Wanxiang). From its humble beginnings as a county government factory producing universal joints, Wanxiang has become one of China's top producers of auto parts with substantial international holdings.[216] After growing in China, in part by supplying U.S. parts makers such as Zeller through exports, Wanxiang invested in a U.S. sales outpost in Kentucky, Wanxiang America, in 1993 and received its first order from GM in 1997.[217] By 2007, Wanxiang America was generating $1 billion in revenues and GM, Ford, and Chrysler were among its top clients.[218] But as Wanxiang's sales were growing, the U.S. parts industry was hemorrhaging red ink. From 1999 to 2006, 36 U.S. parts producers filed for bankruptcy protection.[219] Wanxiang America expanded by purchasing some of these financially distressed firms and shifting a portion of their production to China.[220] Nevertheless, companies purchased by Wanxiang usually continued to operate and Wanxiang reinvested its profits in the U.S. market.[221] In all, the company has purchased or taken stakes in 20 U.S. companies and is believed to employ 5,000 Americans.[222]

The U.S. financial sector has been the major recipient of investments from China. A large portion of this investment occurred in late 2007, when U.S. financial stocks were plummeting due to the bursting of the housing bubble. As noted earlier, CIC purchased 9.9 percent of Morgan Stanley for $5.6 billion. China's CITIC Securities purchase $1 billion stake in Bear Stearns. China's CDB purchased infused $3 billion into Barclays, the firm that eventually purchased the North American assets of Lehman Brothers after its bankruptcy. Though the U.S. financial situation continued to deteriorate after these investments, these and other large infusions from other nations' sovereign wealth funds probably prevented the U.S. financial sector from deteriorating more rapidly.

XII. Comparison of Chinese Investments with Investments from Other Developed Countries

> China's overseas FDI has taken a different form from that of the U.S., Japan, Europe, and the other advanced countries. The latter have shaped their FDI according to the advantages of their domestic industries, using overseas FDI to create a worldwide industrial system. However, China's FDI is chiefly the result of governmental engineering, especially China's strategy of "Going Global".[223]

As the above quotation illustrates, and as discussed in section XIII, the Chinese government has played an important role in directing the pace of Chinese FDI. This section compares Chinese direct investments in the United States to direct investments from OECD countries in terms of job creation and other measures. It then briefly reviews a subset of direct investments and assesses whether their operations reflect market forces, Chinese government policies, or both.

A. Comparison with FDI from Other OECD Countries

The official data on the operations of Chinese-owned firms, collected by BEA, offer the most detailed information on the behavior of Chinese-owned firms. For many years, China's direct investments in the United States were relatively minor and therefore were lumped into a basket category until the early 1990s. Tables covering the operations of U.S. affiliates of foreign multinational corporations are available electronically on the BEA's web site beginning with 1997. The analysis in this section is based on that data, which currently runs through 2009. Because the official data do not capture 2010 and 2011, they leave out many of the investments cited by private sources. However, the official data are the only force for examining the sourcing behavior, job creation trends, profitability, and research and development of Chinese FDI. The official data also include similarly detailed information about investments from countries other than China.

As noted above, Chinese FDI was relatively minor until recently, and is still fairly insignificant when compared to the investment levels of countries whose firms have been long-time investors in U.S. assets. Nearly all of these long-time investors belong to the Organisation for Economic Cooperation and Development (OECD), a grouping that includes many of the word's advanced economies.[224] Several of these OECD countries do not have very large economies and very few of their firms engaged in FDI in the United States. As such, BEA's data did not specify these countries separately for many indicators prior to 2001. The analysis below is confined to OECD countries for which data were available during the entire 1997-2009 period.[225]

Sourcing: One way to compare sourcing patterns is to compare the ratios of affiliate imports to affiliate value added and to sales. High values for these ratios indicate that U.S. affiliates of foreign-owned firms are predisposed to importing rather than to producing in the United States or purchasing U.S.-made inputs. Low values indicate that that the U.S. affiliates concentrate more on adding value in the United States than on importing. An increasing ratio indicates that there is a movement toward increasing imports relative to U.S. production.

During the period covering 1997 to 2009, Chinese majority-owned affiliates did not have an unusual sourcing patter relative to affiliates for other countries. As shown in Figure 22, the median value for affiliates from Japan, New Zealand, and Korea exceeded 200 percent, indicating that affiliates' imports tended to exceed value added by a 2-to-1 ratio. For Korea, the median ratio was a whopping 11.6-to-1. The median value for majority-owned affiliates from China was only 0.7-to-1, about the same as for affiliates owned by Spanish, Italian, and Mexican MNCs. True, affiliates from several other countries had lower median values than affiliates from China, but nothing in the distribution suggests that Chinese firms have an abnormally high propensity to import.

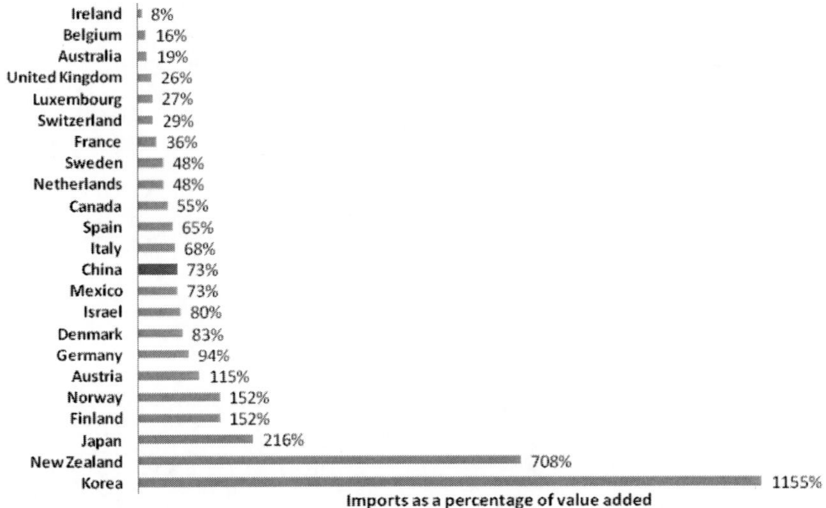

Source: Bureau of Economic Analysis; author's calculations.

Figure 22. Affiliate Imports Relative to Value Added for Majority-Owned U.S. Affiliates, Median Values, 1997-2009.

On the other hand, data shown in Figure 23 definitely indicate that Chinese affiliates as a group were more reliant on imports in 2009. Imports by Chinese affiliates exceeded value added by a ratio of 1.8-to-1, behind only Japanese (2.4-to-1) and Korean (11-to-1) affiliates. The high value in 2009 could be an aberration – this ratio jumped two other times before returning to more typical values – but it bears watching, especially if Chinese affiliates decide to follow the Korean model.

Employment: Although Chinese FDI supports the creation of jobs in the United States, jobs created and supported have been modest when compared with those of most other OECD countries. Figure 24 below compares employment changes over two periods for majority-owned affiliates, 1997 to 2006 and 2007 to 2009.[226] The data are sorted based on additions to employment from 2007 to 2009.

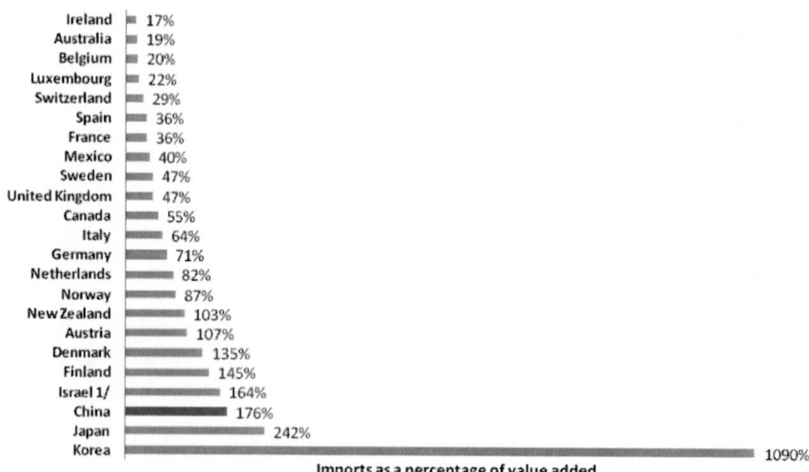

Source: Bureau of Economic Analysis; author's calculations.

Figure 23. Affiliate Imports relative to Value Added for Majority-Owned U.S. Affiliates, 2009.

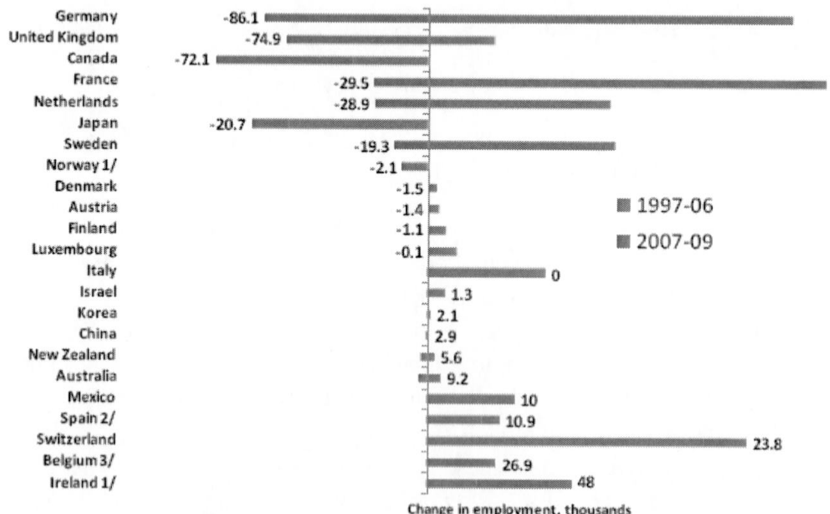

Source: Bureau of Economic Analysis; author's calculations.

Figure 24. Changes in Employment at Majority-Owned U.S. Affiliates, 1997-2006 and 2007-2009.

During this later period, German affiliates showed the largest losses, with employment shrinking by 86,000. Irish-owned affiliates had the largest increase, with employment growing by 48,000. Employment by Chinese affiliates expanded by nearly 3,000 workers from 2007 to 2009, a modest number but still better than majority-owned affiliates from Germany, the United Kingdom, Canada, France, the Netherlands, Japan, Sweden, Norway, Denmark, Austria, Finland, Luxembourg, Italy, Israel, and Korea. The modest gain is all the more impressive given that it occurred during a recession.[227] At least in the aggregate data, there is nothing to suggest a widespread move by Chinese owned affiliates to shut down operations and move production to China, though there are some instances of this happening in the case studies.

Research & Development: Through 2009, there was little R&D activity in Chinese majority-owned U.S. affiliates. In a majority of years, the value of R&D conducted by these affiliates was either not disclosed or zero. In recent years R&D expenditures by Chinese affiliates has risen from nothing to $21 million. However, this level of spending would place China last relative to the 22 other OECD countries whose data was reviewed.

Based on recent increases in investment documented by nongovernment sources, the level of R&D that can be attributed to Chinese affiliates is likely to rise significantly in the coming years' official statistics. Still, it would take very large increases to put China's majority-owned affiliates in the same ballpark as affiliates from Canada ($1.1 billion); the Netherlands ($1.8 billion); France ($5.0 billion); Germany ($5.5 billion); the United Kingdom ($6.6 billion); Japan ($7.1 billion); and Switzerland ($9.1 billion).

Profitability: The BEA's data can be used to calculate return on assets (ROA) for majority-owned affiliates from 1997 to 2009. The figure below plots a distribution, by country of affiliate, showing the first quartile value at the bottom of each line, the third quartile value at the top of each line, and median value, identified with a triangle.

The median profitability measures are depressingly low — ROAs are less than 1 percent for the majority of countries.[228] For Norway, Israel, China, and Spain, the median ROA values are actually negative. This result provides modest support for the view that Chinese affiliates are not driven by profitability. Yet other countries' affiliates also have performed poorly on an ROA basis, so it is difficult to draw any sweeping conclusions from these comparisons. Chinese affiliates are definitely among the laggards, but they have company.

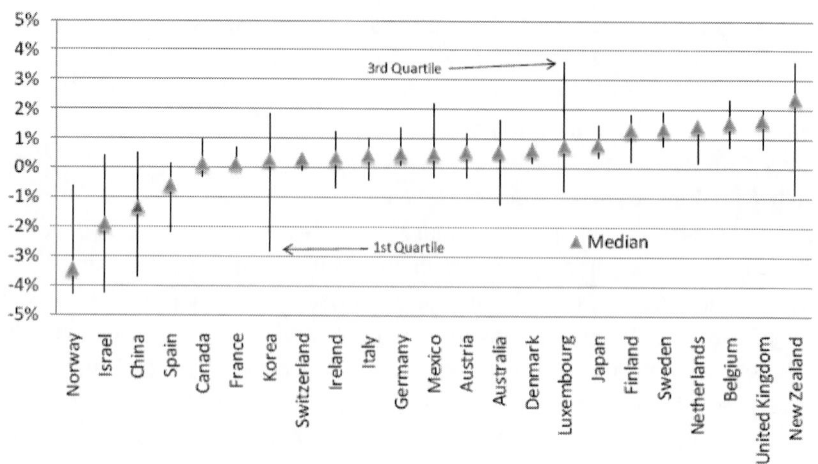

Source: Bureau of Economic Analysis; author's calculations.

Figure 25. Partial Distributions of ROAs for China and Select OECD Countries, 1997- 2009.

B. Are the Official Data Underestimating the Size of China's Investments?

As mentioned earlier, private entities are tracking investments from China and making those data available on the Internet. However, these data sources do not track the operations of affiliates, and therefore do not publish data on employment, value added, imports, income or other data on the operations of foreign-owned affiliates in the United States. Still, it is instructive to compare the different sources, as shown in Table 17. BEA data on capital inflows are relatively low compared to other measures. This disparity is not surprising because the BEA's investment flow and historical cost data only count actual capital flows and do not count any capital obtained from a U.S. source, such as a bank, as FDI. Moreover, certain actions by the U.S. affiliates after the investments are made can either increase or decrease the stock of existing FDI. For example, repayment of a loan borrowed from a foreign parent to make the initial investment, or profit repatriation in excess of actual profits earned during a given year, result in negative capital flows that can offset positive capital inflows and reduce the stock of FDI. Detailed BEA data on capital inflows suggest that from 2002 to 2010, there were several years in which one or both of these components were negative for China. The cumulative impact of these transactions was to depress the headline capital inflow values by nearly one billion dollars through 2010.

Table 17. Comparison of Chinese Investments in 2010, by Data Source and Measure

Source	Measure	Amount $ billion
Bureau of Economic Analysis	Direct investment, historical cost by country of foreign parent	3.2
Bureau of Economic Analysis	Direct Investment, historical cost by ultimate beneficial owner	5.8
Heritage China Global Investment Tracker	Direct investment 1/	11.2
Rhodium Group China Investment Monitor	Direct investment	11.7
Bureau of Economic Analysis 2/	Assets owned by affiliates	19.1
Heritage China Global Investment Tracker	Investment 3/	32.2

1/ Includes only transactions with an ownership stake of 10 percent or more. 2/ Source only covers data through 2009. 3/ Includes all investments in the database.

There are other reasons for the disparity between the official and the privately collected data. The data published in the Heritage Foundation's China Global Investment Tracker include some portfolio investment transactions as well as direct investments. Counting only direct investment transactions, the value of Chinese FDI through 2010 in the Heritage database declines to $11.2 billion, only slightly less than the amount counted in the Rhodium Group's China Investment Monitor. Because the two private sources count the announced purchase value, rather than the actual capital flow, the BEA's tally for assets might be a more appropriate comparison with the privately maintained data. This value actually exceeds the investment values in the private sources, which validates the BEA's accounting of FDI from China. This provides some measure of confidence that the official data on Chinese inward investment and operations of Chinese-owned affiliates are not wildly incorrect—they are just somewhat outdated compared to the private sources whose data are more contemporaneous.

C. Assessment

Are Chinese investments focused on market returns or creating greater demand for Chinese products? Based on the limited pool of official data, no robust conclusions are possible. There are early indications that China may be moving toward the Korean and Japanese approach of using their U.S. affiliates to support high levels of imports relative to value added, but the data remain inconclusive. Korean and Japanese affiliates have consistently taken this approach, while Chinese affiliates, as a group, have not. Thus, it is not possible to conclude that Chinese firms are focused more on creating market demand than affiliates from other OECD countries.

Neither do the data support a conclusion that Chinese firms are, or are not, focused on market returns. Those returns have been awful, but Chinese affiliates are not alone in this regard. It is worth noting that in 2007, just prior to the recession, Chinese affiliates racked up profits of $124 million, by far their best showing.

However, this could have been due to the addition of new affiliates in profitable industries and not better performance by existing affiliates suddenly focused on improved profitability. The answers to these questions may become clearer in the coming years when data for the expanding universe of Chinese firms are included in the BEA's data.

XIII. Motives Underlying Chinese Investments in the United States

This section examines whether China's FDI in the United States is driven by the profit motive, by state policy goals, or both. First, it reviews studies and other information on Chinese ODI in general to see if they offer any clues about the state's role in outward direct investments. Second, it reviews evidence specific to the United States, including policy pronouncements and data trends.

A. Motives for Investing Abroad

The OECD's Investment Policy Review of China in 2008 identified five major motivations underlying China's ODI: 1) acquiring natural resources; 2) obtaining access to markets; 3) acquiring strategic assets (such as advanced technology, brand names, and distribution networks); 4) diversifying business areas; and 5) seeking more efficient distribution of assets and production activities.[229]

These motives are consistent with FDI theory, which was largely developed to explain FDI undertaken by advanced country multinationals that were presumably responding to market force. However, in China's case, state objectives have been at least as important as market force.

Indeed, a review of the history of China's ODI indicates that China's enterprises have always taken cues from government. Although Chinese multinationals existed prior to 1949, during the first 50 years of the People's Republic of China, there was very little outward investment from China.[230] Outward FDI activities began cautiously in 1979, with FDI limited to central SOE trading corporations and to economic and technological cooperation under provincial and municipal governments. The government began to encourage FDI by easing some restrictions from 1986 to 1991, allowing sufficiently deep enterprises to invest in joint ventures.[231] Through 1991, outward investment totaled $680 million, mostly in North American and Oceania resource ventures.[232]

A further acceleration of China's ODI activities began in 1992, as state plans began encouraging internationalization and sub-national governments began to promoting ODI, especially in Hong Kong. Policy-supported investments became more important beginning in 1999, with the government providing incentives to ODI in targeted industries that supported Chinese exports.

The importance of ODI as a policy goal was formalized in 2001 – the year China joined the WTO – with inclusion of the "Go Out" directive in the 10th Five Year Plan.[233] But even before "Go Out," studies of China's FDI concluded that Chinese ODI sought to pursue "national and provincial economic goals and policy objectives" such as supporting the exports of SOEs, stabilizing supplies of scarce natural resources, and acquiring information for other Chinese enterprises about operating abroad.[234]

The government's hand is most evident in resource acquisition. The initial take-off in China's ODI was directed toward resource rich countries, many of which were in Africa. According to one account, by early 2007 there were more than 800 Chinese SOEs invested in, or working on projects in, Africa.[235] The tilt toward Africa and resource-rich developing countries is illustrated below.

The stock of China's ODI in Africa and the Organization of the Petroleum Exporting Countries (OPEC), relative to host country GDP, has been far greater than in either the United States or the European Union.[236] Had China's ODI been geared toward tapping wealthy foreign markets, ratios in the United States and the EU would surely have been higher.

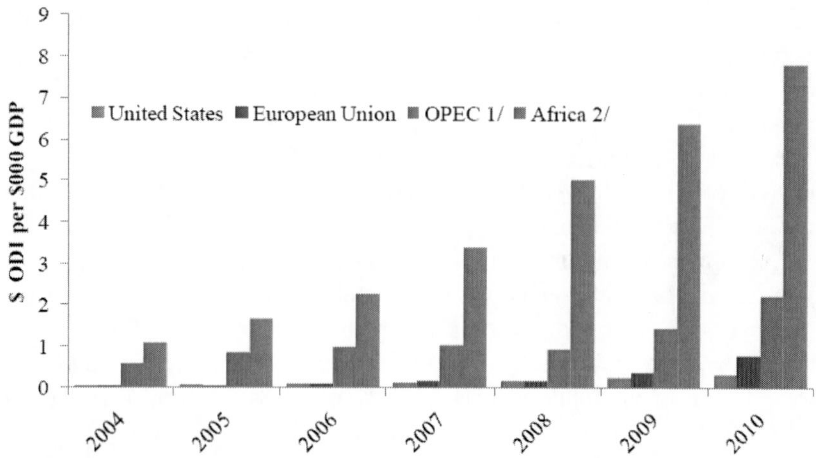

1/ GDP data for Iran, Kuwait, Libya, and Qatar in 2010 were unavailable and were set equal to 2009 values.

2/ GDP data for Djibouti and Libya in 2010 were unavailable and were set equal to 2009 values.

Source: China's Ministry of Commerce; World Bank.

Figure 26. Ratio of China's ODI Stock to Host GDP.

Given the economic reforms in China and the growth of the private sector, there are suggestions that market forces are becoming more pronounced determinants of China's ODI. For example, more recent studies of China's outward investments indicate that the acquisition of technology and other strategic assets, the exploitation of new markets, and diversification are becoming more important motivations.[237] These motivations are viewed as being more market oriented.

While acquiring technology and obtaining access to new markets may be reasonable commercial reasons for investing abroad, in China's case, the demarcation between market forces and state guidance is blurred. The recent surge in Chinese ODI followed policy changes that liberalized, targeted, and supported foreign investments. These trends were detailed in a recent report on outward ODI published by the Commission.[238]

Liberalization: A number of steps have been taken to facilitate outward investments by Chinese enterprises. In July 2006, China's State Administration of Foreign Exchange abolished quotas on the purchase of foreign exchange for overseas investment. Beginning December 2008, the Banking Regulatory Commission allowed commercial banks to make loans for cross-border mergers and acquisitions (M&A). The Ministry of Commerce in

2009 facilitated ODI by reducing approval times, lifting value thresholds, and transferring authority to local ministry branches.

Targeting: A joint circular published by the NDRC and the Ex-Im Bank of China in October 2004 encouraged ODI that would help China cope with domestic shortages of natural resources; promote domestic technologies, products, equipment, and labor; expose Chinese firms to internationally advanced technologies, managerial skills and professionals; and enhance the international competitiveness and market access of Chinese enterprises.

Support: As noted in section VIII, there are a number of central and provincial mechanisms in place to provide support, financial and otherwise, to Chinese investments. Financial support includes "loans made at below market rates, providing investment for infrastructure, and aid to the government of states that produce natural resources."[239]

Moreover, other factors and trends indicate the hand of the state maintains a strong grip on China's recent ODI activities. Many of the technology assets being acquired are related to industries considered important to national and economic security (e.g., the telecommunications services, transportation services, and the aerospace industries). The investors are firms owned by the state and/or supported by the state. The state's industrial blueprint specifically calls for technology acquisition.[240]

It is difficult to divorce motives such as market entry from government policy when a government representative identifies "eliminating excess supply" as a motivation for ODI.[241] In short, despite the existence of multiple motives for Chinese outward investments, the government continues to play a primary role in directing the overall pace and nature of Chinese FDI.

B. Motives for Investing in the United States

> {M}any Chinese SOEs, in a wide array of industries, are cash rich. The goods they produce are becoming globally competitive. These firms will seek opportunities within U.S. borders, and U.S. household and corporate customers will be interested in their products.
>
> -- David F. Gordon, Testimony before the U.S.-China Economic and Security Review Commission, Feb. 15, 2012[242].

The motives underlying China's increased interest in acquiring U.S. assets are extremely important from a policy standpoint. If investments are being undertaken by private firms focused on profit maximization, then there is no strong case for doing anything differently. If, on the other hand, the investments are being conducted by SOEs in strategic industries under the guidance of the government and the investment outcomes are inconsistent with commercial outcomes, then it may be necessary for the United States government to put in place a policy to deal with inward FDI from China.

1. Why Has Chinese FDI in the United States Been So Low?

As described above, Chinese FDI in the United States is rising, a trend that is likely to continue in the coming years. But until recently, Chinese direct investments in the United States – those investments that have resulted in Chinese investors owning 10 percent or more of the recipient's shares – have been minor according to official data sources and more contemporaneous unofficial sources of investment data.[243]

Based on standard theories of FDI, China's direct investments in the United States should be higher. The United States has a large domestic market and is home to abundant natural resources. Efficiency seeking investments may not find the U.S. economy attractive because Chinese wages are already low, but U.S. technologies and management techniques are attractive from an efficiency standpoint.

China's direct investments in the United States have been depressed largely due to the U.S. and Chinese governments. The U.S. government has resisted certain Chinese investments due to national security concerns.[244] Although U.S. government scrutiny and adverse publicity may have made Chinese firms think twice before investing,[245] the primary reason for the paucity of Chinese FDI is Chinese government policy.

China's weak Yuan policy and capital controls ensure that foreign currencies earned by Chinese exporters would be invested primarily by the Chinese government, which invests the vast majority of its currency holdings in U.S. treasury and agency debt. Had these currency earnings been invested by firms responding to market forces, China's FDI would have increased sooner.

Once Beijing began promoting outward investments, those direct investments were directed primarily toward securing energy and raw materials and carried out primarily by SOEs, frequently in countries having good relations with China.[246] For the most part, neither the United States nor other OECD countries were initially attractive to China's SOEs.[247]

2. What Are the Motives Underlying the Current Expansion in Chinese FDI in the United States?

By all indications the trickle of U.S. inward FDI from China is a thing of the past. A number of "push and pull" factors have changed, and FDI from China is now trending higher. This section explores the factors "pushing" Chinese entities to invest in the United States.[248] These factors are both macroeconomic and strategic.

On the macro side, the main motivation for increasing direct investments in the United States is the size of China's holding of U.S. government securities. After years of recycling dollars in government securities, China has reached the point where it is no longer comfortable with the makeup of its portfolio. This unease has been exacerbated by growing U.S. fiscal deficits and government debt. To limit further increases in exposure to government debt, China's financial authorities have been allowing recycling in portfolio investments, largely undertaken by sovereign wealth funds (see Section V) and direct investments. China's portfolio of dollar holdings now includes a higher percentage of U.S. equity and direct investments and a lower percentage of government securities than would have existed otherwise.

China's financial authorities are also allowing the Yuan to appreciate somewhat, which reduces the need to purchase and invest dollars and helps stem the rise of China's current account surplus. The stronger Yuan is another macroeconomic factor underlying the current expansion of China's FDI because it makes dollar assets cheaper in terms of Yuan. For a Chinese firm, one million Yuan at the end of 2011 could purchase nearly 30 percent more in dollar-denominated assets than was the case in June 2005, on the eve of the initial re-evaluation.

Factors affecting individual firms are also motivating China's increased direct investment activity in the United States. These include a desire to maintain or increase market share in the face of trade remedies, such as antidumping and countervailing duties; the desire to acquire technology, and the desire to participate in U.S. sectors deemed important to the Chinese government.

Economic theory holds that policies such as tariffs that limit imports encourage exporters to replace exports with FDI.[249] The best known example of this phenomenon is Japanese investment in the U.S. auto industry.[250] Many Chinese firms, from both the state and non-state sectors, have been subject to numerous antidumping and countervailing duty investigations in the United States in recent years, as shown in Figure 27. There are currently 113 antidumping and countervailing duties orders in affect against Chinese firms, with some dating back to the early 1980s. The majority of these orders went into effect after 2007.[251]

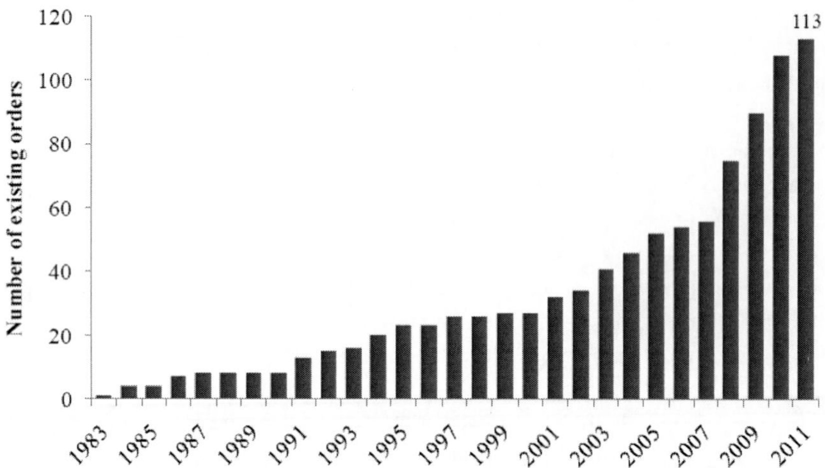

Source: USITC, http://pubapps2.usitc.gov/sunset/.

Figure 27. U.S. Antidumping and Countervailing Duty Orders in Effect against Chinese Firms, Cumulative Totals.

There are several instances of FDI by Chinese firms made in response to trade remedy orders – or proactively in order to avoid potential trade remedy orders – though not all such investments have occurred in the United States. China's steel pipe and tube producers have been subject to antidumping orders in recent years as low prices have led to dramatic increases in imports from China. For example, imports of oil country tubular goods from China expanded by more than 200 percent from 2006 to 2008.[252] With a U.S. antidumping petition on the horizon, and a case already under way in Canada, state-owned Tianjin Pipe in January 2009 announced the largest ever Chinese investment in the United States.[253] Following the imposition of antidumping and countervailing duties against citric acid imports from China in 2009, Chinese investors funded the establishment of a huge citric acid production facility in Thailand set to begin production in 2010.[254] The planned U.S. investment by the Anshan Iron & Steel Group (Anshan), one of China's top central-SASAC-owned steelmakers, is motivated by concerns about trade remedies.[255] Avoiding such duties was also an important motivation of privately owned Shandong Nanshan Aluminum Co. Ltd., which is establishing a production facility in Lafayette, Indiana.[256]

Although resource acquisition remains an important objective of ODI, China is also seeking to expand its U.S. investments into downstream industries favored by government policies. Examples include the steel industry, which has a high level of government ownership in China, and the solar industry, which has a relatively low level of government ownership but is also promoted and supported by the state.

Anshan is a straightforward example of a new phase of Chinese investment that was discussed extensively at the Commission's hearing on *China's State-Owned and State-Controlled Enterprises* in 2012.[257] In May 2010, Anshan announced that it was forming a joint venture to build several new steel plants in the United States. China's 2009 Revitalization Plan specifies that Anshan will receive government support to enhance its international competitiveness and to assist Anshan with investments to acquire strategic resources and establish overseas operations.[258] Anshan's Chinese language material describes its U.S. foray with missionary zeal:

> Anshan's investment in building mills in the U.S. is not only going to fit the need of self-development, it's also Anshan's sacred historic mission of being the 'eldest son of iron and steel' of the world's largest iron and steel country. It will demonstrate China's iron and steel industry's capabilities in international deployment and operations, and their influences on the industry. It is also Anshan's contribution to the realization of transforming China from a big iron and steel country to a strong iron and steel country.[259]

U.S. FDI by Chinese producers of solar panels demonstrates how the intersection of Chinese industrial plans, government support, and FDI can destabilize the U.S. market and harm existing manufacturers. China's 9th Five Year Plan promoted domestic production of alternative energy sources. The 10th Five Year Plan specified wind, solar and geothermal power technologies and indicated that the government would provide financial assistance and preferential taxes. The 11th Five Year Plan and other contemporaneous measures explicitly encouraged production of renewable energy and continued industry incentives. The government also funded national R&D efforts aimed at solar and other renewable technologies.[260] By 2009, the government role had expanded to near epic proportions.[261]

The cumulative effects of these policies are stunning. "In 2003, China had virtually no solar power industry. By 2008, it was making more solar cells than any other country and taking customers away from American and other foreign companies that had originally invented the technology."[262] Chinese firms were raising capital on U.S. stock exchanges and at least one, Suntech Power Holdings (Suntech), had invested in a U.S. facility to modularize crystalline solar photovoltaic cells.[263] By 2011, U.S. imports of crystalline solar cells and modules from China had driven prices to very low levels and several members of the U.S. solar industry had gone bankrupt or exited the industry.[264] In an interview with *The New York Times* in China, Suntech's CEO was quoted saying his firm was building market share by "selling solar panels on the American market for less than the cost of the materials, assembly, and shipping."[265] Although many Chinese producers of crystalline solar photovoltaic cells and modules are private, there are some firms that are affiliated with SOEs. In addition, the industry producing the primary input in solar cells, polysilicon, is dominated by SOEs.[266]

The acquisition of technology is also an overarching motive for the current FDI in the United States.[267] The Chinese government is known to acquire foreign technology from firms investing in China. However, in some industries, the government seems reluctant to allow FDI. Steel and telecommunications services are two such industries. In other cases, the technology China wants is being developed by U.S. firms that are too small to invest in China. Small firms in internet-related and energy industries are thus attractive to Chinese investors. In these industries, it appears that FDI in the United States is to some degree motivated by the desire to acquire foreign technology.

Steel: According to a study on FDI by SOEs that was prepared by the law firm Wiley Rein in 2011, Anshan's Chinese language explanations for its U.S. investments include "acquiring advanced technology and returning the technology to China, and enhanc[ing] the internationalization of Anshan."[268] The technology of interest is electric arc furnace technology.[269]

Telecommunications/software: As noted above, the telecom giant Huawei recently tried to obtain certain intellectual property assets from 3Leaf and some of its employees. The technology in question was related to cloud computing. In this instance, the target was clearly the intellectual property because no other assets appear to have been part of the deal.

Auto parts—lithium battery: In November 2010, *Automotive News China* reported that Zhuhai Yintong Energy Co., Ltd. (ZYTE) had announced plans to purchase Altair Nanotechnologies (Altair Nano), a U.S. producer of lithium titanate batteries. The same month the planned acquisition was announced, ZYTE's parent, Yintong Group (Yintong), was visited by Premier Wen Jiabao and various CCP luminaries.[270] In March 2011, even before the deal with Altair Nano had been consummated, Yintong was touting its "Industrialization of High-efficient Energy Storage Lithium Titanate Battery," noting that it is one of the technologies listed in China's 863 Technology Plan.[271] The investment was finalized in the summer of 2011 by Canon Investment Holding Co., Ltd., an investment arm of China's Yintong Group.[272] Yintong's New Energy Vehicle Development Plan for 2011-2020 makes clear that the Altair Nano investment was undertaken with the state's development objectives in mind and to obtain Altair Nano's lithium titanate battery technology for China.[273] Yintong also has a subsidiary in the aerospace equipment supply chain and the development plan indicates that the technology acquired through the Altair deal has defense-related applications.

> At present, lithium batteries in market widely adopt {sic} graphite as cathode. Through holding shares of American Altairnano Company, Yintong Group has introduced the globally most advanced cell anode material technology --- lithium titanate technology into Chinese market. Yintong Group purchases dedicated lithium titanate material of Altairnano for production of cell cells {sic} in China. Lithium titanate cell has the features such as extremely-long service life (up to more than thirty years, and 20 thousand of cycles), incredibly high safety performance and so on. The batteries can be assembled together in a large scale to serve as an energy storage power station, which can save energy during idle time for peak time, store wind energy, solar energy and tidal energy, etc.; it has high-current charging and discharging capacity under either high or low temperature, broader application scope for both the areas with pleasant climate and the areas with cold and bad weather; it possesses superior reliability in applications of national defense, national infrastructure and other equipment.[274]

It is notable that although Yintong is probably not an SOE, the Chinese government clearly was a major player in Yintong's U.S. acquisition. According to Frank Gibbard, CEO of Altair, Altair's buyer has "excellent" government contacts in China.[275] Moreover, when his group visited China, it "was hosted by senior government officials at the national, provincial and municipal levels in China. Everywhere we went, we experienced a tide of enthusiasm for alternative energy technology projects and manufacturing plants."[276]

Alternative energy: In February 2007, the U.S. firm Syntroleum signed a deal with Sinopec, the listed arm of the SOE China Petroleum and Chemical Corporation.[277] As part of the deal, Syntroleum received $20 million and other benefits and transferred its gas-to-liquid Catoosa Demonstration Facility (CDF) to China, where it began operations in August 2011.[278] The CDF, Fischer-Tropsch (FT) technology, had been developed with funding from Syntroleum, Marathon Oil, and the Department of Energy, which provided $16 million in funding.[279] The facility, which was the only fully integrated FT plant operating in the United States, provided fuels purchased by the government and used to run buses in Washington, DC, as well as jet engines on B-52s.[280] However, Syntroleum abruptly shut the CDF in October 2006 soon after fulfilling its commitment to produce 100,000 gallons of ultra-clean aviation fuel for the military, eliminating 46 positions.[281]

Based on these case studies, it is difficult to make the case that these investments were undertaken solely for profit. In Anshan's case, the firm is clearly interested in accessing the U.S. procurement market, which is currently hampered by Buy American provisions. However, Anshan's primary motives appear to be expanding the reach of the Chinese steel industry beyond the country's borders and acquiring electric arc furnace technology.[282] In Huawei's case, the driving motive was obviously the cloud computing technology, as the purchase does not appear to have included any tangible assets. Yintong's investment was also clearly related to the acquisition of Altair Nano's technology, not incremental profitability from U.S. sales. Indeed, Altair Nano had lucrative business with the U.S. military, but has had to sever those ties because of the Yintong acquisition.[283] The Altair Nano saga also indicates that even though the investing firm was privately owned, the ultimate beneficial owner is a Chinese firm that is actively pursuing the Chinese government's industrial policy.

This is not to say that profitability is not part of the equation at all. Obviously, if Anshan's joint venture is profitable, the SOE will make money. The fact that a profit maximizing firm is jointly investing suggests that neither party views the venture as a loss leader.[284] A proximate impact of the Yintong's investment in Altair Nano was the loss of lucrative business, but the transaction may ultimately make money for Yintong if the lithium titanate technology it purchased becomes widely used in China. As noted by Li Zhaoxi of the State Council's research arm, these investments are intended to benefit both the business making the investment and China as well.

Based on the above, it is also possible to assess the motivations of the various investing entities by mode of investments. The results are summarized in the table below. The categories are not meant to be mutually exclusive — for example, the product of a merger could engage in a greenfield investments

— but are meant to provide a tool for assessing the goals of state actors based on the type of investments they make.

Table 18. Investment Goals by Type of State-Controlled Entity and Mode of Investment

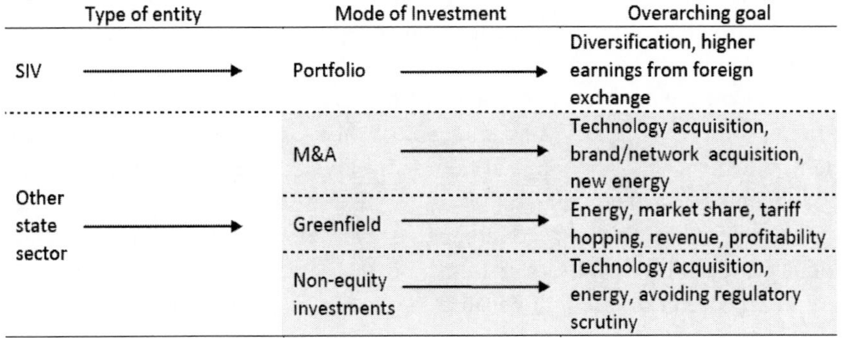

Type of entity	Mode of Investment	Overarching goal
SIV	Portfolio	Diversification, higher earnings from foreign exchange
Other state sector	M&A	Technology acquisition, brand/network acquisition, new energy
	Greenfield	Energy, market share, tariff hopping, revenue, profitability
	Non-equity investments	Technology acquisition, energy, avoiding regulatory scrutiny

SIVs were created to achieving greater profitability for Chinese foreign exchange holdings. There is little indication thus far that they are anything other than passive investors.

Other firms from the state sector, including private firms that closely hew to state goals, tend to have different goals that can be associated with certain types of investment. M&A transactions are often undertaken to acquire technology (e.g., Altair Nano, Syntroleum, Boston Power) or acquire an existing brand or network (e.g., LenovoIBM). Greenfield investments tend to occur when the goal is to gain or, in the case of tariff hopping, maintain market share in the U.S. market (e.g., TIPCO and Anshan). Although the firms making such investments may not be profit maximizers, they are seeking to maintain revenues in the face of trade remedies.

Many are also seeking to penetrate U.S. markets by combining high value imports with some U.S. value added, and to create channels for unloading excess capacity existing in China (e.g., Suntech and Goldwind USA). A third category of investment, referred to as non-equity investments, is not considered to be FDI in the official sense because the arrangement does not lead to ownership. However, Chinese firms appear to utilize this mode to acquire technology and access to energy while minimizing the regulatory scrutiny that comes with ownership (e.g., Huawei-3Leaf and CNOOC-Chesapeake).

XIV. Chinese Purchases of Financially Distressed Companies

FDI from China appears to have accelerated in the wake of the U.S. financial crisis and subsequent recession. The weak economy coincided with deteriorating financial conditions for U.S. firms. This section reviews instances in which Chinese firms took advantage of this weakness to increase their ownership of U.S. firms.

Based on the analysis presented in this report, it is clear that there are many reasons why Chinese FDI increased in the United States. As such, the extent to which U.S. economic weakness motivated the increase in Chinese investments is unclear. Nevertheless, a review of Chinese investments suggests that many of the target companies were having difficulties, and thus welcomed the influx of Chinese funds. At the same time, Chinese investors were in a position of strength because they were less scarred by the financial crisis and because U.S. assets had become a bargain. Economic weakness led to lower valuations in the United States, while several years of slow appreciation had increased the Yuan's purchasing power. After years of growing national income and wealth in China, U.S. assets went on sale, and Chinese investors jumped at the opportunity,[285] just as Japanese investors had done during the 1980s and 1990s.

The Chinese government recognized the implications of U.S. economic weakness and took steps to facilitate Chinese acquisitions.[286] In December 2008 the Chinese bank regulators instituted policy changes to facilitate domestic and foreign investments. The changes included making loans more accessible for firms engaging in M&A, providing low interest loans, and generally looking to provide additional support to the "Go Out" policies already in place. Banks were allowed to extend an additional RMB 900 billion (approximately $130 billion) to finance M&A transactions.[287]

More recently, according to the U.S. investment firm FINNEA Group, the Chinese Government earmarked another $60 billion dollars for acquisitions and mergers aimed specifically at acquiring U.S. industrial assets and technology.[288]

Thus, the Chinese government not only encouraged Chinese enterprises to purchase relatively cheap U.S. companies and assets during the financial crisis, but also funded the purchases.

A. Examples of Distressed or Capital Starved Firms That Obtain Investment from China

A review of Chinese investments finds many instances of such bargain hunting. The most prominent example is CIC's purchase of nearly ten percent of Morgan Stanley, discussed in sections VI and XI. When CIC made its first large equity purchase of Morgan Stanley in December 2007, CIC was buying into a firm that had just experienced its first quarterly loss and had declined approximately 40 percent from highs achieved earlier that year.[289] Chinese investors also made significant purchases of U.S. real estate, where distress has been acute. CIC has been particularly active. For example, in November 2010, CIC invested $1.02 billion for a 7.6 percent stake in General Growth Properties (GGP), the second largest commercial mall company in the United States, which was going through bankruptcy.[290] In January 2011, CIC took an undisclosed equity stake in a 27 story Manhattan office building at 650 Madison Avenue (headquarters of Polo Ralph Lauren Co.), whose owners required assistance with refinancing. A CIC subsidiary through control of the Beijing Bank of China recently agreed to invest $800 million to refinance an office building on Park Avenue.[291] In addition to these more publicized moves, CIC has invested more than $1 billion into the real estate funds of Morgan Stanley, Blackstone, AREA Property Partners, and Brookfield Asset Management Inc.[292] CIC is not alone in investing in Manhattan real estate; SouFun Holding Ltd and HNA Property also have made significant purchases.[293] Aside from large purchases in finance and real estate, Chinese investors have also purchased distressed assets in the U.S. solar and auto parts industries, though purchases in the latter took place both before and after the financial crisis.

Solar industry: Evergreen Solar, once the third largest U.S. producer of solar panels and beneficiary of subsidies from the state of Massachusetts, ran into financial troubles as excess Chinese production and exports 'cratered' industry prices. Evergreen entered into a joint venture with Chinese solar panel companies and agreed in March 2011 to move its major manufacturing facilities to China. The firm entered bankruptcy in August 2011 and most of its core assets were sold to Evergreen's Chinese joint venture for a mere $9.2 million.[294]

Auto parts industry: This report has already reviewed two examples of Chinese investors, PCM and Wanxiang America, which purchased distressed auto parts producers. Looking to raise cash in the aftermath of its government bailout, GM was willing to shut Nexteer's facilities if it did not find a buyer.

Aside from PCM, there was only one other suitor. Wanxiang America's U.S. acquisitions include several U.S. firms that were at or near bankruptcy, including Zeller, Universal Automotive Industries (UAI), and Rockford Powertrain. In 2000, Wanxiang America bought the intangible assets of its former customer, Zeller, for a mere $420,000 after Zeller suffered major losses.[295] Wanxiang America took 20 percent of UAI in 2001 and subsequently came to control 58.8 percent after losses during the recession had UAI on the verge of being delisted from NASDAQ. [296] Similarly, Wanxiang took control of 33.3 percent of Rockford, a significant U.S. player in the U.S. automotive and defense industries, after that firm began experiencing financial troubles during the late 1990s.[297]

Automobile industry: Chinese purchases were not limited to distressed parts makers. For example, Zhejiang Geely Holding Group, part of China's 12th largest automaker, acquired Volvo Motors from Ford in 2010 for $1.8 billion.[298] Sichuan Tengzhong Heavy Industrial Machines attempted to purchase GM's Hummer division for $100 million, but Chinese regulators rejected the transaction.[299]

Chinese FDI as an Alternative Source of Funding

Boston Power is a lithium car battery producer based in Massachusetts. After failing to secure to secure significant funding from the U.S. government, Boston Power obtained funds from China. GSR Ventures, a venture capital company with offices in Beijing, Hong Kong, and Silicon Valley, funded Boston Power with a combination of private capital and low-interest loans, grants, and tax exemptions from the Chinese government that totaled $125 million. As a result of this funding, Boston Power dialed back plans to produce its batteries in Massachusetts, and instead chose to relocate and expand its production and R&D capabilities in China. According to Boston Bower's CEO, "And China is doing something that's so cool. It's inviting players from all over the world to be in their sandbox."

(Bullis, 2011); (Freedman, 2011); and (Sedgwick, China State-Owned Suppliers Seek US Acquisitions, 2012).

New battery technology: China is trying to develop and/or acquire automotive technologies, which are promoted under China's 12th Five Year Plan.[300] Both Altair Nano and Boston Power were distressed firms when they attracted investments from Chinese firms. Altair Nano's financial performance had been disappointing and its stock price had plummeted to less than one dollar per share. In the case of Boston Power, it had failed to obtain a U.S. government loan.[301] The market's verdict on both these firms has been negative, but Chinese investors with government support have stepped in to save the firms and bring production to China.

B. Assessment

It is no accident that the increase in Chinese investment coincided with a period of U.S. economic weakness. The financial crisis brought down the prices of U.S. industrial, financial, and real estate assets to levels that were more attractive to Chinese investors, both state-owned and private. The Chinese government promoted and financed purchases of these assets at a time when potential U.S. investors, current owners, or U.S. governments were unwilling or unable to provide investment funds or loans.

The non-financial investments examined above share certain characteristics. First, they occurred in industries (solar panels and auto parts) that have experienced significant increases in imports from China. Second, they occurred in industries (automotive and new energy) that have been promoted in China's five-year planning documents. Third, they have resulted in some production shifting to China. In the case of auto parts, a more established industry, the investors sought to maintain a significant level of U.S. production even as some production was (or is likely to be) shifted to China. However, in the new energy sector (Evergreen, Altair Nano, and Boston Power), where technology acquisition was clearly a goal, the foreign investment is leading to a much larger shift in production to China.

But what was the alternative? Two possible outcomes for a distressed firm are illustrated in Figure 28. In the case of Nexteer, at least, the alternative was closure and job loss. At least some of the firms purchased by Wanxiang faced continued economic uncertainty and potential closure as well. For these Chinese investments, the influx of Chinese investment appears to have been positive for the local workforce and communities, despite the shift of some production to China. For the new energy investments, the analysis is less straight-forward. Based on its stock price and financial results, Altair Nano was a struggling firm with uncertain prospects. If its battery technology were a certain winner, surely its stock price would be much higher. Chinese investors, with the support of government, are clearly willing to take a risk on this technology, whereas private investors in the United States are not, at least based on the company's current valuation.[302] In the case of Boston Power, the precipitating factor was its failure to win a $100 million stimulus grant, which went to a player in Michigan.[303] It is not known whether Boston Power had other potential non-Chinese investors. With government support, Chinese investors are providing $125 million and China is getting all the potential employment and other benefits that would have occurred in Massachusetts. On the other hand, China is taking on the risk as well, as not all new energy firms succeed.

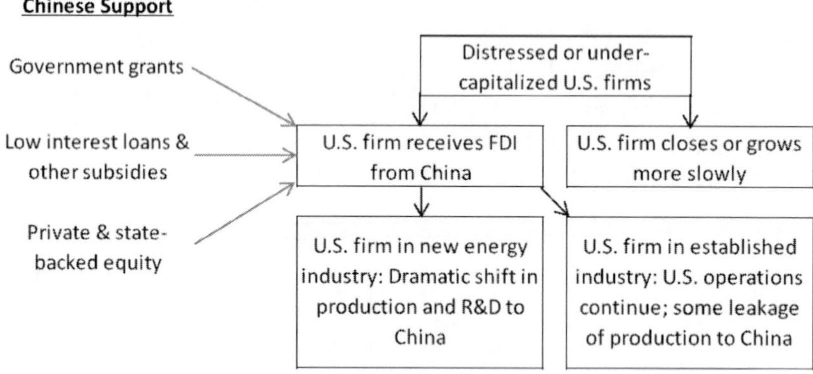

Figure 28. Illustration of Chinese FDI in distressed U.S. firm.

XV. Efforts by U.S. Entities to Attract Chinese Investments

There is an inherent tension among the different levels of U.S. government regarding FDI from China. On the one hand, the federal government tends to be concerned with the big picture. On the economic front, this means maintaining the attractiveness of the U.S. economy by providing non-discriminatory, rules-based access to foreign investors who are interested in investing in the U.S. economy. On the national security front, the federal government is primarily concerned with making certain that Chinese investments – and foreign investments in general – do not have adverse consequences for national security.

As discussed above, the SOE prevalence in U.S. investments from China, particularly in sectors that have a bearing on national security and/or are considered to be important to America's economic future, is of particular concern to many stakeholders in the federal government. This concern has been exacerbated by China's latest five-year plan and related policy pronouncements, which all but declare "open season" on many industries which are at a more advanced stage of development in the United States. For example, the 12th Five-Year Plan emphasizes the development of new strategic industries, including energy-saving and environment-friendly new-generation information technology, biology, high-end equipment manufacturing, new energy sources, new materials and new energy automobiles. The plan also specifies a number of goods and services (e.g., cloud computing) and instructs that the value added of these new industries should reach eight percent of GDP.[304] China's *modus operandi* has been to create production capacity well in excess of its ability to consume, and then to crash global prices by exporting the surplus. Aggressive, state-funded forays into emerging industries could short-circuit their development in the United States, harming not only near-term job creation, but also long-term economic performance.

For many U.S. stakeholders, this issue is particularly vexing because China does not provide reciprocal access to U.S. investments in strategic sectors, and has been using subsidies and a variety of other policies to give Chinese firms competitive advantages in markets in China and beyond. These policies are widely seen as contributing to the dramatic decline in U.S. manufacturing employment above and beyond levels that can be explained by productivity gains and GDP fluctuations.[305]

In contrast, state governments are less concerned with national strategic issues and more concerned with state economic performance. In recent years, state economies have lost manufacturing jobs due to outsourcing and the recession. State officials are thus anxious to create jobs, and attracting foreign capital, including capital from China, helps to accomplish this goal. Indeed, a 2008 study by the Kiel Institute found strong evidence of favorable FDI effects on output and employment in U.S. states.[306] There is also evidence that politicians' promotional activities at the state level are rewarded at the polls.[307]

In practice, this dichotomy between national and state-officials does not always hold. For states that had fewer manufacturing jobs to lose in the first place, or produced capital goods that have benefitted from growing exports to China, the relationship with China has been largely profitable. Like their counterparts at the state level, these states' federal representatives are more prone to put aside concerns about national economic security and focus instead on the near-term economic benefits to be gained from Chinese investments.

Likewise, federal agencies concerned with the overall economy do undertake activities to encourage FDI, including FDI from China.

A. Federal Efforts to Attract Chinese FDI

As noted in section IV, the legal framework in the United States is set up to facilitate inward investment and provide transparency for investors. The major exception has been FDI aimed at sectors related to national security, which falls under the purview of CFIUS, which was created in 1975. CFIUS has hardly been a stumbling block to inward FDI.[308]

However, recent changes brought about by FINSA provide the body with more authority, and its review process is believed to have been instrumental in the withdrawal of at least two transactions involving China.

Source: Department of Commerce, ITA, Attracting Chinese FDI to the United States.

Figure 29. Excerpt from Department of Commerce presentation on Attracting FDI from China.

Nevertheless, the federal government does promote Chinese FDI in the United States. China represents the largest mission of the U.S. Foreign Commercial Service (FCS). The China Office is three times larger than the next largest Commercial Service office. Among other things, the FCS provides assistance to Chinese firms looking to sell as well as invest in the United States. SelectUSA (formerly InvestAmerica), based in the Department of Commerce, also promotes FDI.

SelectUSA provides a venue for U.S. states interested in meeting with potential Chinese investors.[309] SelectUSA's pitch to support Chinese FDI includes a sharp 32 page PowerPoint that trumpets the virtues of the U.S. economy, provides guidance on relevant federal programs and promoted sectors, and offers assistance to foreign investors.[310] The slide below, taken from the presentation, summarizes bilateral efforts to enhance investment flows between the United States and China, including a memorandum on investment signed in October 2009 and a memorandum of understanding signed in December 2010.

Federal efforts to attract FDI from China are not limited to the Department of Commerce. For example, Montana Senator Max Baucus was instrumental in attracting Goldwind to construct a 20 megawatt wind farm in Montana.[311]

B. State Efforts to Attract FDI

States are even more active than the federal government in seeking Chinese FDI. The American Chamber of Commerce in Shanghai estimates that over 30 U.S. state overseas trade offices were registered in China in 2010.[312] CNN Money reports that 33 states, ports and municipalities have sent representatives to China to lure jobs to the United States.[313] State governments have viewed attracting FDI to their states as central to their economic development strategies.

During President Hu Jintao's visit to the United States in January, 2011 a U.S.-China Memorandum of Understanding was signed that sought to strengthen cooperation between U.S. governors and Chinese Provincial Leaders. The memorandum supports the establishment of a China-U.S. Governors Forum by the Chinese People's Association for Friendship with Foreign Countries (CPAFFC) and the National Governors Association (NGA) of the U.S.[314] The National Governor's Association announced July 15, 2011 that it convened a U.S. – China Governors Forum. Chinese provincial party secretaries and governors met with U.S. governors and business leaders to exchange ideas and enter into partnerships in areas including, but not limited to, trade and investment, energy, educational exchange, and environment.[315] In October six U.S. state governors traveled to China to meet with their counterparts.[316]

Several states have translated their investment slogans on their websites into Chinese.[317] In the Midwest, twelve states have banded together to form the MidWest US-China Association ("MWCA"). The MCWA is focused on helping attract Chinese government and business leaders to explore the opportunities offered by the region.[318] New York State has had a yearly trade delegation to China under its "Invest in New York" program since 2003. The New York trade mission grew out of the Asian American Business Development Corporation (AABDC) that initially promoted Asian American business and has grown to promote business opportunities in both countries. It operates a New York in China Center in Beijing as well as its own center in New York.[319] Los Angeles County maintains its own economic development department, the Los Angeles County Economic Development Corporation (LAEDC). While LA County is home to two large ports, it also has high levels of FDI. While not specifically focused on Chinese investment it has translated its website into Chinese and has put together a 147 page report on ties between Los Angeles County and China. In the report it notes that China and Hong Kong rank #9 in terms of FDI into the region.[320] The desire to attract Chinese FDI is not just limited to governments. Non-profit business organizations are also involved in fostering FDI. The American Chamber of Commerce in the People's Republic of China (AmCham-China) is a non-profit organization which represents US companies and individuals doing business in China. Papers on FDI have been published by both AmCham-Shanghai and the AmCham-China in Beijing. U.S. Chamber of Commerce in the U.S. has promoted Chinese/U.S. business relationships by hosting dialogues between CEOs and Former Senior Officials.[321] The financial community is also interested in attracting Chinese capital in the form of portfolio investment. U.S. brokerages firms and investment banks have a presence in China, but Chinese capital controls render attracting Chinese capital for foreign portfolio investment difficult. As noted at section IX, U.S. hedge funds are involved in funneling Chinese direct investments into shell companies listed in the United States. However, these transactions are ultimately aimed at attracting U.S. capital to finance businesses whose real assets are located in China, not the United States. U.S. investment funds and law firms play an important role in guiding Chinese companies through the process of investing through M&A. Until recently, China had little experience investing in the U.S. and other advanced country markets. China's "Go Out" policy, combined with the new focus on advanced country markets, has led to significant and profitable business opportunities for the U.S. law firms and investment advisory services with offices in Asia. However, these firms are not the driving forces behind the investments, but rather the beneficiaries of China's recent urge to invest in U.S. market and expanding U.S. efforts to attract Chinese FDI.

C. Assessment

At first blush, U.S. policies toward FDI from China seem ad hoc and disjointed: some government resources are trying to attract FDI from China, while others are urging caution or even discouraging it. There does appear to be a method to this madness. The United States has historically welcomed FDI for its economic benefits, with a few exceptions, and governments at all levels have efforts in place to attract FDI. From an economic perspective, greenfield investments stimulate local economic activity and create jobs, whether they are domestic or foreign, and it makes sense for governments, national and local, to pursue these benefits. In contrast, the economic benefits of M&A are ambiguous. There generally are no surges in employment and output resulting from M&A, so the economic benefits are less pronounced than for greenfield investments. However, from the standpoint of the U.S. economic security there are potential pitfalls from M&A. The new owners can shift production to another country. They can acquire strategic assets, such as raw materials and use those assets in ways that do not reflect market forces or U.S. economic interests. They can acquire important technologies for use outside the United States. These more strategic concerns are best handled by the federal government through an agency such as CFIUS.

CONCLUSION

This study has examined five major topics regarding foreign investments from China: the magnitude of FDI from China, FDI from the state-sector, U.S. regulations and oversight of investment from China, the motives underlying China's increase in FDI, and the economic benefits of FDI from China. What has been learned?

Chinese investments in U.S. businesses have been extremely modest but have been growing sharply. Until recently, Beijing's capital controls and long-held preference for investing in U.S. government securities had depressed Chinese investment in privately owned U.S. assets, even after the inauguration of China's "Go Out" policy in 2000. Thus, the value of Chinese direct investment in the United States has significantly lagged the growth in China's economy and trade. Both official and non-government data sources, as well as the business press, indicate that China's purchases of U.S. assets have grown significantly in recent years. These investments have been in the form of direct investments, in which the Chinese investors are able to exert full or partial control over corporate management, and indirect financial investments in which Chinese investors exert no formal management control.

Contemporaneous estimates of the value of Chinese investments range up to $30 billion through the end of 2011, compared to official estimates of $5.8 billion through 2010. Official FDI data are better indicators of actual capital flows, while the unofficial data likely provides a better indication of China's investment footprint. Both numbers suggest that FDI from China, through 2011, was relatively modest. This is likely to change.

Absent significant changes in current economic and policy trends, FDI from China is likely to increase significantly. The Chinese government is looking to diversify China's asset holdings away from Treasuries. China's industrial policy goals like technology acquisition, brand development, emerging industries, and market penetration favor FDI to advanced countries like the United States.

China's trade surplus, corporate profitability, and greater comfort level with FDI also point to higher levels of FDI from China. These and other trends suggest that the annual level of FDI from China is likely to approach levels associated with major OECD countries. Policy changes in the United States and China could hasten or slow this convergence but given current trends, convergence seems inevitable. All regions of the country are likely to see increased interest from China, though the Southwest, Great Lakes, and Southeast regions have been the most attractive thus far. The financial industry; petroleum and chemicals; manufacturing industries such as automotive, industrial machinery, and information technology; and emerging and new energy industries are likely to see continued interest from Chinese investors.

Investment from China is dominated by the state sector. China's SOEs remain important in China's economy and have been the main source of FDI, both overall and in the United States. China is also using well funded state investment vehicles to invest foreign exchange earnings in U.S. equities and private firms. These investments have been the largest source of China's major

U.S. investments, and are likely to remain important given Beijing's plans to increase funding for vehicles focused on U.S. and European investments. FDI has also come from China's private-sector. Beijing has been supportive of private-sector investments and they are likely to expand as well.

The U.S. regulatory system is evolving to deal with challenges posed by Chinese FDI. The United States is very open to FDI. Foreign-owned businesses are subject to many of the same legal restrictions as domestic businesses regarding antitrust, export controls, and listing requirements. China's goals for its outward FDI, articulated in planning documents and by government officials, raise a number of issues regarding U.S. national and economic security. CFIUS, the U.S. agency responsible for screening inward FDI for national security purposes, has reviewed some Chinese purchases, and a few potential transactions have terminated as a result of this process. Changes to CFIUS have expanded the types of transactions it can examine. There have been concerns that state-owned firms could theoretically act in collusion to acquire corporate assets important to national security. While SEC disclosure requirements and the transparency of U.S. markets render an under-the-radar acquisition of an important large U.S. firm unlikely, acquisitions of smaller firms with important technology assets will be difficult to control. Some Chinese firms have taken obvious steps to avoid the regulatory scrutiny associated with traditional FDI. Others have purchased smaller U.S. businesses with novel technologies and shifted production and research activities to China. Given such concerns, it may make sense for the United States to apply an economic benefits test to certain types of FDI similar to the approach taken by Canada.

Reverse mergers by scores of Chinese companies have allowed them to list on U.S. exchanges and raise funds from U.S. investors. While none of these mergers allowed Chinese firms to acquire important assets, many U.S. investors were burned when the Chinese firms were found to be much less than advertised. The SEC and the PCAOB have responded quickly to protect U.S. investors.

In short, the U.S. regulatory apparatus is already adjusting to the influx of Chinese investment in ways that will protect U.S. interests. Some observers believe the current system needs to be strengthened further to ensure U.S. economic interests are not harmed by investments responding to Chinese government policies rather than market forces. Congress has considered stronger measures in the past but has failed to enact them.

The growth in China's U.S. investments reflects efforts by governments on both sides of the Pacific. Responding to changes in China's "Go Out" policy and financial incentives provided by government-owned financial institutions, Chinese firms have in recent years turned their sights on advanced country markets, with the goals of acquiring brands, technologies, and markets for Chinese goods. These are frequently accomplished through M&A with U.S. firms. Washington and state capitals have actively promoted inward FDI from China, particularly in the form of greenfield investments that are more likely to generate jobs. U.S. business groups have also been actively seeking to attract FDI from China.

On an aggregate basis, the economic benefits of Chinese investments have been relatively modest compared to investments from other OECD countries. Based on public and private sources, it is reasonable to conclude that jobs in Chinese-owned affiliates in the United States increased by 10,000 to 20,000 workers during the past five years. While hardly significant relative to overall U.S. employment and even to jobs in other countries' U.S. affiliates, any job creation is welcome given continued slackness in the U.S. labor market. The number of workers employed by Chinese-owned firms is likely to increase significantly in the coming years as Chinese investments grow.

Chinese FDI in U.S. companies has helped stabilize some financially troubled firms. Portfolio investments by sovereign wealth funds also have helped the economy by solidifying the financial system and providing liquidity to certain property markets.

Chinese investments have occurred in all U.S. regions and in many sectors. According to one private data source, they have been especially prominent since 2007 in the Southwest, Great Lakes, Southeast, and Far West regions, and in the fossil fuels and chemicals, industrial machinery, and information technology industries. According to another private source, as well as government data, the financial sector is also a major recipient of Chinese FDI.

These economic benefits from Chinese investments are counterbalanced by policy challenges. First, U.S. affiliates of Chinese companies are not pure market actors and may be driven by state goals, not market forces. China's outward investments are dominated by China's SOEs, their subsidiaries, and SIVs. These entities are potentially disruptive because they frequently respond to policies of their owners, the Chinese government. Likewise, the government behaves like an owner, providing overall direction to SOE investments, including encouragement on where to invest, in what industries, and to what ends.

Second, SOEs may have unfair advantages relative to private firms when competing to purchase U.S. assets. SOEs benefit from substantial subsidies in

China and their investments in developing countries also receive ample financial support from the national and sub-national governments, state-owned financial institutions and local governments. Government pronouncements out of China suggest that investments in the United States and other advanced countries will also receive ample financial support. This raises the possibility that Chinese largesse could determine market outcomes for purchases of U.S. businesses.

Third, an increased SOE presence may be harmful to the U.S. economy. In China, SOEs are a major force in China, but as a group they are less efficient and profitable than private firms. To the extent that SOEs purchase U.S. companies on the basis of artificial advantages and operate inefficiently, they may not be beneficial to long-term U.S. economic performance.

Fourth, Chinese investments will create tensions related to economic security and national security if they behave in accordance with China's industrial policy as articulated in the 12th Five Year Plan, government pronouncements, and official investment guidance.

China's current policy guidance directs firms to obtain leapfrog technologies to create national champions in key emerging industries, while investment guidance encourages technology acquisition, energy security, and export facilitation. Based on this juxtaposition, some will conclude that Chinese FDI in the United States is a potential Trojan horse. Indeed, this study describes three new energy related investments after which production utilizing the desired technology was shifted to China.

ATTACHMENT 1: DESCRIPTION OF SELECT CHINESE INVESTORS IN U.S. COMPANIES

Wanxiang Group (Wanxiang) formed Wanxiang America as a Kentucky corporation in 1993, primarily to sell auto parts made in China to existing and new U.S. customers. The firm soon moved its main operations to Chicago, and became a major supplier to U.S. automakers and parts producers. Wanxiang America gained U.S. business at a time when U.S. parts producers were going bankrupt. Wanxiang America expanded its U.S. footprint by purchasing financially troubled U.S. firms and shifting some production to China. However, the firms purchased by Wanxiang America continued some production activities in the United States. The firm is believed to own or hold stakes in 20 U.S. firms that employ 5,000 Americans.

Lenovo Group Limited (Lenovo)[322] purchased IBM's personal computer (PC) business in 2005 for $1.7 billion. At the same time, IBM also purchased shares in Lenovo. Ten thousand of IBM's employees from the PC business joined the company, which initially kept space at IBM's headquarters in Armonk, NY. A number of changes have taken place to Lenovo's U.S. operations since 2005. The firm moved its headquarters to Morrisville, North Carolina, near Raleigh, and several IBM executives left the company. The firm's sales have thrived in Asia, especially in China, and it has expanded production in Mexico and other locations outside the United States. Currently, its main U.S. facilities are the headquarters and development facility in Morrisville and a fulfillment center in Whitsett, North Carolina, near Greensboro. The bulk of Lenovo's U.S. employment is in the North Carolina, where there are approximately 2,000 workers. The number of Lenovo's workers in other U.S. states is not known. Also, it is not known how many of the 10,000 IBM employees that joined Lenovo were employed in the United States.

China Investment Corporation (CIC) purchased a 9.9 percent share in Morgan Stanley in December 2007, just below the 10 percent share that officially constitutes FDI. The agreement dictated that CIC would be a passive financial investor with no special rights of ownership, no role in management, and no right to designate a member of the Board of Directors. In subsequent months, CIC bought and sold shares, including an additional $1.2 billion purchase of newly issued shares in June 2009, the proceeds of which Morgan Stanley used to repay U.S. government funds borrowed during the depths of the financial crisis. It is unclear how these investments affected jobs at Morgan Stanley, though it is clear that the funds were beneficial relative to the alternative of no investment. CIC has earned significant dividends on its investment, but has endured large paper losses because Morgan Stanley's stock is currently (i.e., the Spring of 2012) trading at one-third of the price that prevailed when CIC first invested.

CNOOC International Limited (CIL) has invested in two energy exploration projects with Chesapeake Energy: a 33.3 percent equity interest in Chesapeake's Eagle Ford Shale project in south Texas ($2.2 billion) in November 2010; and a 33.3 percent interest in Chesapeake's 800,000 oil and natural gas leasehold acres in northeast Colorado and Wyoming ($570 million) in early 2011. These investments were structured in a way that leaves CIL with no management control.

According to one Chesapeake official, his company is "in complete control of this acquisition. Our new partner, under no circumstances, will be allowed to operate any wells. We'll be driving that operation, and it's a very unique transaction...." These deals were attractive to Chesapeake because they allow it to derive revenues from the project more quickly. The employment affects of these transactions are likely positive.

Pacific Century Motors (PCM), a joint venture between the Aviation Industry Corporation and the investment arm of the Beijing municipal government, purchased Nexteer Automotive from GM in November 2010 for $450 million. Nexteer is the second largest employer in Michigan's Saginaw County.

GM was reportedly planning to close the facility if it did not find a buyer, and the only other buyer besides PCM was the Korean parts producer, Mando Corp. Since the investment occurred, equipment has been upgraded and 600 jobs have been added, though the economic recovery may partly explain the expansion in employment. Nexteer has also announced a new investment in India.

Attachment 2: Yintong Group Receives Praise and Important Visitors after Purchasing Altair Nano

The Yintong Group is a Chinese enterprise focused on new energy storage products. The following excerpts from the "People in Yintong" section of its Web site provide a sense of the role played by government plans and government officials in the new energy industry.

In March 2010, the industrialization of lithium titanate energy storage batteries was included on Guangdong Provinces list of top industrial projects. In November, Yintong announced its intention to acquire Altair Nanotechnologies, a struggling U.S. producer of lithium titanate batteries. That month, it received Premier Wen as a visitor, as well as other Party dignitaries.

In March 2011, according to Yintong, lithium titanate battery development was designated as special project in Guangdong and listed in the 863 Technology Plan, China's National High Technology Program, sure indications that the project will receive some form of state support.

In March 2010

The "R&D and Industrialization of High-performance Lithium Iron Phosphate Power Battery and High-efficient Lithium Titanate Energy Storage Battery" were listed in the Top 500 projects of modern industries in Guangdong Province. Technologies demonstrate concepts while quality reflects value.

On November 15, 2010

Wen Jiabao, Premier of the State Council, visited Guangdong Yintong New Energy Industrialization Base, and encouraged scientific research personnel to assume the historic mission of developing Chinese electric automobiles industry while seizing opportunities.

In the same month, Li Yi, the former Minister of Ministry of Industry and Information, visited Yintong; Wang Yang, Member of the Political Bureau of the Central Committee of the CPC and Secretary of Guangdong Provincial Committee of the CPC and Wan Gang, Vice Chairman of the Chinese People's Political Consultative Conference and Minister of Ministry of Science and Technology successively visited the exhibition area of Zhuhai Yintong Energy Co., Ltd. during EVS25, and highly appraised the battery technologies of Yintong. Care from leaders is the driving force for our growing.

In March 2011

Yintong's "Industrialization of Energy-type Lithium Ion Battery", "New Battery Structure" and "Industrialization of High-efficient Energy Storage Lithium Titanate Battery" were regarded as the industry research and significant special projects in Guangdong Province.

In April, "High-efficient Energy Storage Lithium Titanate Battery" and "High-performance Lithium Iron Phosphate Power Battery" were listed in the State "863" Technology Plan. The development of new energy automobile industry has gradually become the hot topic in society, and will become the national strategy.

ATTACHMENT 3: NEW ENERGY VEHICLE DEVELOPMENT PLAN OF GUANGDONG YINTONG INVESTMENT HOLDING GROUP COMPANY LIMITED (2011-2020)

The following excerpts from the "Development Plan" section of the Yintong Group's Web site provide a sense the role played by technology acquisition in Yintong's current and future plans. In China's planning cycle, the Party proposes five-year plans that are drafted by the State Council and approved by the National People's Congress. These plans serve as economic and industrial blueprints for China's planning agencies, sub-national governments, banks, SOEs, and private enterprises. The Yintong Group's Web site contains the group's New Energy Vehicle Development Plan covering 2011 to 2020. The plan references various provincial planning documents as well as the "national energy policy." Yintong's plan includes specific capacity targets, references to the government's role in targeting and funding, and plans for "international cooperation," including domestic production using Altair Nano's equipment and future plans with Dow Chemical.

Chapter 1 Cell industry development plan

III. Cell Materials

At present, lithium batteries in market widely adopt graphite as cathode. Through holding shares of American Altairnano Company, Yintong Group has introduced the globally most advanced cell anode material technology --- lithium titanate technology into Chinese market. Yintong Group purchases dedicated lithium titanate material of Altairnano for production of cell cells in China.

Lithium titanate cell has the features such as extremely-long service life (up to more than thirty years, and 20 thousand of cycles), incredibly high safety performance and so on. The batteries can be assembled together in a large scale to serve as an energy storage power station, which can save energy during idle time for peak time, store wind energy, solar energy and tidal energy, etc.; it has high-current charging and discharging capacity under either high or low temperature, broader application scope for both the areas with pleasant climate and the areas with cold and bad weather; it possesses superior reliability in applications of national defense, national infrastructure and other equipment.

Chapter 5 International Cooperation

The company will strengthen international scientific and technological cooperation and accelerate new energy industry development, which is of great significance for adjusting national energy structure, safeguarding energy safety, promoting energy saving and consumption reduction, reducing greenhouse gas emission, developing low-carbon economy, and realizing economic and social sustainable development. Adhering to the principle of Mutual Benefits and Win-Win, Intellectual Property Rights Protection, Advanced Technology Sharing, Advantageous Resources Integration, and Technical Innovation in international cooperation, the company aims to promote in-depth international scientific and technological cooperation in new energy sector, solve key and urgent problems in China's energy utilization, and strengthen technical innovation capability of China's new energy industry so as to form new energy technical development capability with independent intellectual property rights and drive international society to participate in new energy development and to share innovation achievements.

1. Integration of international key part technologies of electric vehicles, in particular, motor, electric control and module technologies. The company will introduce integrated technologies to China and other areas throughout the world, and promote actively the development and popularization of electric vehicle industry. The company has got in touch with companies with relevant technologies in USA, Japan, Germany, Italy, and Australia, and will integrate these companies through technical cooperation, joint market development, or international capital operation in the coming 5 – 10 years.
2. Promotion and cooperation of energy storage system. Through acquisition of Altairnano, the company has possessed world-advanced energy storage system technologies and owned two types of energy storage systems including lithium iron phosphate and lithium titanate simultaneously and because of this, the company can turn out energy storage system products covering medium- and low-end market and high-end market. It actively makes cooperation with large wind and solar power generation enterprises and large contractors throughout the world, thus promoting energy storage products to sell overseas in large quantities.
3. In terms of lithium titanate and lithium iron phosphate cell production, the company actively introduces new equipment, new materials and

new technologies in an attempt to unceasingly improve battery technologies and quality. The company has contacted nano-fiber companies in Korea and Japan to discuss technologies for prolonging battery life span and boosting battery safety. It is excepted that, in the coming 5 – 10 years, the company will develop new materials and new technologies that can greatly raise battery life span and safety, and will use them in the production of batteries.

4. The company will procure the research and development and industrialization of lithium titanate materials by Altairnano Inc. (USA) in China, and make efforts to reach the goal of annual yield of 3000 tons of lithium titanate anode materials.
5. The company will further strengthen the cooperation with Dow Chemical Company (USA) to design, produce, evaluate and optimize the preparation of lithium ion batteries by using Dow Chemical Company's LMP or NMC (2nd generation) as cathode materials and Yintong's LTO as anode materials. According to relevant regulations:
   (1) Conduct 1st phase bench-scale test and pilot test.
   (2) Reach the goal of annual yield of 3000 tons of cathode materials in 2012.
   (3) Build a Sino-US lithium ion cell material base for the mass production of cell anode and cathode materials, ceramic diaphragm and electrolyte.

BIBLIOGRAPHY

Data Sources

China

National Bureau of Statistics, http://www.stats.gov.cn/english/statisticaldata/yearlydata/and Haver Analytics.

Ministry of Commerce, http://english.mofcom.gov.cn/statistic/statistic.html State Administration of Foreign Exchange, via Haver Analytics.

United States

Bureau of Economic Analysis, http://www.bea.gov/iTable/index_MNC.cfm

Federal Reserve Bank of St. Louis, *Federal Reserve Economic Data*, http://research.stlouisfed.org/fred2/

United States International Trade Commission,

http://pubapps2.usitc.gov/sunset/
Yahoo Finance, http://finance.yahoo.com/

Other
Haver Analytics
Sovereign Wealth Fund Institute, http://www.swfinstitute.org/
United Nations Conference on Trade and Development, http://archive.unctad.org/Templates/Page.asp?intItemID=4979
World Bank, *World dataBank*, http://databank.worldbank.org/ddp/home.do?Step=12&id=4&CNO=2

REFERENCES

Abrami, R. M., & Zhang, W. (2011). *China Construction America (A): The Road Ahead.* Cambridge: Harvard Business School.

Abrami, R. M., Kirby, W. C., McFarlan, F. W., Wong, K. C.-H., & Manty, T. (2008). *Wanxiang Group: A Chinese Company's Global Strategy.* Cambridge: Harvard Business School and Ivey Publishing.

Aguilar, L. A. (2011). Facilitating Real Capital Formation. *Council of Institutional Investors Spring Meeting.* Washington, DC.

Ajaga, E., & Nunnekamp, P. (2008, May). *Inward FDI, Value Added and Employment in US States: A Panel Approach.* Kiel, Germany: Kiel institute for the World Economy. Retrieved from Kiel Institute for the World Economy.

Alpert, B., & Norton, L. P. (2010, August 20). Beware This Chinese Export. *Barrons's*, pp. 21-24.

Altair Nanotechnologies. (2011). *Q3 2011 Altair Nanotechnologies Inc Earnings Conference Call.* New York: Thomson Street Events.

American Chamber of Commerce in Shanghai. (2011, June). Chinese FDI in the U.S.-- Causes, Case Studies and the Future. *Viewpoint*. Shanghai, China.

American Lorain Corporation. (2011). *Form 10-K for 2010.*

Announcement of U.S.-China Governors Forum in Utah. (2011, July 15). Retrieved December 8, 2011, from U.S. Department of State: http://iipdigital.usembassy.gov/st/english/texttrans/2011/07/20110715132232s u9.554034e-02.html#axzz1k1dOZHvC

Areddy, J. T. (2010, May 18). Anshan to Invest in the U.S. *Wall Street Journal Online*. Retrieved from Wall.

Asia Pulse. (2005, June 24). *CNOOC bids US$67 per share for Unocal.* Retrieved May 10, 2012, from Asia Times Web site: http://www.atimes.com/atimes/China/GF24Ad01.html

Aucoin, M. (2002, June 1). Syntroleum, Marathon Expand Synthetic Fuels Demo Plant. *Daily Oklahoman (via Highbeam Research).*

Bathon, M. (2011, November 11). Bankruptcy Judge Approve Asset Sales by Evergreen. *Boston Globe.*

Baucus Announces New Wind Farm near Shawmut. (2012, January 19). Retrieved February 29, 2012, from States news Service, via Highbeam Research: http://www.highbeam.com/doc/1G1-277547494.html

Beene, R. (2010, February 1). Finalist: Best Deal - Large -- Beijing West Industries/Delphi Corp. *Crain's Detroit Business.*

Bergsten, C. F., & Noland, M. (1993). *Reconcilable Differences?* Washington, DC: Institute for International Economics.

Bradsher, K. (2009, August 25). China Racing Ahead of U.S. in the Drive to Go Solar. *The New York Times.*

Bradsher, K. (2010, March 28). Ford Agrees to Sell Volvo to a Fast Rising Chinese Company. *The New York Times.*

Brightbill, T. C. (2012, February 15). Written Testimony before the U.S.-China Economic and Security Review Commission. *Hearing on Chinese State-Owned and State-Controlled Enterprises.* Washington, DC: U.S.-China Economic and Security Review Commission.

Brown, K. (2008). *The Rise of the Dragon: Inward and outward investment in China in the reform period 1978-2007.* Oxford: Chandos Publishing.

Buckley, P. J., Clegg, J. L., Cross, A. R., Voss, H., Rhodes, M., & Ping, Z. (2008). In K. P. Sauvant, *The Rise of Transnational Corporations from Emergin Markets: Threat or Opportunity?* (pp. 107-157). Cheltenham: Edward Elgar.

Buckley, P. J., Clegg, L. J., Cross, A., Xin, L., Voss, H., & Ping, Z. (2010). The Determinents of Chinese Outward Direct Investment. In P. J. Buckley, *Foreign Direct Investment, China and the World Economy* (pp. 81-118). Basingstoke: Palgrave Macmillan.

Buckley, p. J., Cross, A., Tan, H., Liu, X., & Voss, H. (2010). Historic and Emergent Trends in Chinese Outward Direct Investment. In P. J. Buckley, *Foreign Direct Investment, China, and the World Economy* (pp. 119-162). New York: Palgrave Macmillan.

Bullis, K. (2011, December 6). Why Boston Went to China. *Technology Review (MIT).*

Bunkley, N. (2010, November 29). G.M. Sells Parts Maker to a Chinese Company. *The New York Times.*

Bureau of Economic Analysis. (2011, June 16). *Foreign Direct Investment in the United States (FDIUS).* Retrieved January 25, 2012, from Bureau of Economic Analysis: http://www.bea.gov/international/di1fdiop.htm

Bureau of Economic Analysis. (2012). *Direct Investment & Multinational Companies (MNCs).* Retrieved from Bureua of Economic Analysis Interactive Data Web site: http://www.bea.gov/iTable/index_MNC.cfm

Bureau of Foreign Trade of Guangzhou Municipality. (n.d.).

Byrnes, N., & Browning, L. (2011, August 1). Special Report: China's Shortcut to Wall Street. *Reuters*, pp. 1-6.

Caves, R. E., Frankel, J. A., & Jones, R. W. (1993). *World Trade and Payments: An Introduction* (Sixth ed.). New York: Harper Collins.

Certain Oil Country Tubular Goods from China, Investigation Nos. 701-TA-463 and 731- TA1159 (Preliminary) Publication 4081 (June 2009).

Chavez, J., & Linkhorn, T. (2011, November 17). *Chrysler outlines plans for $1.7 billion investment.* Retrieved February 8, 2012, from toledo.Blade.com: http://www.toledoblade.com/Automotive/2011 /11/17 /Chrysler-outlines-plansfor-1-7-billion-investment.html

Chediak, M. (2009, November 6). *AES to Sell Stock, Wind-Power Stake to China's CIC.* Retrieved February 9, 2012, from Bloomberg Web site: http://www.bloomberg.com/apps/news?pid=newsarchive&sid=aoCzEbLi3umI

Chen, A. (2011, April 20). *Special Report: China set to unearth shale power.* Retrieved March 1, 2012, from Reuters.com: http://www.reuters.com/article/2011/04/20/us-china-shaleidUSTRE73J12F20110420

Chesapeake Energy Corporation. (November 18, 2011). *Form 8-K.*

Chesapeake Energy, China team up for Niobrara play. (2011, February 1). Retrieved March 1, 2012, from Wyoming Business Report: http://www.wyomingbusinessreport.com/article.asp?id=55837

China Cablecom Holdings, Ltd. (2011). *Form 20-F for 2010.*

China Development Bank. (2011). *2010 Annual Report: Overview of Operations (3).* Retrieved February 16, 2012, from China Development Bank Web site: http://www.cdb.com.cn/english/Column. asp? Column Id=217

China Development Bank. (2012). *2011 Annual Report.*

China 'to block' Hummer takeover. (2009, June 26). Retrieved February 29, 2012, from BBC Web site: http://news.bbc.co.uk/2/hi/8120231.stm

China to create new $300 billion FX vehicle. (2011, December 9). Retrieved December 9, 2011, from Reuters.com: http://www.reuters.com /assets /print?aid=USTRE7B80N620111209

China-Africa Development Fund. (2012). Retrieved March 7, 2012, from Sovereign Wealth Fund Institute Web site: http://www.swfinstitute.org /swfs/china-africadevelopment-fund/

China's Ministry of Commerce. (2011). *2010 Statistical Bulletin of China's Outward Foreign Direct Investment.*

CIC gets Fed approval about the purchase of the 10% voting stake in Morgan Stanley. (2010, September 1). Retrieved February 24, 2012, from SWF Institute: http://www.swfinstitute.org/swf-article/cic-gets-fed-approval-about-thepurchase-of-the-10-voting-stake-in-morgan-stanley/

CIC gets Fed approval about the purchase of the 10% voting state in Morgan Stanley. (2010, September 1). Retrieved February 9, 2012, from SWF Intsitute Web site: http://www.swfinstitute.org/swf-article/cic-gets-fed-approval-about-thepurchase-of-the-10-voting-stake-in-morgan-stanley/

CIC to Expand Morgan Stanley Stake. (2010, September 1). Retrieved February 29, 2012, from Dailymarkets.com: http://www.dailymarkets.com /stock/2010/09/01/cicto-expand-morgan-stanley-stake/

Citric Acid and Certain Citrate Salts from Canada and China, Investigation Nos. 701-TA456 and 731-TA-1151-1152 (Final) Publication 4076 (United States International Trade Commission May 2009).

Clement, C. (2011, May 26). *Attracting Chinee FDI to the United States.* Retrieved December 28, 2011, from Invest in America: http://www.mitc. com/PDFs/ClementChinaTradeDayMay2011.pdf

CNOOC Limited. (2012). *Annual Report 2011.*

Crystalline Silicon Photovoltaic Cells and Modlues from China, Investigation Nos. 701-TA481 and 731-TA-1190 (Preliminary) Pub. 4295 (United States International Trade Commission December 2011).

Davis, B. (2012, February 23). New Push for Reform in China. *The Wall Street Journal*, p. A1.

de la Merced, M. J., & Bradsher, K. (2007, December 20). China fund invests in Morgan Stanley First quarterly loss and 2nd write-down lead to sale of 9.9% stake in company. *International Herald Tribune*.

de Swaan, J. (2010, April 29). *China Goes to Wall Street.* Retrieved February 27, 2012, from Foreign Affairs: <http://www.foreignaffairs.com/articles /66398/jc-deswaan/china-goes-to-wall-street?page=2>

Delegation to China. (n.d.). Retrieved December 1, 2011, from Asian American Business Development Center: http://www.aabdc.com/aabdcz /program/delegation-tochina/

Deng, Y., Morck, R., Wu, J., & Yeung, B. (2011, March). Monetary and Fiscal Stimuli, Ownership Structure, and China's Housing Market. *NBER Working Paper Series(Working Paper 16871)*. Cambridge, MA: National Bureau of Economic Research.

Department of Commerce. (2007, June 15). *Commerce Department Announces Updated Export Controls for China*. Retrieved January 2012, from Bureau of Industry and Security Web sit: http://www.bis.doc.gov /news/2007/06-15-07-export-rulepress-release---final.pdf

Department of Foreign Trade and Economic Cooperation of Guangdong Province. (n.d.).

Department of Justice. (2010, April 12). *Foreign Corrupt Practices Act: An Overview*. Retrieved February 16, 2012, from Fraud Section: Home: http://www.justice.gov/criminal/fraud/fcpa/

Department of the Treasury. (2011, March 12). *Covered Transactions, Withdrawals, and Presidential Decisions, 2008-2010*. Retrieved January 11, 2012, from CFIUS: Resource Center: Reports and Tables: http://www.treasury.gov/resourcecenter/international/foreign-investment/Documents/CoveredTransactions2008- 2010.PDF

Department of the Treasury. (2011, March 12). *The Committee on Foreign Investment in the United States (CFIUS)* . Retrieved 30 2012, January , from Treasury Web site: Resource Center: http://www.treasury.gov /resourcecenter/international/Pages/Committee-on-Foreign-Investment-in-US.aspx

Dewey & Leboeuf LLP. (2010). *China's Promotion of the Renewable Electric Power Equipment Industry*. Washington, DC: National Foreign Trade Council.

Drake, E. J. (2012, February 15). Policy Options for Addressing Chinese State-Owned Enterprises. *Testimony before the U.S.-China Economic and Security Review Commission*. Washington, DC: U.S.-China Economic and Security Review Commission.

Economist Intelligence Unit. (2011, November 27). *China: FDI Outflows as a Percent of GDP (%) (A924OUDF@EIUIASIA)*. Retrieved February 7, 2012, from Haver Analytics: http://www.haverselect.com/dlx/home.htm

Engardio, P. (2005, August 22). *"Online Extra: "China Is a Private-Sector Economy"*. Retrieved August 17, 2011, from Businessweek.com: http://www.businessweek.com/magazine/content/05_34/b3948478.htm

Exclusive: China's CIC to get $50 billion boost. (2011, December 23). Retrieved December 23, 2011, from Reuters Web site: http://www.reuters.com/article/2011/12/23/us-china-sovereignidUSTRE7BM09A20111223

Export.gov. (2011, September 21). *Chinese Overseas Investment Fair--Expo and SelectUSA Smeinar.* Retrieved March 6, 2012, from SelectUSA: http://export.gov/china/selectusa/eg_cn_039446.asp

Export-Import Bank of China. (2011). *2010 Annual Report.*

Export-Import Bank of the United States. (June 2011). *Report to the U.S. Congress on Export Credit Competition and the Export-Import Bank of the United States.*

Fagan, D. N. (2009). The US regulatory and institutional framework for FDI. In K. P. Sauvant, *Investing in the united States* (pp. 45-84). Northampton, MA: Edward Elgar.

Freedman, D. (2011, September 27). *China Beckons for clean Energy Startups.* Retrieved February 16, 2012, from Technology Review: http://www.technologyreview.com/energy/38678/page2/

Freeman III, C. W., & Yuan, W. J. (2011, November). China's Investment in the United States--National Initiatives, Corporate Goals and Public Opinion.

FTC pre-merger Notification Office. (2008). *To File or Not to File.* Washington, DC: Feteral Trade Commission.

Fund Rankings. (2012, February 9). *SWF Institute.*

Going Public, Chinese Style. (2007, March 5). *Bloomberg Business Week.*

Gordon, D. F. (2012, February 15). Testimony before the U.S.-China Economic and Security Review Commission. *The Competitive Challenges Posed by China's State-Owned Enterprises.* Washington, DC: U.S.-China Economic and Security Review Commission.

Guangdong Yintong Investment Holding Group Company Limited New Energy Vehicle Development Plan (2011-2020). (n.d.). Retrieved February 22, 2012, from Yintong Group Web site: http://en.yintonggroup.com/culture /&FrontComContent_list01- 1319886598334ContId=6a02ab93-70e2-4268-b82fc52604d6e5a5&comContentId=6a02ab93-70e2-4268-b82f-c52604d6e5a5.html

Hainan Group. (Unk). *HNA: Our History.* Retrieved February 29, 2012, from HNA Group Web site: http://en.hnagroup.com /HnaGroupWebUI /Company/wfmHistory.aspx

Hamilton, J. (2011, December 1). *U.S. Regulators Push Chinese to Resume Auditor-Inspection Talks.* Retrieved December 28, 2011, from Bloomberg

Businessweek: http://www.businessweek.com/news/2011-12-01/u-s-regulators-push-chineseto-resume-auditor-inspection-talks.html

Hammer, A., & Jones, L. (2012, January). China's Emerging Role as a Global Source of FDI. *USITC Executive Briefings on Trade*. Washington, DC: United States International Trade Commission.

Hilzenrath, D. S. (2012, February 22). SEC: China-based coal mining company Puda an empty shell, defrauded investors. *Washington Post.*

Historical Prices. (2012). Retrieved February 29, 2012, from Google Finance: http://www.google.com/finance

Hou, R. (2011, June). *Sub-National Contacts Deepen Chinese-U.S. Relations*. Retrieved December 8, 2011, from Chinatoday.com: http://www. chinatoday.com.cn/ctenglish/se/txt/2011- 06/10/content_366273.htm

Huang, Y. (2008). *Capitalism with Chinese Characteristics.* New York: Cambridge University Press.

Huawei. (2012, February 5). *Huawei Horth American Fact Sheet*. Retrieved March 6, 2010, from Huawei Web site: http://www.huawei.com/ucmf /groups/public/documents/webasset/hw_090310 .pdf

Huaweil Piled Up 3Leaf Acquisition on Neglect of Reporting. (2011, March 7). *AsiaInfo Services.*

Hubbard, P. (2007, September). Aiding Transparency: What We Can Learn About China ExIm Bank's Concessional Loans. Center for Global Development.

Implications of Sovereign Wealth Fund Investments for national Security: Statement of Sen. Evan Bayh. (2008, February 7). *Hearing of the U.S.-China Economic and Security Review Commission*. Washington, DC.

International Cooperation Department of China Industrial Overseas Development and Planning. (n.d.).

International Monetary Fund. (2011, September 20). China: Current Account Balance (% of GDP) Series A924BCDS@IMFWEO. *World Economic Outlook.*

Jackson, J. K. (2006, February 23). *CRS Report for Congress: "The Exon-Florio National Security Test for Foreign Investment" February 23, 2006 at CRS-3 http://www.fas.org/sgp/crs/natsec/RS22197.pd.* Retrieved Janaury 12, 2012, from http://www.fas.org/sgp/crs/natsec/RS22197.pdf

Jensen, N. M., & Malesky, E. J. (2010). *FDI incentives pay--politically.* New York: Vale Columbia Center on Sustainable International Investment.

Jones, A. (2011, November 6). China and US in standoff over auditors. *Financial Times.*

Jones, H. (2011, May 20). China's Auto Industry Shows Signs of Impending Gridlock. *Forbes.*

Karmin, C., & Wei, L. (2012, February 16). Real-Estate Chief Exits from China Wealth Fund. *Wall Street Journal*, p. C3.

Kingold Jewelry, Inc. (2011). *Form 10-K for 2010.*

Legend Holdings Limited. (n.d.). *Legend Holding: Company Profile.* Retrieved February 29, 2012, from Legend Holding Web site: http://www.legendholdings.com.cn/intro_en.asp

Lenovo Group Limited. (2011). *2010/2011 Annual Report.*

Li, S. (2011, June 27). Property firm lands second US deal. *South China Morning Post.*

Li, X. (2010). *China's Outward Foreign Investment.* Lantham, MD: United Press of America.

Li, Z. (2009). China's Go Global Policy. In J.-P. Larçon, *Chinese Multinationals* (pp. 31-48). Singapore: World Scientific.

Li, Z. (2009). China's Outward Foreign Direct Investment. In J.-P. Larcon, *Chinese Multinationals* (pp. 49-76). Singapore: Mainland Press.

Li, Z., Schwartz, S., & Xu, G. (2011, October 12). *BBVA Research.* Retrieved February 7, 2012, from Economic Watch: China's outward FDI expands: http://www.bbvaresearch.com/KETD/fbin/mult/111014_ChinaWatch_ofdi _tcm3 48-272185.pdf?ts=722012

Lumsden, A., & Knight, L. (2012, April 19). *New SASAC Rules Signal Greater Transparency and Accountability.* Retrieved May 10, 2012, from Corrs Chambers Wesgarth Web site: http://www.corrs.com.au /thinking/insights/new-sasac-rules-signalgreater-transparency-and-accountability/

Lyne, J. (2009, January). *$1 Billion in the Texas Pipeline.* Retrieved February 21, 2012, from Siteselection.com: http://www.siteselection.com/ssinsider /bbdeal/Billionin-Texas-Pipeline.htm

Margin & Safety. (2011, October 31). *Harbin Electric Buyout Approved: Implications For U.S. Listed Chinese Stocks.* Retrieved February 13, 2012, from Seeking Alpha: http://seekingalpha.com/article/303735-harbin-electric-buyout-approvedimplications-for-u-s-listed-chinese-stocks

Mayer Brown LLP. (2010, November 23). US Government Forces Parties to a Completed Transaction to Submit to Review by the Committee on Foreign Investment in the United States. *Monday Business Briefing.*

McCoy, K., & Chu, K. (2011, December 26). Merger of U.S., Chinese Firms is Cautionary Tale. *USA Today.*

Min, X. (2011, July 19). *U.S. States Fight it out for Chinese Investment.* Retrieved December 6, 2011, from Business China: http://en.21cbh.com /HTML/2011-7- 19/3NMjM1XzIxMDU3NA.html

Ministry of Commerce. (2009, March 19). Measures for Overseas investment Management.

Ministry of Finance. (2003). Provisional Administrative Measures on Special Venturing Fund for Letters of Guarantee on Foreign Contracting Projects.

Mobley, J. (2010). Chesapeake Energy Corporation (Final Transcript). *Bank of America Merrill Lynch Credit Conference.* Thomson StreetEvents.

Moore, M. (2010, July 28). *CIC Sells Morgan Stanley Shares for Total of $396.5 Million in Past Week.* Retrieved February 24, 2012, from Bloomberg: http://www.bloomberg.com/news/2010-07-28/cic-sells-morgan-stanley-sharesfor-total-of-396-5-million-in-past-week.html

Morgan Stanley. (December 27, 2007). *Form 8-K.*

Murray, B. (2012, February 12). Chinese Firm HNA Property Holding Spends $130M on NYC's Cassa Hotel. *Copmmercial Property Executive.*

National Development and Reform Commission. (2011). *12th Five-Year Plan for National Economic and social Development.*

National Development and Reform Commission. (2011, February 14). Notice Relating to Delegation of Examination and Approval Authority for Overseas Investment Projects.

National Social Security Fund. (2010, June 4). Retrieved February 9, 2012, from SWF Institute Web site: http://www.swfinstitute.org/swfs/national-social-securityfund/

Ng, L., & Cheng, W.-G. (2005, June 27). *CNOOC Gets Cheap China Government Loan for $18.5 Bln Unocal Bid.* Retrieved May 10, 2012, from Bloomberg Web site: http://www.bloomberg.com/apps/news?pid=newsarchive&sid=a4J4nnu9fwOA& refer=top_world_news

Niran--We Innovate Green. (2009). Retrieved October 8, 2010, from Niran (Thailand) Co., Ltd.: http://www.niran.co.th/company.html

O'Brien, K. J. (2006, March 9). Lenovo steps out onto global stage. *International Herald Tribune.*

Of Emperors and Kings: China's state-owned enterprises are on the march. (2011, November 12). *The Economist.*

Ondrey, G. (2007, march 1). CTL/GTL cooperation. *Chemical Engineering (via Highbeam Research).*

Organisation for Economic Cooperation and Development. (2008). OECD Investment Policy Reviews: China 2008.

Organisation for Economic Cooperation and Development. (2010, September 28). *Arrangement on Export Credits: About*. Retrieved May 4, 2012, from OECD Web site: http://www.oecd.org/about/0,3347,en_2649_34171 1 1 1 1 1,00.html

Organization for Economic Cooperation and Development. (2000, November 8). OECD

Declaration and Decisions on International Investment and Multinational Enterprises.

Oxford Economic Forecasting. (2011, April 14). China: Current Account Balance (Bil.US$) Series A924BCUD@OEFAMACR.

Oxford Economics. (2011, April 14). *China: Foreign Direct Investment: Exports (Bil.US$) (A924FDXD@OEFAMACR).* Retrieved February 7, 2012, from Haver Analytics: htpp://http://www.haverselect.com /dlx/home.htm

Payne, D., & Yu, F. (2011, June). *Foreign Direct Investment in the United States*. Retrieved from U.S. Department of Commerce: Economics and Statistics Administration: http://www.esa.doc.gov/sites/default/files /reports/documents/fdiesaissuebrief no2061411final.pdf

People's Bank of China. (1990, April 13). Procedures for the Administration of Chinese Financial Institutions Abroad.

Pomfret, J. (2011, January 19). A plan for new U.S. jobs, from China. *The Washington Post*, p. A1.

Prasso, S. (2010, May 7). *American Made, Chinese Owned*. Retrieved 12 6, 2011, from CNNMoney.com: http://money.cnn.com/2010/05/06/news /international/china_america.fortune/i ndex.htm

Prestowitz, C. (2010). *The Betrayal of American Prosperity*. New york: Free press. Prestowitz, C. V. (1988). *Trading Places*. New York: Basic Books.

Price, A. H., Brightbill, T. C., Weld, C. B., & El-Sabaawi, L. (2011). *Facing the Challenges of SOE Investment Abroad.* Washington, DC: North American Steel Trade Committee.

Quijano, A. M. (1990, February). A Guide to BEA Statistics on Foreign Direct Investment in the United States. *Survey of Current Business*, pp. 29-37.

Raice, S., & Dowell, A. (2011, February 22). Huawei Drops U.S. Deal Amid Opposition. *The Wall Street Journal.*

Rasiah, R., Gammeltoft, P., & Yang, J. (2010). Home Government Policies for Outward FDI from Emerging Economies: Lessons from Asia. *International Journal of Emerging Markets, 5*(3/4), 333-357.

Richter, W. (2011, December 29). China is Steadily Buying Up the US Auto Industry. *Business Insider.*

Roberts, K. R. (2006, December 12). *Syntroleum FT Process and Fuels.* Retrieved February 24, 2012, from Center for Strategic and International Studies Web Site: http://csis.org/files/media/csis/events /061212_ roberts. pdf

Rosen, D. H., & Hanemann, T. (2011, May). An American Open Door? Washington, DC: Asia Society.

Rosen, D. H., & Hanemann, T. (2012). *China Investment Monitor.* Retrieved from

Rhodium Group: http://rhgroup.net/interactive/china-investment-monitor

Salidjanova, N. (2010). *Going Out: An Overview of China's Outward Foreign Direct Investment.* Washington, DC: U.S.-China Economic & Security Review Commission.

Santangel, B., Stein, G., Suh, S.-H., White, P. H., & Friedman, W. I. (2011, January 18). *Government Launches FCPA Inquiry into Investments by Sovereign Wealth Funds in U.S. Banks and Private Equity Firms.* Retrieved February 6, 2012, from Shulte Roth & Zabel Web site: http://www.srz.com/files/News/537c575a-9da6-4076-9457-130b10d603d3/Presentation/NewsAttachment/b6cc579f-56e6-4874-9e9c-19cbdc79b7b8/011811_Government_Launches_FCPA_Inquiry_Into_Investments _by_Sovereign_Wealth_Funds.pdf

Scissors, D. (2010, August 17). *Where China Invests, and Why It Matters.* Retrieved December 1, 2011, from Forbes.com: http://www.forbes.com /2010/08/17/china-spending-investment-overseasmarkets-economy-china-tracker.html

Scissors, D. (2011, February 3). *China's Investment Overseas in 2010.* Retrieved September 16, 2011, from The Heritage Foundation Web Memo: http://www.heritage.org/research/reports/2011/02/chinas-investmentoverseas-in-2010

Scissors, D. (2012). *China Global Investment Tracker Interactive Map.* Retrieved from The Heritage Foundation: http://www.heritage.org /research/projects/chinaglobal-investment-tracker-interactive-map

Securities and Exchange Commission. (2011, November 9). *SEC Approves New Rules to Toughen Listing Standards for Reverse merger Companies.* Retrieved February 13, 2012, from SEC Web site: http://sec.gov/news/press/2011/2011-235.htm

Securities and Exchange Commission. (2011, June 8). Self-Regulatory Organizations; The NASDAQ Stock Market LLC; Notice of Filing of Proposed Rule Change to Adopt Additional Listing Requirements for

Reverse Mergers. *Release No. 34-64633; File No. SR-NASDAQ-2011-073.*

Securities and Exchange Commission. (2012, February 8). Retrieved February 16, 2012, from Form 20-F.

Securities and Exchange Commission. (unk). Retrieved February 20, 2012, from Forms 3, 4, and 5: http://www.sec.gov/answers/form345.htm

Securities and Exchange Commission: What we do. (2010, January 20). Retrieved February 20, 2012, from Securities and Exchange Commission Web site: http://www.sec.gov/about/whatwedo.shtml

Sedgwick, D. (2011, February 21). How a Chinese Owner Took Root in the Rust Belt. *Automotive News.*

Sedgwick, D. (2012, January 12). *China State-Owned Suppliers Seek US Acquisitions.* Retrieved February 23, 2012, from Automotivenews.com: http://www.autonews.com/apps/pbcs.dll/article?AID=/20120112/OEM09/1201 19906

Show Me State Worth a Look. (2011, July 1). Retrieved December 1, 2011, from MidWest US-China Association: http://pitchengine.com/midwest uschinaassociation/showmestateworthalookdelegationfromchinamakesst louisitsmidweststoponauseconomictour

Shu, J., & Wang, J. (2006). *Wanxiang Group: Exploring the International Market.* Ontario: China Europe International Business School and Ivey Management Services.

Sidhu, N. D., Guerra, F., Ritter, K., & Kyser, J. (2010). *China and los Angeles County: Growing Together.* Los Angeles, CA: Los Angeles County Economic Development Corporation and Kyser Center for Economic Research.

Sinopec and Syntroleum Announce Grand Opening of Coal to Liquids Demonstration Plant. (2011, August 1). Retrieved February 24, 2012, from Globe News Wire: http://www.globenewswire.com/

Socialism with Chinese Characteristics. (2007, September 30). Retrieved July 2011, from englishpeoplesdaily.com: http://english.peopledaily.com.cn /90002/92169/92211/6275043.html#

Springut, M., Schlaikjer, S., & Chen, D. (2011). *China's Program for Science and Technology Modernization.* Washington, DC: U.S.-China Economic and Security Review Commission.

Stanford Law School and Cornerstone Research. (2012, January 19). Securities Class Action Filings: 2011 Year in Review.

Sub-Prime Report. (2008, April). *Sovereign Wealth Quarterly.*

Sun, W., & Bo, J. (2011). *How Chinese Investors Go Out.* Retrieved from China Law Information: http://article.chinalawinfo.com/ArticleHtml /Article_64555.shtml

SWF Institute. (2011, January 4). *CIC and Manhattan Real Estate.* Retrieved February 28, 2012, from SWF Institute Web site: http://www.swfinstitute. org/swf-article/cicand-manhattan-real-estate/

Syntroleum (SYNM) to Suspend Operations of Catoosa. (2006, September 7). Retrieved February 24, 2012, from StreetInsider.com: http://www. streetinsider.com/

Syntroleum Corporation. (2009). *Q1 2009 Syntroleum Earnings Conference Call.* Thomson Street Events. Retrieved from Thomson Street Events.

Szamosszegi, A. (2007). *How* Chinese *Government Subsidies and Market Intervention Have Resulted in the Offshoring of U.S. Auto Parts Production: A Case Study.* Washington, DC: Capital Trade, Inc.

Szamosszegi, A., Anderson, C., & Kyle, C. (2009). *An Assessment of China's Subsidies to Strategic and Heavyweight Industries.* Washington, DC: U.S.-China Economic and Security Review Commission.

Tafara, E. (2008, April 24). *Testimony Concerning The Regulatory Framework for Sovereign Investments.* Retrieved February 15, 2012, from Securities Exchange Commission Web site: http://www.sec.gov/news /testimony/2008/ts0342408et.htm

The World Bank and Development Research Center of the State Council. (2012). *China 2030.* Washington, DC: The World Bank.

The World Bank and Development Research Center of the State Council. (2012). *China 2030: Building a Modern, Harmonious, and Creative High-Income Society.* Washington: World Bank.

Top 20 Largest Hedge Funds 2012. (2012, January 2). Retrieved Fubruary 16, 2012, from Hedge Fund Blog Man: http://hedgefundblogman. blogspot.com/2012/01/top20-largest-hedge-funds-2012.html

Trina Solar Limited. (2011). *Form 20-F for 2010.*

Trindle, J. (2011, November 10). SEC Tightens Rules for 'Reverse Merger' Listings. *Wall Street Journal.*

U.S. Chamber Continues U.S.-China CEO Dialogue to Highlight Importance of Bilateral Relationship. (2011, November 15). Retrieved December 1, 2011, from U.S. Chamber of Commerce: http://www.uschamber.com /press/releases/2011/november/us-chambercontinues-us-china-ceo-dialogue-highlight-importance-bilater

U.S. Department of the Treasury. (2011, March 31). *About Us: Office of Foreign Assets Control.* Retrieved February 9, 2012, from U.S. Treasury

Web site: http://www.treasury.gov/about/organizational-structure/offices /Pages/Officeof-Foreign-Assets-Control.aspx

U.S.-China Economic and Security Review Commission. (2011, September 9). Investments made in the united States by investors from the People's Republic of China, and potential impacts on future U.S. economic and national security. *Request for Proposals*. Washington, DC.

U.S.-China Economic and Security Review Commission. (2011). *The National Security Implications of Investments and Products from the People's Republic of China in the Telecommunications Sector.* Washington, DC: USCC.

U.S.-China Economic Security and Review Commission. (October 2011). *An Analysis of State-Owned Enterprises and State Capitalism in China.* Washington, DC: Capital Trade, Inc.

U.S.-China Governors Forum Continue in Beijing. (2011, October 18). Retrieved December 8, 2011, from U.S. Department of State: http://www.state.gov/r/pa/prs/2011/10/175781.htm

Unirule Institute of Economics. (2011). *The Nature, Performance, and Reform of the State-Owned Enterprise.* Beijing: Unirule.

United Nations Conference on Trade and Development. (2011). *World Investment Report 2011*. New York: United Nations.

United States Trade Representative. (2008, December). *United States Files WTO Case Against China Over Illegal Support for Chinese "Famous Brands"*. Retrieved May 3, 2012, from USTR Web site: http://www.ustr. gov/about-us/press-office/pressreleases/archives/2008/december/united-states-files-wto-case-against-chi

Visclosky, P. J. (2012, February 15). Testimony on Congressional Perspectives. *Hearing on China's State-Owned and State-Controlled Enterprises*. Washington, DC: U.S.- China Economic and Security Review Commission.

von Reppert-Bismarck, J. (2011, January 13). *EU prepares to challenge China export credit.* Retrieved May 10, 2012, from Reuters Web site: http://af.reuters.com/article/energyOilNews/idAFLDE70C2G220110113? pageNu mber=3&virtualBrandChannel=0&sp=true

Walter, C. E., & Howe, F. J. (2011). *Red Capitalism: The Fragile Financial Foundation of China's Extraordinary Rise.* Singapore: John Wiley & Sons (Asia).

Wang, Y. (2009). Corporate Culture and Organization of Chinese Multinationals. In J.-p.

Larcon, *Chinese Multinationals* (pp. 167-191). Singapore: Mainland Press.

Watts, J. (2012, February 4). China Plots Path for Green Growth Amid a Boom Built on Dirty Industry. *The Guardian*, p. 2012.

Wei, J. (2009, March 6). Survery: Chinese Companies Keen on Foreign Buys. *China Daily.*

Weiss, M. (2011, January 4). *CIC Backs Carlyle's Manhattan Tower in U.S. Push.* Retrieved February 28, 2012, from Bloomberg: http://www.bloomberg.com/news/2011-01-03/cic-backs-manhattan-tower-aschina-steps-up-u-s-real-estate-investments.html

White, J. B., & Shirouzu, N. (2012, February 11). In the Heart of the Rust Belt, Chinese Funds Provide the Grease. *The Wall Street Journal*, p. A1.

World Bank. (2011, December 15). *World Development Indicators*. Retrieved February 20, 2012, from World Bank Web site: http://databank. worldbank.org/ddp/home.do?Step=1&id=4

Wu, S. (2009). *Chinese Multinationals in historical Perspective.* Lexington, KY: VDM Verlag Dr. Muller.

Xinhua. (2012, February 12). *Changes in Chinese Companies' Overseas Investments.* Retrieved February 13, 2012, from Chinascope: http://chinascope.org/main/content/view/4288/107

Yang, Z. (2009, April 20). Easier Loans Lead to More Mergers and Acquisitions. *China Daily*, p. 4. Retrieved February 24, 2012, from Chinadaily.com: www.chinadaily.com.cn/bw/2009-04/20/content_ 7693 323.htm

Zacks Investment Research. (2010, September 1). *CIC gets Fed approval about the purchase of the 10% voting stake in Morgan Stanley*. Retrieved February 9, 2012, from daily markets.com: http://www.dailymarkets. com/stock/2010/09/01/cicto-expand-morgan-stanley-stake/

Zeller Jr., T., & Bradsher, K. (2010, December 15). China's Push into Wind Worries U.S. Industry. *The New York Times*, p. B1.

Zhang, Q. (2011, May 12). *Nanshan Aluminum to open US plant*. Retrieved February 23, 2012, from China Daily Web site: http://www.chinadaily. com.cn/bizchina/2011- 05/12/content_12496676.htm

Zhang, W., & Alon, I. (2010). *A Guide to the Top 100 Companies in China.* Singapore: World Scientific.

Zheng, Z. (2010, December 1). Leverage: How Youngor Succeeds in the Clothing Industry. *Nan Feng Chuang (The South Window)*, p. http://en.youngor.com/news.do?action=detail&cid=20081190204341243 &id=2 009091710485567624.

Zhuhai Yintong Energy: About us. (n.d.). Retrieved February 22, 2012, from Zhuhai Yintong Energy: http://en.yintonggroup.com/energy_index.html

Zoom Technologies, Inc. (2011). *Form 10-K for 2010.*

End Notes

[1] According to the OECD, China's inward direct investment position in Germany was a mere one million dollars in 1984.

[2] Given that many investments from tax haven economies and Hong Kong are likely undertaken by Chinese-owned firms, it is likely that Chinese FDI is even higher than official totals suggest.

[3] (Socialism with Chinese Characteristics, 2007)

[4] A direct investment is one in which the investor acquires an ownership stake in a foreign firm that is sufficient to allow the investor to exercise influence over the management of the acquired enterprise. In the United States, the Bureau of Economic Analysis considers this ownership threshold to be 10 percent. (Quijano, 1990, p. 29) A portfolio investment is one in which the foreign investor's ownership share is insufficient to allow the investor to exercise managerial control. Portfolio investment also includes purchases of debt.

[5] The current account considers trade in goods and services as well as income flows from foreign investments, government grants, and worker remittances.

[6] The identity is $S - I = X - M$. where S is national savings, I is national investment, X is total exports, and M is total imports. A country that exports more than it imports (i.e., $X > M$) must also save more than it invests domestically (i.e., $S > I$).

[7] Note that we are not attributing China's current account surplus to excess savings, but pointing out that when a country runs a current account surplus, it has foreign exchange available for foreign investments.

[8] A country's foreign investments, including FDI, are treated as debits, which are analogous to imports. In this presentation, capital account incorporates both the capital and financial accounts.

[9] In this explanation, the errors and omissions term is assumed to be zero.

[10] One might ask how, if China runs surpluses in both its capital and current accounts, it can achieve balance in its international payments? The answer is that Chinese monetary authorities must purchase large amounts of foreign currency. This stockpile of currency is then used to purchase foreign assets, which traditionally have been dominated by purchases of U.S. government debt.

[11] (Rosen & Hanemann, An American Open Door?, 2011, pp. 81-82).

[12] (Scissors, China Global Investment Tracker Interactive Map, 2012).

[13] (Rosen & Hanemann, China Investment Monitor, 2012).

[14] Some state-specific data stopped being published in 2007. Although BEA does identify the investors in some large investments in *Survey of Current Business*, it only does so if the source of the investment has been made public.

[15] Chinese statistics on outward FDI prior to 2003 were not calculated in accordance with international standards and are believed to have undercounted China's ODI. Nevertheless, the current statistics are also believed to undercount ODI because private investors do not always seek official approval. (Organisation for Economic Cooperation and Development, 2008, p. 71).

[16] (United Nations Conference on Trade and Development, 2011, pp. 7, 9).

[17] (United Nations Conference on Trade and Development, 2011, pp. 30-31).

[18] (Salidjanova, 2010, pp. 19-24).

[19] (Huang, 2008, p. 6) As Huang puts it, "Hong Kong is a safe harbor for some of the talented Chinese entrepreneurs and an alternative to China's poorly functioning financial and legal systems."

[20] The Organisation for Economic Cooperation and Development (OECD) is a grouping of the world's so-called advanced economies.

[21] (U.S.-China Economic and Security Review Commission, 2011, pp. 28-30).

[22] The stock of Chinese FDI in Australia was only $434 million in 2006, indicating that the increase in Chinese inward investment there has been quite dramatic during the past four years.

[23] (United Nations Conference on Trade and Development, 2011, p. 48).

[24] OECD statistics on ODI stock from China are not reported for Belgium or Luxembourg though yearly FDI inflows have been reported since 2002. Prior to 2002, the OECD combined the FDI data for Belgium and Luxembourg. Summing together the annual data on FDI inflows is not a valid methodology for calculating FDI stock. Still, this methodology at least provides some indication of FDI from China in these two countries. From 1987 to 2004, total FDI inflows from China reported by Belgium and Luxembourg were $256 million. From 2005 to 2010, there was an additional $2,448 million in inflows from China, the bulk of which were directed to Luxembourg. The data on annual flows suggest that Luxembourg has been one of the more attractive destinations for Chinese FDI in OECD countries, consistent with the Chinese proclivity for investing in haven economies.

[25] Some changes were made to the categories in the CIT categories used by China Global Investment Tracker. Manufacturing consists of chemicals, transport equipment, computer manufacturing, and other manufacturing industries. Transport and communications services were separated from their original categories and combined. Transactions in all remaining service industries were lumped together.

[26] (International Monetary Fund, 2011). This estimate is based on the IMF's update of September 2011 on Haver Analytics.

[27] (Oxford Economic Forecasting, 2011). This estimate is based on Oxford Economics update of April 2011 on Haver Analytics.

[28] This estimate, which includes inflation, reflects the compound average growth rate implied by the IMF's estimate of China's GDP through 2016.

[29] An appreciating currency implies that the purchasing power of each Yuan will increase from current levels.

[30] The value of China's ODI varies depending on the source. For example, According to China's State Administration of Foreign Exchange, China's ODI on a balance of payments basis was $60.2 billion in 2010.

[31] (Li, Schwartz, & Xu, 2011, p. 3); and (Rosen & Hanemann, An American Open Door?, 2011).

[32] This scenario also assumes that the U.S. share of ODI from China reflects the 2009-2010 experience.

[33] Through the third quarter of 2011, the latest data available at the time this report was being drafted, net inward FDI capital flows from China were $164 million (-46 million in the first quarter, $135 million in the second quarter, and $75 million (preliminary) in the third quarter), suggesting that actual capital inflows from China for full year 2011 may be less than in 2010.

[34] (Li, Schwartz, & Xu, 2011, p. 3)

[35] According to BEA, the ultimate beneficial owner ("UBO") is that person, proceeding up a U.S. affiliate's ownership chain, beginning with and including the foreign parent, that is not

owned more than 50 percent by another person. The country of ultimate beneficial owner is often the same as that of the foreign parent, but it may be a different country (or the United States). In theory, this measure should capture investments by Chinese-owned firms that make their investments through offshore tax havens.

[36] The BEA's regional definitions are as follows. New England consists of Connecticut, Maine, Massachusetts, New Hampshire, Rhode Island, and Vermont. Mideast consists of Delaware, District of Columbia, Maryland, New Jersey, New York, and Pennsylvania. Great Lakes consist of Illinois, Indiana, Michigan, Ohio, and Wisconsin. Plains consist of Iowa, Kansas, Minnesota, Missouri, Nebraska, North Dakota, and South Dakota. Southeast consist of Alabama, Arkansas, Florida, Georgia, Kentucky, Louisiana, Mississippi, North Carolina, South Carolina, Tennessee, Virginia, and West Virginia. Southwest consist of Arizona, New Mexico, Oklahoma and Texas. Rocky Mountain consists of Colorado, Idaho, Montana, Utah, and Wyoming (5). Far West consists of Alaska, California, Hawaii, Nevada, Oregon, and Washington.

[37] Approximately 10 percent of the deals reported by the China Investment Monitor do not include a valuation either because the underlying source did not provide a value or the value could not be confirmed by the Rhodium Group.

[38] "Famous brands" refers to Chinese government efforts "to promote the development of global Chinese brand names and to increase sales of Chinese- branded merchandise around the world." See (United States Trade Representative, 2008). These efforts included export subsidies and other preferences conferred by various levels of government. While China agreed to eliminate dozens of famous brands subsidies in December 2009, the promotion of "famous brands" remains a goal of Chinese economic policy.

[39] (National Development and Reform Commission, 2011).

[40] (Xinhua, 2012).

[41] (The World Bank and Development Research Center of the State Council, 2012).

[42] (Davis, 2012).

[43] (The World Bank and Development Research Center of the State Council, 2012, pp. 63, 420-421).

[44] (The World Bank and Development Research Center of the State Council, 2012, pp. 419-421).

[45] (National Development and Reform Commission, 2011).

[46] Statistics on corporate bonds also includes state and local government securities, securities of U.S. government agencies, corporations, and issues of new debt securities sold abroad by U.S. corporations organized to finance direct investments abroad.

[47] (Exclusive: China's CIC to get $50 billion boost, 2011).

[48] Still, it is possible that China will use these funds to stabilize the ongoing Euro Zone crisis.

[49] (The World Bank and Development Research Center of the State Council, 2012, pp. 428-433). The liberalization of capital controls does not seem imminent as of this writing. Indeed, the World Bank report indicates that the Yuan's exchange rate would have to be liberalized first. (The World Bank and Development Research Center of the State Council, 2012, p. 433).

[50] (Hammer & Jones, 2012). According to the USITC's analysis, the auto sector was the third most attractive sector for ODI, accounting for 9 percent of ODI.

[51] (Organisation for Economic Cooperation and Development, 2008, p. 75).

[52] (Bradsher, China Racing Ahead of U.S. in the Drive to Go Solar, 2009). "Even organizing a united American response to Chinese exports could be difficult. Suntech has encouraged executives at its United States operations to take the top posts at the two main American industry groups, partly to make sure that these groups do not rally opposition to imports,

{CEO} Dr. Shi said." (Bradsher, China Racing Ahead of U.S. in the Drive to Go Solar, 2009).

[53] (The World Bank and Development Research Center of the State Council, 2012, p. 420).

[54] The BEA belongs to the Economics and Statistics Administration of the Department of Commerce. In addition to data on inward FDI, the BEA maintains the national income and product accounts, including GDP; data on other international transactions, such as those involving services, and economic data specific to industries and regions.

[55] (Quijano, 1990, p. 29). Data collection occurs pursuant to the International Investment and Trade in Services Survey Act, 22 USC Sec. 3101.

[56] (Quijano, 1990, p. 33). The BEA can perform statistical analyses of company data and share company data with other agencies.

[57] (Rosen & Hanemann, China Investment Monitor, 2012); and (Scissors, China Global Investment Tracker Interactive Map, 2012).

[58] Capital Trade's experience with commercial databases based on corporate announcements, or press reports of those announcements, is that the reported data are frequently estimates based on other transactions in the same industry. The China Investment Monitor, which is based on proprietary databases, indicates that it performs careful due diligence on the projects it includes in its database. (Rosen & Hanemann, An American Open Door?, 2011, p. 84)

[59] (Rosen & Hanemann, An American Open Door?, 2011, p. 83).

[60] (Payne & Vu, 2011).

[61] See Pub.L.-203, H.R. 4173.

[62] (Securities and Exchange Commission, unk) and (Securities and Exchange Commission: What we do, 2010).

[63] (Securities and Exchange Commission, 2012).

[64] (Tafara, 2008).

[65] (Fagan, 2009, p. 52).

[66] 47 U.S.C. §310. However, the FCC has some discretion in applying this regulation. As Fagan notes, "{F}oreign entities may acquire, directly or indirectly, up to 100 percent of the stock of a US company owning or controlling an FCC licensee if the FCC does not find the foreign ownership to be inconsistent with the public interest." (Fagan, 2009, p. 53)

[67] (Fagan, 2009, p. 53).

[68] (Aguilar, 2011).

[69] Companies that have gone public through a reverse merger must complete a one-year "seasoning period" by trading in the U.S. over-the-counter market for one year once all transactions disclosure if submitted to the SEC. Companies hoping to list on the NASDAQ, NYSE and NYSE Amex must have filed audited financial statements and maintained a minimum bid price. (Securities and Exchange Commission, 2011).

[70] (Hamilton, 2011) and (Jones A. , 2011).

[71] (Hilzenrath, 2012).

[72] (Fagan, 2009, p. 56).

[73] (Department of the Treasury, 2011).

[74] For example, from 2008 to 2010, there were 313 transaction notifications to CFIUS. Only 13 (4.1 percent) resulted in transaction withdrawals, all of which occurred prior to the presidential review (Department of the Treasury, 2011).

[75] 50 USC app 2170.

[76] (Jackson, 2006, pp. CRS-3).

[77] (Fagan, 2009, p. 56).

[78] In 2005 CNOOC made an all-cash 18.5 billion offer to buy the American oil company Unocal. Democrats and Republicans in Congress organized opposition to the CNOOC bid. Congress argued that it was not a free market transaction and questioned the motives of the CNOOC. CNOOC withdrew its bid.

[79] (Fagan, 2009, p. 60).

[80] (Committee on Foreign Investment In the United States, December 2011, p. 20).

[81] (Committee on Foreign Investment In the United States, December 2011, p. 20).

[82] (Committee on Foreign Investment In the United States, December 2011, p. 21). Monitoring reports generally occur on a quarterly basis.

[83] (Committee on Foreign Investment In the United States, December 2011, p. 34).

[84] See discussion of Huawei in Section IX.B.

[85] (Drake, 2012, pp. 9-10) and (Brightbill, 2012, p. 14). It should be noted that prior Congressional efforts to strengthen CFIUS considered, but failed to adopt, this approach.

[86] 15 U.S.C. § 18a.

[87] (FTC pre-merger Notification Office, 2008).

[88] 15 U.S.C. §§ 78dd-1, et seq.

[89] See 15 U.S.C. § 78m.

[90] (Department of Justice, 2010).

[91] (Fagan, 2009, p. 50); and 15 U.S.C. § 78dd-3(a).

[92] (Santangel, Stein, Suh, White, & Friedman, 2011).

[93] Title 15 § 730.1.

[94] Title 15 § 730.3.

[95] (Department of Commerce, 2007).

[96] Title 22 §121.1 Et. Seq.

[97] (U.S. Department of the Treasury, 2011).

[98] (Brightbill, 2012).

[99] (U.S.-China Economic and Security Review Commission, 2011, p. 2).

[100] The version used was updated on January 15, 2012.

[101] Not all deals covered in the Rhodium database include a value. The averages computed in Figure 19, Table 7, and Table 8 are based on the number of deals for which values were known.

[102] (Lenovo Group Limited, 2011, p. 45).

[103] (Lenovo Group Limited, 2011, p. 62) and (O'Brien, 2006) All of Lenovo's founders came from CAS. (Huang, 2008, p. 3) The SOE holds 36 percent of Legend's equity, its Employee Shareholding Society holds 35percent, and China Oceanwide, a private investment firm, holds the remaining 29 percent. (Legend Holdings Limited).

[104] (Bunkley, 2010) and (Sedgwick, How a Chinese Owner Took Root in the Rust Belt, 2011).

[105] (Beene, 2010).

[106] (Hainan Group, Unk).

[107] (Murray, 2012) and (Li S. , 2011).

[108] This share likely understates the true SOE footprint because firms with significant, but not majority, SOE ownership would not be considered government or government-related entities.

[109] (Wang, 2009, p. 188) and (Huawei, 2012).

[110] State-controlled Legend Holding Limited only holds 42 percent of Lenovo. Since no other entity owns 50 percent of Lenovo, Lenovo would be deemed the ultimate beneficial owner in the BEA's data and the investment would be associated Hong Kong, not China.

[111] According to its listing documents, the firm two parcels of industrial land in Minnesota as of the end of the first quarter, 2010, which were being used for the demonstration project, the Uilk Wind Farm.

[112] The investments by CNOOC and selected other investors mentioned in this study are described in Attachment 1.

[113] (Zhang & Alon, 2010, p. 87).

[114] (Szamosszegi, Anderson, & Kyle, An Assessment of China's Subsidies to Strategic and Heavyweight Industries, 2009, p. 95).

[115] (Zhang & Alon, 2010, p. 87). Actually, CNOOC has a fully-owned subsidiary in Bermuda. That entity fully owns another entity in the British Virgin Islands, CNOOC (BVI) Limited; which is technically owned 64.41 percent of CNOOC Limited's shares as of March 31, 2011.

[116] (CNOOC Limited, 2012, p. 95).

[117] (National Development and Reform Commission, 2011, p. 11). "Strengthen the exploration and development of petroleum and natural gas resources, stabilize domestic petroleum output, and promote the rapid growth of natural gas output, and the development and utilization of unconventional oil and gas resources, such as coal-bed gas and shale gas."

[118] (Chen, 2011, p. 2).

[119] (Chesapeake Energy Corporation, November 18, 2011, p. 2).

[120] (Chesapeake Energy, China team up for Niobrara play, 2011).

[121] (Chen, 2011, p. 2).

[122] (Chen, 2011, p. 2).

[123] Indeed, it appears that the transaction was set up to avoid a replay of the UNOCAL investment. According to Chesapeake Senior Vice president Jeff Mobley, "We recently closed our transaction with CNOOC. It's kind of a groundbreaking transaction for the industry, and we think it's a better way for our new partner to implement a US investment that's different from one that was contemplated a few years ago. And the key distinction is that we're in complete control of this acquisition. Our new partner, under no circumstances, will be allowed to operate any wells. We'll be driving that operation, and it's a very unique transaction, and we're excited about our opportunity set to ramp up in that particular play." (Mobley, 2010, p. 3).

[124] (Walter & Howe, 2011, pp. 129-130).

[125] (Walter & Howe, 2011, pp. 132-133).

[126] (China-Africa Development Fund, 2012).

[127] (Morgan Stanley, December 27, 2007).

[128] (National Social Security Fund, 2010).

[129] (China to create new $300 billion FX vehicle, 2011).

[130] (CIC gets Fed approval about the purchase of the 10% voting state in Morgan Stanley, 2010).

[131] (Zacks Investment Research, 2010).

[132] (Chediak, 2009).

[133] (Weiss, 2011).

[134] In the 1970s, the concessional element of trade finance became too large, causing significant losses in export credit agencies, including the U.S. Export-Import Bank. The OECD's Arrangement on Export Credit was created to limit the concessional element for trade finance and to tie ECA interest rates to fluctuations in market interest rates.

[135] (Organisation for Economic Cooperation and Development, 2010).

[136] (Organization for Economic Cooperation and Development, 2000, p. 2).

[137] (Organisation for Economic Cooperation and Development, 2008, p. 90).

[138] (China Development Bank, 2012, p. 2).

[139] (China Development Bank, 2011).

[140] (China Development Bank, 2011).

[141] (Export-Import Bank of the United States, June 2011, p. 112).

[142] (Export-Import Bank of the United States, June 2011, p. 97).

[143] (Organisation for Economic Cooperation and Development, 2008, p. 91) and (Export-Import Bank of China, 2011, p. 26).

[144] (Export-Import Bank of China, 2011, pp. 21-22). Not all loans are at the two percent discounted rate.

[145] (Export-Import Bank of the United States, June 2011, p. 111).

[146] (Export-Import Bank of the United States, June 2011, p. 111).

[147] (Asia Pulse, 2005) and (Ng & Cheng, 2005). CNOOC Ltd. was to receive zero or below market rates from its parent, state-owned CNOOC. Although the Bloomberg article concludes that additional funding from the state-owned Industrial and Commercial Bank of China was at a market rate, it is likely that the funds $7 billion in subsidized lending from the parent would have been funded by state-owned financial services firms as CNOOC Ltd. holds most of CNOOC's major assets.

[148] (Zheng, 2010).

[149] (Bullis, 2011) and (Freedman, 2011). Boston Power has reduced its U.S. headcount and is expanding in China.

[150] (Export-Import Bank of the United States, June 2011, p. 107).

[151] (von Reppert-Bismarck, 2011).

[152] China has unified its tax system and benefits from several tax programs are being phased out.

[153] For similar reasons related to non-market finance, SOE have been shown to bid up prices in China's urban real estate markets. (Deng, Morck, Wu, & Yeung, 2011) However, a subsidized loan would not enable the investing firm to charge lower prices in the marketplace, because interest costs are fixed costs.

[154] Such projects are often associated with FDI.

[155] Put differently, access to favorable finance leads to an outward shift in the government's demand curve for the Chinese bundle.

[156] (Unirule Institute of Economics, 2011).

[157] (Of Emperors and Kings: China's state-owned enterprises are on the march, 2011).

[158] (Abrami & Zhang, China Construction America (A): The Road Ahead, 2011, pp. 3-10).

[159] (Zeller Jr. & Bradsher, 2010).

[160] With a traditional initial public offering, the SEC and the public receive, review and consider robust disclosures and underwriters and auditors perform due diligence. In addition, there are legal liabilities potentially arising from false statements made by the people best positioned to ensure accuracy. (Aguilar, 2011).

[161] (Going Public, Chinese Style, 2007).

[162] (Alpert & Norton, p. 23).

[163] (Byrnes & Browning, 2011).

[164] According to a Stanford Law School report, 17.6% (33 out of 188) of all class action cases in 2011 were filed against Chinese companies. All of the 42 reverse merger Chinese litigation cases since 2010 were pursued on the grounds of GAAP violations, unreliable financial records, restatements, and 97.5% of the cases include allegations of rule 10b-5 violations (acts or omissions resulting in security fraud). (Stanford Law School and Cornerstone Research, 2012).

[165] (Aguilar, 2011).

[166] (Alpert & Norton, 2010).

[167] (McCoy & Chu, 2011).

[168] For example, Harbin Electric, which listed in the U.S. through a reverse merger, was partially owned by a group of former SOEs. (Margin & Safety, 2011).

[169] (Trindle, 2011).

[170] (American Lorain Corporation, pp. 4, F-25).

[171] (China Cablecom Holdings, Ltd., pp. 25-27).

[172] (Kingold Jewelry, Inc., p. 13).

[173] (Zoom Technologies, Inc., p. 3).

[174] (Byrnes & Browning, 2011).

[175] (Top 20 Largest Hedge Funds 2012).

[176] For example, the market capitalizations of 3M and Chesapeake Energy in mid-February 2012 were approximately $61.0 billion and $15.6 billion, respectively.

[177] (Tafara, 2008).

[178] (Alpert & Norton, p. 24).

[179] (Huaweil Piled Up 3Leaf Acquisition on Neglect of Reporting, 2011).

[180] (Mayer Brown LLP, 2010).

[181] (Raice & Dowell, 2011).

[182] (Committee on Foreign Investment In the United States, December 2011, p. 34)

[183] (Li Z. , China's Go Global Policy, 2009, p. 41).

[184] (Salidjanova, 2010, pp. 5-6) and (Li Z. , China's Go Global Policy, 2009, p. 42).

[185] (Li Z. , China's Go Global Policy, 2009, p. 42).

[186] (Sun & Bo, 2011); (National Development and Reform Commission, 2011); and (International Cooperation Department of China Industrial Overseas Development and Planning).

[187] (Sun & Bo, 2011); (Ministry of Commerce, 2009); (Department of Foreign Trade and Economic Cooperation of Guangdong Province); and (Bureau of Foreign Trade of Guangzhou Municipality).

[188] (Sun & Bo, 2011).

[189] (Sun & Bo, 2011) and (People's Bank of China, 1990).

[190] (Li X. , 2010, p. 11).

[191] "At this time of energetically expanding exports, , we shall, with proper steps and leadership, organize and support a group of enterprises with advantages and strengths to go abroad to make investments and set up factories there, particularly in Africa, Central Asia, the Middle East, Eastern Europe and South America." Jiang Zemin, 2001, quoted in the *Almanac of China's Foreign Economic Relations and Trade 2001*. (Li X. , 2010, p. 120).

[192] (Li X. , 2010, pp. 12-13).

[193] (Li Z. , China's Go Global Policy, 2009, p. 31).

[194] (Li Z. , China's Go Global Policy, 2009, pp. 31-33).

[195] (Unirule Institute of Economics, 2011); (Of Emperors and Kings: China's state-owned enterprises are on the march, 2011); and (Szamosszegi, Anderson, & Kyle, An Assessment of China's Subsidies to Strategic and Heavyweight Industries, 2009).

[196] (Ministry of Finance, 2003).

[197] (Li Z. , China's Go Global Policy, 2009, p. 44).

[198] (Bullis, 2011) and (Freedman, 2011).

[199] (United Nations Conference on Trade and Development, 2011, pp. 47-48).

[200] Banned investments also include those that violate Chinese laws, laws in the host country, or treaties that China has signed.

[201] (United Nations Conference on Trade and Development, 2011, p. 48).
[202] (Li X. , 2010, p. 120).
[203] (Li Z. , China's Outward Foreign Direct Investment, 2009).
[204] (Li, Schwartz, & Xu, 2011, p. 3).
[205] The groups putting forth suggested reforms include the China Democratic League Guangdong Provincial Commission, the Global Environmental Institute in Beijing, and the China Center for International Economic Exchange. See, for example, http://www.gdmm.org.cn /Article/class3/class22/201101/2669.html; http://www.chinaassn.com/55022.html; and http://www.21cbh.com/HTML/2010-5- 31/1NMDAwMDE3OTc1Ng.html.
[206] (The World Bank and Development Research Center of the State Council, 2012, pp. 62-63).
[207] (Buckley, Cross, Tan, Liu, & Voss, 2010, pp. 131-153).
[208] (Lumsden & Knight, 2012).
[209] (Chavez & Linkhorn, 2011).
[210] BEA does not present capital inflow data on a UBO basis. Capital inflows are presented for foreign parent groups, and therefore exclude capital flows arising from Chinese-owned firms based in third countries. However, even accounting for this omission, it is likely that China's share of capital inflows was less than 1 percent during the period.
[211] Data on assets and expenditures for PPE are presented on a UBO basis and therefore are meant to capture the assets and expenditures of firms whose ultimate owner is based in China.
[212] It is possible, due to the convoluted ownership structures of many Chinese-owned firms, that foreign investments controlled by Chinese investors would be treated as BVI, Cayman, or Hong Kong investments. However, no effort was made to adjust for changes in Chinese-owned firms incorporated in tax havens because net employment for firms ultimately owned by investors in Caribbean UK islands and Hong Kong actually declined from 2007 to 2009.
[213] Delphi was a major investor in China. Delphi Saginaw Steering (Suzhou) Co., Ltd. began production in the Suzhou Industrial Park in 2007, less than two years after Delphi's U.S. corporate entity filed for bankruptcy. (Szamosszegi, How Chinese Government Subsidies and Market Intervention Have Resulted in the Offshoring of U.S. Auto Parts Production: A Case Study, 2007, pp. 22, 25-27).
[214] (White & Shirouzu, 2012, p. A1). The only other interested buyer was a Korean firm.
[215] (White & Shirouzu, 2012, p. A1).
[216] (Shu & Wang, 2006, p. 2).
[217] (Shu & Wang, 2006, p. 4). The main office was soon moved to Chicago.
[218] (Abrami, Kirby, McFarlan, Wong, & Manty, 2008, p. 7).
[219] (Abrami, Kirby, McFarlan, Wong, & Manty, 2008, p. 6).
[220] (Abrami, Kirby, McFarlan, Wong, & Manty, 2008, p. 8). Wanxiang's founder was guided by the principle of "producing at China's cost, selling at U.S. prices."
[221] (Abrami, Kirby, McFarlan, Wong, & Manty, 2008, pp. 7, 9).
[222] (Pomfret, 2011, p. A1).
[223] (Li X. , 2010, p. 39).
[224] The OECD's 34 member countries are Australia, Austria, Belgium, Canada, Chile, the Czech Republic, Denmark, Estonia, Finland, France, Germany, Greece, Hungary, Iceland, Ireland, Israel, Italy, Japan, Korea, Luxembourg, Mexico, the Netherlands, New Zealand, Norway, Poland, Portugal, Slovak Republic, Slovenia, Spain, Sweden, Switzerland, Turkey, the United Kingdom, and the United States.
[225] Data for Chile, the Czech Republic, Estonia, Greece, Hungary, Iceland, Poland, Portugal, the Slovak Republic, Slovenia, and Turkey were not part of the analysis.

[226] Data for the two periods are not comparable. Beginning to 2007, BEA began reporting data for bank and non-bank affiliates. Prior to 2007, only data for nonbank affiliates were reported.

[227] It should be noted that job additions and reductions at these affiliates include both changes in employment at existing firms, as well as the addition of new foreign affiliates.

[229] (Organisation for Economic Cooperation and Development, 2008, pp. 93-94).

[230] (Wu, 2009, p. 121) and (Brown, p. 145).

[231] (Buckley P. J., et al., p. 89).

[232] (Brown, p. 147).

[233] (Buckley P. J., et al., pp. 89-90).

[234] (Buckley P. J., et al., 2008, pp. 111-2). This study contains a useful literature review on the topic of China's ODI.

[235] (Brown, p. 160).

[236] The table was derived based on Chinese statistics. The official data have been criticized because they consist of approved projects, not actual investments. (Scissors, Where China Invests, and Why It Matters, 2010). Indeed, using the Heritage Foundation's *China Global Investment Tracker*, the disparity between Africa, OPEC, the EU and the United States from 2005 to 2010 (the *Investment Tracker* data only goes back to 2005). was much narrower, though the tilt toward Africa remains. Many of the U.S. investments in the database would not count as direct investments by the U.S. definition because their ownership shares are less than 10 percent.

[237] (Buckley P. J., et al., p. 112).

[238] (Salidjanova, 2010, pp. 4-6).

[239] (Li X. , 2010, p. 126).

[240] (Salidjanova, 2010, p. 4).

[241] (Li Z. , China's Go Global Policy, 2009, pp. 31-3)

[242] (Gordon, 2012).

[243] Although private-sector sources indicate the official data understate the level of Chinese investments, these sources sometimes include portfolio investments, and therefore potentially overstate the level of direct investment from China.

[244] CNOOC's planned purchase of UNOCAL and Huawei's backdoor investment in 3Leaf Systems are two instances in which Chinese firms backed off certain investments in the wake of political opposition.

[245] (Gordon, 2012).

[246] (Salidjanova, 2010); (Scissors, China's Investment Overseas in 2010, pp. 2-3); and (Brown, pp. 154, 164).

[247] Though that changed in 2008 as resource-rich Australia and Canada began attracting significant amounts of FDI.

[248] The factors "pulling" in FDI from China will be discussed in section XIV.

[249] (Caves, Frankel, & Jones, pp. 187-8).

[250] Japan proposed voluntary export restrains in the face of congressional proposals to impose quotas. (Prestowitz C. V., 1988, pp. 252-3) Following the Auto Agreement of 1981, Japanese producers began establishing facilities in the United States. (Bergsten & Noland, 1993, p. 110).

[251] Beginning in mid 2008, the Department of Commerce modified its longstanding practice and began applying countervailing duties against subsidized imports from China. Since then, U.S. industries petitioning for relief against imports from China under Title VII of U.S. trade law have filed antidumping and countervailing duty petitions concurrently. However,

as noted in Commission testimony, a recent decision by the U.S. Court of Appeals for the Federal Circuit has ruled that the United States cannot apply its antisubsidy law against China because it is treated as a non-market economy (NME) under the antidumping law. (Drake, p. 4) The U.S. Congress recently passed, and President Obama signed, changes to U.S. law enabling the United States to apply countervailing duties to imports from NMEs such as China.

[252] (Certain Oil Country Tubular Goods from China, 2009, pp. IV-5). The import average unit value for imports from China were, on average $300-to-$400 less per ton than imports from the rest of the world.

[253] (Lyne, 2009). The U.S. industry filed its antidumping and countervailing duty petitions on April 8, 2009. (Certain Oil Country Tubular Goods from China, p. 1).

[254] (Niran--We Innovate Green, 2009) and (Citric Acid and Certain Citrate Salts from Canada and China, 2009, p. 1).

[255] (Price, Brightbill, Weld, & El-Sabaawi, p. 10).

[256] (Zhang Q. , 2011).

[257] (Brightbill, 2012) and (Visclosky, 2012).

[258] (Price, Brightbill, Weld, & El-Sabaawi, 2011, pp. 9-10).

[259] (Price, Brightbill, Weld, & El-Sabaawi, 2011)

[260] (Dewey & Leboeuf LLP, 2010, pp. 18-24) and (Brightbill, 2012, p. 9)

[261] "Chinese governments at the national, provincial and even local level have been competing with one another to offer solar companies ever more generous subsidies, including free land, and cash for research and development. State-owned banks are flooding the industry with loans at considerably lower interest rates than available in Europe or the United States." (Bradsher, China Racing Ahead of U.S. in the Drive to Go Solar, 2009).

[262] (Prestowitz C. , 2010, p. 201)

[263] Trina Solar Limited listed on the New York Stock Exchange in December 2006. (Trina Solar Limited, 2011, p. 1)

[264] (Crystalline Silicon Photovoltaic Cells and Modlues from China, 2011, pp. 24-8; III-3).

[265] (Bradsher, China Racing Ahead of U.S. in the Drive to Go Solar, 2009).

[266] (Brightbill, 2012, pp. 8-9).

[267] (United Nations Conference on Trade and Development, 2011, p. 50).

[268] (Price, Brightbill, Weld, & El-Sabaawi, 2011, p. 10)

[269] (Areddy, 2010).

[270] See Attachment 2.

[271] The 863 Program is shorthand for China's National High Technology Program, which was created in 1986 to target key deficiencies in sectors crucial to China's long-term competitiveness and national security. (Springut, Schlaikjer, & Chen, p. 24).

[272] (Zhuhai Yintong Energy: About us). Canon is a Hong Kong registered holding company with authorized share capital of $HK 10,000. Its sole director is Wei Yangcai, who is now on Altair Nano's board of directors.

[273] See Attachment 3.

[274] (Guangdong Yintong Investment Holding Group Company Limited New Energy Vehicle Development Plan (2011-2020)).

[275] (Altair Nanotechnologies, 2011, p. 2).

[276] (Altair Nanotechnologies, 2011, p. 3).

[277] (Ondrey, 2007).

[278] (Syntroleum Corporation, p. 2) and (Sinopec and Syntroleum Announce Grand Opening of Coal to Liquids Demonstration Plant, 2011). Syntroleum's equipment is being used,

however, for coal-to-liquid conversion. Syntroleum CEO and President Gary Roth describes the deal as follows. "The Sinopec arrangement is important in a number of ways, including technology payments totaling $20 million net of Chinese taxes, establishment of a 10 year technology partnership including Research and Development paid for by Sinopec as well as the six month CDF run time obligation. Syntroleum retains the right to use the CDF in China for 10 years. We have access to Sinopec's vast network of competitive Research and Development and engineering services, including catalyst manufacturing. We have a 50/50 royalty sharing arrangement for licensing of technology improvements in China. And finally, we believe we have a path to commercialization of the Syntroleum FT technology." (Syntroleum Corporation, 2009). Initial press reports of $20 million in payments annually for five years were incorrect.

[279] (Aucoin, 2002).

[280] (Roberts, 2006).

[281] (Syntroleum (SYNM) to Suspend Operations of Catoosa, 2006).

[282] China's steel producers use blast furnaces to make steel from iron ore. Electric arc furnace (EAF) technology enables steel producers to manufacture steel from scrap metal. This technology is widely used in the United States and other countries, and equipment can be purchased from unrelated parties. By investing in a U.S. minimill with a U.S. partner, Anshan can acquire minimill technology while also gaining access to the U.S. market.

[283] (Altair Nanotechnologies, 2011, p. 3 and 7).

[284] (Revisited: US steel sector falls out over Anshan-SDC jv, 2010). Anshan became a 14 percent owner of Steel Development Company in September 2010.

[285] (de Swaan, 2010) and (Wei, 2009).

[286] (Rasiah, Gammeltoft, & Yang, 2010).

[287] (Yang, 2009).

[288] (Sedgwick, China State-Owned Suppliers Seek US Acquisitions, 2012).

[289] (de la Merced & Bradsher, 2007).

[290] (Weiss, 2011).

[291] (SWF Institute, 2011).

[292] (Karmin & Wei, 2012).

[293] (Murray, 2012).

[294] (Bathon, 2011). Most of Evergreen's operations are now housed in a Wuhan warehouse where the Chinese government purportedly conducted mass executions during the Cultural Revolution.

[295] (Wang, 2009, p. 182) and (Abrami, Kirby, McFarlan, Wong, & Manty, 2008, p. 6).

[296] (Wang, 2009, pp. 182, 185-186). However, Wanxiang failed to revive UAI and exited the business. UAI went bankrupt and was subsequently liquidated in September 2005. See (Abrami, Kirby, McFarlan, Wong, & Manty, 2008, p. 1).

[297] (Wang, 2009, p. 186) and (Shu & Wang, 2006, p. 1).

[298] (Bradsher, Ford Agrees to Sell Volvo to a Fast Rising Chinese Company, 2010). Ford had acquired Volvo in 1999 for $6 billion.

[299] (China 'to block' Hummer takeover, 2009).

[300] (Watts, 2012).

[301] (Bullis, 2011) and (Freedman, 2011).

[302] True, China could have purchased the batteries from Altair Nano, but current policies in China favor the acquisition and development of foreign technology over importation.

[303] (Bullis, 2011).

[304] (U.S.-China Economic Security and Review Commission, October 2011, p. 65).

[305] Disagreements on non-economic matters likely exacerbate U.S. concerns, but are beyond the scope of this study.

[306] (Ajaga & Nunnekamp, 2008, p. 11).

[307] (Jensen & Malesky, 2010) The Vale Columbia Center on Sustainable International Economics found that politicians who use tax incentives to take credit for investment flowing into their districts, or to deflect blame for losing the competition for mobile firms, gained a 5.6 percentage point vote bonus.

[308] Indeed, then Senator Evan Bayh, testifying before the Commission in 2008, likened CFIUS to a toothless watchdog. (Implications of Sovereign Wealth Fund Investments for national Security: Statement of Sen. Evan Bayh, 2008).

[309] (Export.gov, 2011).

[310] (Clement, 2011)

[311] (Baucus Announces New Wind Farm near Shawmut, 2012). Said Baucus, "I am pleased to welcome Goldwind to Montana, along with the local tax revenue and jobs this project will bring, and I'm hopeful the Shawmut wind farm will be just the beginning for our new partnership."

[312] (American Chamber of Commerce in Shanghai, 2011, p. 7).

[313] (Prasso, 2010).

[314] (Hou, 2011).

[315] (Announcement of U.S.-China Governors Forum in Utah, 2011).

[316] (U.S.-China Governors Forum Continue in Beijing, 2011).

[317] (Min, 2011).

[318] (Show Me State Worth a Look, 2011).

[319] (Delegation to China).

[320] (Sidhu, Guerra, Ritter, & Kyser, 2010).

[321] (U.S. Chamber Continues U.S.-China CEO Dialogue to Highlight Importance of Bilateral Relationship, 2011).

[322] Because of its ownership structure, Lenovo is likely considered a Hong Kong owned firm in official U.S. statistics on FDI.

In: Chinese Investments in the U.S. Economy ISBN: 978-1-62618-833-4
Editor: Zackary A. Michaud

Chapter 2

CHINA'S HOLDINGS OF U.S. SECURITIES: IMPLICATIONS FOR THE U.S. ECONOMY*

Wayne M. Morrison and Marc Labonte

SUMMARY

Given its relatively low savings rate, the U.S. economy depends heavily on foreign capital inflows from countries with high savings rates (such as China) to meet its domestic investment needs and to fund the federal budget deficit. The willingness of foreigners to invest in the U.S. economy and purchase U.S. public debt has helped keep U.S. real interest rates low. However, many economists contend that U.S. dependency on foreign savings exposes the U.S. economy to certain risks, and some argue that such dependency was a contributing factor to the U.S. housing bubble and subsequent global financial crisis that began in 2008.

China's policy of intervening in currency markets to limit the appreciation of its currency against the dollar (and other currencies) has made it the world's largest and fastest growing holder of foreign exchange reserves, especially U.S. dollars. China has invested a large share of these reserves in U.S. private and public securities, which include long-term (LT) Treasury debt, LT U.S. agency debt, LT U.S. corporate debt, LT U.S. equities, and short-term debt. As of June 2011, China was the largest holder of U.S. securities, which totaled $1.73 trillion. U.S. Treasury securities constitute the largest category of China's

* This is an edited, reformatted and augmented version of Congressional Research Service, Publication No. RL34314, dated December 6, 2012.

holdings of U.S. securities—these totaled $1.16 trillion as of September 2012, but were down from their peak of $1.31 trillion in July 2011.

China's large holdings of U.S. securities have raised a number of concerns in both China and the United States. For example, in 2009, Chinese Premier Wen Jiabao stated that he was "a little worried" about the "safety" of China's holdings of U.S. debt. The sharp debate in Congress over raising the public debt ceiling in the summer of 2011 and the subsequent downgrade of the U.S. long-term sovereign credit from AAA to AA + by Standard and Poor's in August 2011 appears to have intensified Chinese concerns. In addition, Chinese officials have criticized U.S. fiscal monetary policies, such as quantitative easing by the U.S. Federal Reserve, arguing that they could lead to higher U.S. inflation and/or a significant weakening of the dollar, which could reduce the value of China's U.S. debt holdings in the future. Some Chinese analysts have urged the government to diversify its reserves away from U.S. dollar assets, while others have called for more rapid appreciation of China's currency, which could lessen the need to hold U.S. assets.

Many U.S. policymakers have expressed concern over the size of China's holdings of U.S. government debt. For example, some contend that China might decide to sell a large share of its U.S. securities holdings, which could induce other foreign investors to sell off their U.S. holdings as well, which in turn could destabilize the U.S. economy. Others argue that China could use its large holdings of U.S. debt as a bargaining chip in its dealing with the United States on economic and non-economic issues. In the 112th Congress, H.R. 2166 and S. 1028 would seek to increase the transparency of foreign ownership of U.S. debt instruments, especially China's, in order to assess if such holdings posed potential risks for the United States. The conference report accompanying the National Defense Authorization Act of FY2012 (H.R. 1540, P.L. 112-81) included a provision requiring the Secretary of Defense to conduct a national security risk assessment of U.S. federal debt held by China. Many analysts argue that China's holdings of U.S. debt give it little leverage over the United States because as long as China continues to hold down the value of its currency to the U.S. dollar, it will have few options other than to keep investing in U.S. dollar assets. A Chinese attempt to sell a large portion of its dollar holdings could reduce the value of its remaining dollar holdings, and any subsequent negative shocks to the U.S. (and global) economy could dampen U.S. demand for Chinese exports. They contend that the main issue for U.S. policymakers is not China's large holdings of U.S. securities per se, but rather the high U.S. reliance on foreign capital in general, and whether such borrowing is sustainable.

INTRODUCTION

Because of its low savings rate, the United States borrows to finance the federal budget deficit and its private capital needs. It therefore depends on countries with high savings rates, such as China, to invest some of their capital in the United States. Such investments help to keep U.S. interest rates relatively low and enable the United States to consume more than it produces. According to the International Monetary Fund (IMF), in 2011, the United States was the world's largest importer of foreign capital (at 38.5% of global total), while China was the largest exporter of capital (at 12.5%).[1] From 2002 to 2011 (yearend), the amount of U.S. public debt that is privately held grew from $3.0 trillion to $8.8 trillion; as a share of GDP, this level rose from 28.4% to 57.9%.[2] Of the U.S. public debt that is privately held, more than half is held by foreigners.[3] Many analysts argue that heavy U.S. reliance on foreign savings is not sustainable and may undermine U.S. economic interests over time. China's central bank is a major purchaser of U.S. financial assets, largely because of its exchange rate policy. [4] In order to limit the appreciation of China's currency, the renminbi (RMB), against the dollar, China must purchase U.S. dollars. This has led China to amass a huge level of foreign exchange (FX) reserves, which totaled nearly $3.3 trillion as of September 2012. Rather than hold dollars (and other foreign currencies), which earn no interest, the Chinese central government has converted some level of its foreign exchange reserve holdings into U.S. financial securities, including U.S. Treasury securities, U.S. agency debt, U.S. corporate debt, and U.S. equities.

U.S. Treasury securities, which are used to finance the federal budget deficit, constitute the largest category of U.S. securities held by China. As of September 2012, these totaled $1.16 trillion and accounted for 21.8% of total foreign holdings of U.S. Treasury securities. Some U.S. policymakers have expressed concern that China's large holdings of U.S. securities could pose a risk to the U.S. economy, especially if China attempted to divest itself of a large share of its holdings. Others argue that China's large and growing holdings of U.S. securities give it leverage over the United States on economic and noneconomic issues. On the other hand, many analysts contend that, given the current state of the global economy, China has few options for investing its FX holdings, other than to buy U.S. securities. They further argue that any attempt by China to sell off a large share of its current holdings would diminish the value of its remaining holdings and could further destabilize the global economy, which would likely negatively impact China's economy. Hence, it is argued, China's large holdings of U.S. securities give it very little leverage over U.S. policy. This report examines the importance to the U.S. economy of China's investment in U.S. securities, as well as the policy implications of its holdings for both the United States and China.[5] For the United States, the issue of China's large holdings of U.S. securities is part of a broader question that has been raised by many economists: what are the implications of the heavy U.S. reliance on foreign investment in U.S. securities to maintain healthy economic growth and to finance the budget deficit?[6] Since 2008, private savings in the United States has risen but public savings has declined (i.e., the budget deficit has grown). Borrowing from abroad fell by $681 billion in 2009 over the previous year, but then rose by $1,050 billion in 2011 and by $1,749 billion in 2011.[7] Thus, economic imbalances in the United States have become less of an issue of inadequate private saving and more of an issue of high government borrowing since the financial crisis began. It remains to be seen whether the rise in private savings was a permanent shift or a temporary response to the recession, however. The broader issue for China is whether its current unbalanced economic policies, especially those that have contributed to its large savings rate, over-reliance on exports for its economic growth, and accumulation of huge FX reserves, are sustainable in the long-run, especially given economic slowdowns in Europe and the United States. Some have argued that these factors may induce China to accelerate efforts to boost consumer demand and improve domestic living standards, which could include further appreciation of the RMB against the dollar. Such policies could lessen China's need to buy U.S. securities.

China's Foreign Exchange Reserves

China's economic policies, including those that induce high levels of domestic savings and promote export-related activities as the main engine of China's economic growth, have contributed to a surge in China's FX reserves over the past decade, as indicated in Table 1. China's exchange rate policies attempt to slow (and sometimes halt) the appreciation of the RMB against the dollar. This makes Chinese exports less expensive and foreign imports into China more expensive than would occur if China maintained a floating currency. The main purpose of this policy is to promote China's export industries and encourage foreign investment. To that end, the Chinese central bank must intervene heavily in currency markets by buying up as many dollars as necessary to meet the government's targeted RMB-dollar exchange rate.[8] Chinese policies that induce high savings rates dampen domestic consumption and demand for imports, while shifting financial resources (i.e., low-cost bank credit) largely to export-oriented industries. As a result, China consumes much less than it produces. Such policies have contributed to China's large annual trade surpluses. The combination of China's large merchandise trade surpluses ($185 billion in 2010), inflows of foreign direct investment into China ($106 billion in 2010), and inflows of "hot money" into China have been the main components of China's rapid accumulation of FX reserves.[9]

According to Chinese government figures, its FX reserves rose from $216 billion in 2001 to $3,290 billion as of September 2012, a $3 trillion increase.[10] From 2001 to 2011 (year-end), China's FX reserves grew at an annual average rate of 28.7%. However, from September 2011 to September 2012, its reserves increased by only 2.8%.[11] China's reserves as a percent of nominal GDP grew from 16.3% in 2001 to 48.4% in 2010—an unusually high level for a large economy. That level dropped to 44.1% in 2011 and is projected to fall to 40.8% in 2012. A listing of the world's top holders of FX reserves as of the third quarter of 2012 is shown in Figure 1. Not only was China by far the world's largest holder of FX reserves, its reserves were greater than the combined reserves of Japan, Saudi Arabia, Switzerland, Russia, and Taiwan. (Besides Japan, these countries had much smaller economies than China.)

Table 1. China's Foreign Exchange Reserves: Totals and as a Percent of GDP, 2001-2011 and Estimates for 2012

Year	Billions of U.S. Dollars	As a % of Chinese GDP
2001	215.6	16.3
2002	291.1	20.0
2003	403.3	24.6
2004	609.9	31.6
2005	818.9	36.5
2006	1,068.5	40.2
2007	1,528.2	45.2
2008	1,946.0	45.0
2009	2,399.2	48.1
2010	2,847.3	48.4
2011	3,181.1	44.1
2012 (projected)	3,300.0	40.8

Source: Global Insight, Economist Intelligence Unit, and the Chinese State Administration of Foreign Exchange.

Note: Year-end values. Data for 2012 are projections.

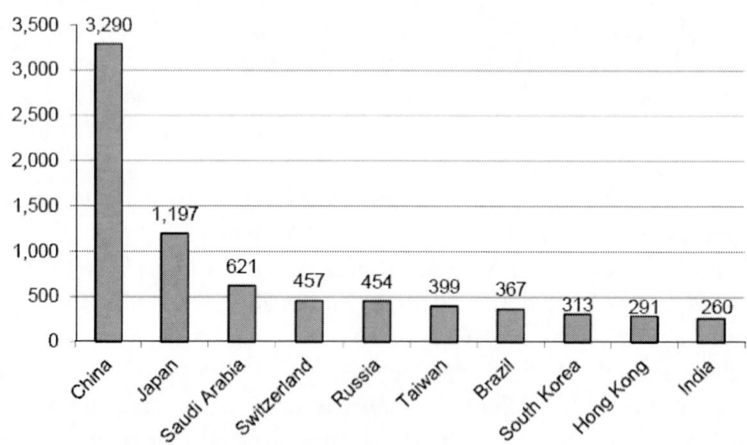

Sources: IMF International Financial Statistics, and Central Bank of the Republic of China (Taiwan).

Notes: Data for Saudi Arabia include gold reserves. Data for China, Russia, Saudi Arabia, Hong Kong, and Switzerland are through September 2012. Data for Japan, Brazil, India, South Korea, and Taiwan are through October 2012.

Figure 1. Major Holders of Foreign Exchange Reserves Through 3rd Quarter 2012.

CHINA'S HOLDINGS OF U.S. SECURITIES[12]

Although the Chinese government does not make public the dollar composition of its FX holdings, many analysts estimate this level to be around 70%.[13] U.S. assets have generally been favored by China for its investment needs for a number of reasons. First, in order to maintain the exchange rate effects that lay behind the acquisition of U.S. dollars, those dollars must be invested in dollar-denominated securities. Second, the United States is the world's largest economy and has the biggest capital market. In 2009, the combined value of U.S. private and public debt securities was $31.7 trillion (compared with $11.9 trillion for Japan and $5.7 trillion for Germany) and accounted for 34.4% of global debt securities. Many analysts contend that the U.S. debt securities market is the only global market that is big enough to absorb a big part of China's large and growing FX holdings. U.S. securities have also been favored by China because, historically, they have been considered to be safe and liquid (i.e., easily sold) relative to other types of investments.[14] Finally, U.S. Treasury securities are backed by the full faith and credit of the U.S. government, which guarantees that interest and principal payments will be paid on time. The global economic slowdown and the European sovereign debt crisis may have also boosted the attractiveness of U.S. securities for China.[15] According to China's State Administration of Foreign Exchange (SAFE), its main principles for administrating China's FX reserves are "security, liquidity, and increases in value, among which security is the primary principle."[16] U.S. financial securities consist of a mix of securities issued by the U.S. government and private sector entities and include long-term (LT) U.S. Treasury securities (which are discussed in more detail in the next section), LT U.S. government agency securities,[17] LT corporate securities (some of which are asset-backed), equities (such as stocks), and short-term debt. LT securities are those with no stated maturity date (such as equities) or with an original term to maturity date of more than one year. Short-term debt includes U.S. Treasury securities, agency securities, and corporate securities with a maturity date of less than one year.[18] The Department of the Treasury issues an annual survey of foreign portfolio holdings of U.S. securities by country and reports data for the previous year as of the end of June.[19] The latest Treasury survey of portfolio holdings of U.S. securities was issued on April 30, 2012.[20] The report indicates that China's total holdings of U.S. securities as of June 2011 were $1.7 trillion. Treasury data indicated that China's holdings of U.S. securities have increased much faster than those of any other country. From 2006-2011, China's holding increased by over $1 trillion (or 147%).[21] China overtook Japan as the largest holder of U.S. securities in 2009, and, as June 2011, its holdings were 9.0% higher than that those of Japan. As indicated in Figure 2, as China's FX reserves have risen rapidly, so has its holdings of U.S. securities. Table 2 lists the top three holders of U.S. securities as of June 2010, broken down by the type of securities held and Figure 3 provides a breakdown of China's holdings of U.S. securities by category. These data indicate that as of June 2011:

- China accounted for 13.9% of total foreign-held U.S. securities (compared with 4.1% in 2002).
- LT Treasury securities constituted the bulk of China's holdings of U.S. securities (at 75.3% of total), followed by long-term agency debt (14.2%) and U.S. equities (9.2%).[22]
- China was the largest foreign holder of LT Treasury debt (32.2% of the foreign total) and the second largest holder of U.S. agency debt (23.8%) after Japan.[23]
- China was the 8th largest holder of U.S. equities at $159 billion, which was 4.2% of total foreign holdings.

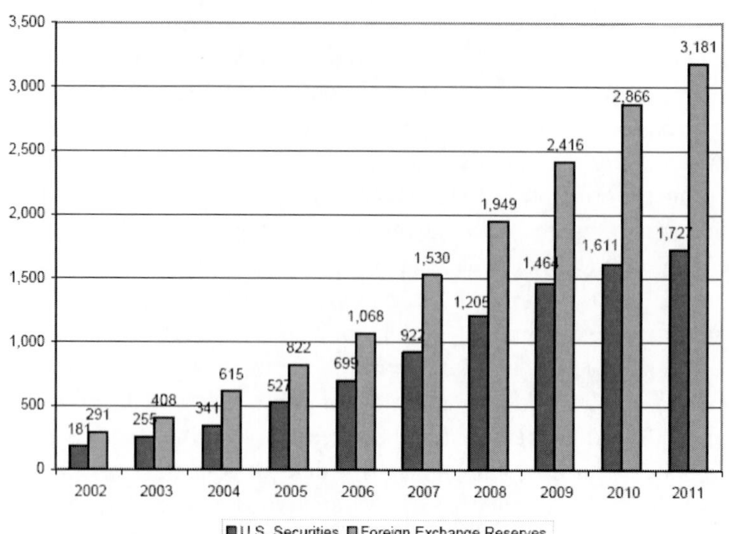

Sources: U.S. Treasury Department, *Report on Foreign Portfolio Holdings of U.S. Securities as of June 30, 2011*, April 2012, and Global Insight Database.

Note: Data on foreign exchange reserves are end of year values while data on holdings of U.S. securities are through the end of June.

Figure 2. China's Holdings of Foreign Exchange Reserves and Public and Private U.S. Securities: 2002-2011.

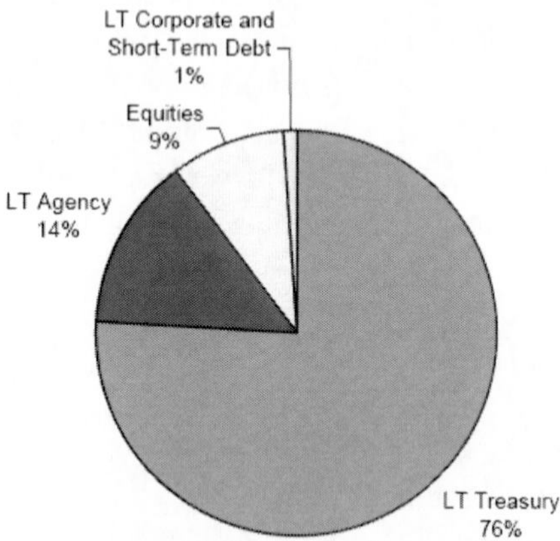

Source: U.S. Department of the Treasury, Report on Foreign Portfolio Holdings of U.S. Securities as of June 30, 2011, April 2012.

Figure 3. China's Holdings of U.S. Securities by Major Category as a Percent of Total Holdings as of June 2011.

Table 2. Top Three Foreign Holders of U.S. Securities and China's Share of These Holdings by Category as of June 2011 ($ billions)

Type of Security	Total	LT Treasury	LT Agency	LT Corporate	Equities	Short Term Debt
China	**1,727**	**1,302**	**245**	**16**	**159**	**5**
Japan	1,585	818	258	140	302	67
United Kingdom	982	118	12	394	441	16
Foreign Total	12,440	4,049	1,031	2,651	3,830	878
China's June 2011						
Holdings as a Percent of Total	13.9%	32.2%	23.8%	0.6%	4.2%	0.6%
Foreign Holdings						

Source: U.S. Department of the Treasury, Report on Foreign Portfolio Holdings of U.S. Securities as of June 30, 2011, April 2012.

Note: LT securities are those with no stated maturity date (such as equities) or with an original term to maturity date of more than one year. Short term securities have a maturity period of less than one year. Data on China exclude Hong Kong and Macau.

China's Ownership of U.S. Treasury Securities[24]

U.S. Treasury securities are the largest category of U.S. securities and are main vehicle the U.S. government uses to finance the federal debt, which totaled $14.3 trillion at the end of March 2011.[25] As indicated in Table 3, China's holdings increased rapidly from 2003 to 2010, both in dollar terms and as a percent of total foreign holdings. In September 2008, China overtook Japan to become the largest foreign holder of U.S. Treasury securities (it was 7th largest in 1997). From 2003 to 2010, China's holdings increased by nearly $1 trillion, which were by far the largest dollar increase in holdings of any country, and accounted for 34% of net new foreign holdings of U.S. Treasury securities over this time. As indicated in Figure 4, China's purchases of new Treasury securities from 2008 to 2010 averaged about $224.2 billion per year. China's share of foreign holdings of U.S. Treasury securities rose from 10.4% in 2002 to 26.1% in 2010. However, China's holdings of U.S. Treasury securities fell $8.2 billion in 2011 over the previous year. China's holdings as of September 2012 were $114.7 billion less than they were in September 2011.[26] China's share of foreign holdings of U.S. securities dropped to 23.0%

at yearend 2011 and as of September 2012 they declined to 21.8%, indicating that the importance of China as a holder (purchaser) of U.S. Treasury securities has declined somewhat. A listing of the top 10 foreign holders of U.S. Treasury securities as of September 2012 is shown in Table 4. China was the largest holder of U.S. Treasury securities (at $1.16 trillion), followed by Japan, major oil producers, Brazil, and Caribbean Banking Centers.

Table 3. China's Year-End Holdings of U.S. Treasury Securities: 2003-2011 and Holdings as of September 2012 ($ billions and as a percent of total foreign holdings)

	2003	2005	2007	2009	2010	2011	Sept 2012
China's Holdings ($billions)	159.0	310.0	477.6	894.8	1,160.1	1,151.9	1,155.6
Holdings as a % of Total Foreign Holdings	10.4%	15.2%	20.3%	24.2%	26.1%	23.0%	21.8%

Source: Department of Treasury, Major Foreign Holders of Treasury Securities Holdings, November 16, 2012.

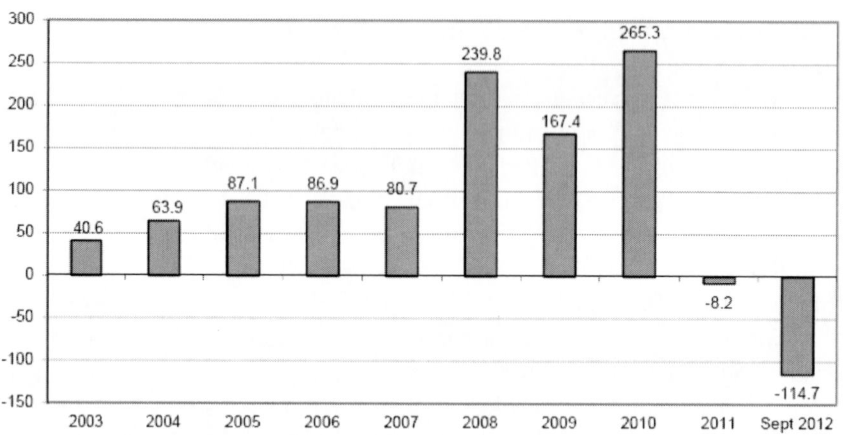

Source: U.S. Department of the Treasury.

Figure 4. Annual Change in China's Holdings of U.S. Treasury Securities: 2002-2011 and Year-on-Year Change in September 2012.

Table 4. Top 10 Foreign Holders of U.S. Treasury Securities as of September 2012

	Total Foreign Holdings ($ billions)	Country Holdings as a Share of Total Foreign Holdings (%)
China	1,155.6	21.8
Japan	1,130.7	20.7
Oil Exporters	267.0	4.9
Brazil	250.5	4.6
Caribbean Banking Centers	240.4	4.4
Taiwan	200.4	3.7
Switzerland	195.8	3.6
Russia	162.8	3.0
Luxembourg	148.1	2.7
Hong Kong	135.7	2.5
Belgium	133.7	2.5
Total Foreign Holdings	5,455.0	100.0

Source: Department of Treasury, Major Foreign Holders of Treasury Securities Holdings, November 16, 2012.

CONCERNS OVER CHINA'S LARGE HOLDINGS OF U.S. SECURITIES

The growing U.S. dependency on China to purchase U.S. Treasury securities to help fund the U.S. budget deficit has become a major concern to many U.S. policymakers. Some have raised concerns that China's large holdings may give it leverage over the United States on economic as well as noneconomic issues. Others have expressed concern that China might lose faith in the ability of the United States to meet its debt obligations, and, thus, might seek to liquidate such assets or significantly cut back on purchases of new securities, a move some contend could damage the U.S. economy. Still others contend that China's purchases of U.S. securities was a major contributing factor to the U.S. sub-prime mortgage crisis and subsequent global economic slowdown because such purchases helped to keep real U.S. interest rates very low and increased global imbalances. [27] Some warn that similar bubbles could occur in the future if imbalances between the United States and China are not addressed.[28] Chinese officials, on the other hand, have expressed concerns over the safety of their large holdings of U.S. debt, and some have argued that China should either diversify away from U.S. Treasury securities or implement policies that slow the accumulation of FX reserves, which would lessen the need to buy U.S. assets.

Growing Bilateral Tensions over the U.S. Public Debt

Since the beginning of the global financial crisis in 2008, U.S. government officials have increasingly sought to offer assurances to Chinese officials regarding the safety of China's holdings of U.S. government debt securities and to encourage China to continue to purchase U.S. securities. For example, during her first visit to China on February 21, 2009, Secretary of State Hillary Rodham Clinton was quoted as saying that she appreciated "greatly the Chinese government's continuing confidence in the United States Treasuries," and she urged the government to continue to buy U.S. debt.[29] However on March 13, 2009, Chinese Premier Wen Jiabao at a news conference stated: "We've lent a huge amount of capital to the United States, and of course we're concerned about the security of our assets. And to speak truthfully, I am a little bit worried. I would like to call on the United States to honor its words, stay a credible nation and ensure the safety of Chinese assets."[30] On March 24, 2009, the governor of the People's Bank of China, Zhou Xiaochuan, published a paper calling for replacing the U.S. dollar as the international reserve currency with a new global system controlled by the IMF.[31]

The recent contentious U.S. debate over raising the debt ceiling and over how to address longterm U.S. debt issues, along with the downgrade of the long-term sovereign credit rating of the United States from AAA to AA + by Standard and Poor's in August 2011, appear to have intensified China's concerns over its U.S. debt holdings.[32] Several government-controlled Chinese newspapers issued sharp criticism of U.S. economic policies (as well as the U.S. political system). For example:

- A July 28, 2011, Xinhua News Agency (Xinhua) editorial stated: "With its debt approximating its annual economic output, it is time for Washington to revisit the time-tested common sense that one should live within one's means."
- An August 3, 2011, a Xinhua editorial stated: "Should Washington continue turning a blind eye to its runaway debt addiction, its already tarnished credibility will lose more luster, which might eventually

detonate the debt bomb and jeopardize the well-being of hundreds of millions of families within and beyond the U.S. borders."

- A Xinhua August 6, 2011, editorial said: "The U.S. government has to come to terms with the painful fact that the good old days when it could just borrow its way out of messes of its own making are finally gone. International supervision over the issue of U.S. dollars should be introduced and a new, stable and secured global reserve currency may also be an option to avert a catastrophe caused by any single country."
- A Xinhua editorial on August 8, 2011, stated: "The days when the debt-ridden Uncle Sam could leisurely squander unlimited overseas borrowing appeared to be numbered as its triple A-credit rating was slashed by Standard & Poor's (S&P) for the first time on Friday. China, the largest creditor of the world's sole superpower, has every right now to demand the United States to address its structural debt problems and ensure the safety of China's dollar assets."

The U.S. debt issue was a major topic during Vice President Joe Biden's trip to China in August 2011. At a meeting with Chinese Premier Wen Jiabo on August 19, 2011, Vice President Biden stated that "we appreciate and welcome your concluding that the United States is such a safe haven because we appreciate your investment in U.S. treasuries. And very sincerely, I want to make clear that you have nothing to worry about in terms of their—their viability."[33] In a speech at Sichuan University, he stated that "the concern that we will not make good on the investments that people have made—in your case up to $1.7 trillion total out of a very large economy is not to worry about. We could not afford—we could not afford not to make good on that requirement."[34]

Some analysts contend that China's main concern is not a possible U.S. default on its debt, but rather U.S. monetary policies that have been utilized by the Federal Reserve in recent years to stimulate the economy, namely the purchases of U.S. Treasury securities, agency debt, and agency mortgage-backed securities. Such measures, often referred to as "quantitative easing" (QE), have led the Federal reserve to purchase over $2 trillion in U.S. securities since March 2009 in an effort to lower long-term interest rates.[35] An August 25, 2011, editorial in China Daily stated that "China is not worried that Standard & Poor's has downgraded the U.S. credit rating from AAA to AA+. Rather it is concerned about the Fed announcing QE3. If the U.S. administration chooses to make the irresponsible choice of devaluating the dollar further, China would not only stop buying U.S. debt, but also gradually decrease its holdings, which would certainly not be in the interests of the U.S. or in accordance with Biden's wishes."[36] Chinese officials have expressed concerns that actions by the Federal Reserve to boost the U.S. money supply will undermine the value of China's holdings of U.S. dollar assets, either by causing the dollar to depreciate against other major currencies or by significantly increasing U.S. inflation. To date, quantitative easing has not led to a noticeable increase in U.S. inflation, and the Federal Reserve has argued that it has sufficient tools to maintain low inflation in the future.

Does China's Holdings of U.S. Debt Give it Leverage?

It is difficult to determine whether China's holdings of U.S. securities give it any leverage over U.S. policies.[37] The importance of China's debt holdings to the U.S. economy can be measured in a number of different ways (see text box below). During his confirmation hearing to become U.S. Ambassador to China before the Senate Foreign Relations Committee in May 2011, Gary Locke, in response to a question on this issue, stated that China's holdings of U.S. Treasury securities did not "in any way influence U.S. foreign policy."[38]

Indicators of the Size of China's Ownership of U.S. Public Debt

China's ownership of U.S. Treasury securities, or U.S. federal debt, is significant, but the relative importance of those holdings to the overall U.S. federal debt can be measured in different ways. The U.S. public debt totaled $14.8 trillion and the end of FY2011. Of this amount, 43% was held by U.S. government trust funds and 57% was privately held. Of the total level of privately-held U.S. Treasury securities ($8.4 trillion), foreigners owned 58% of the total ($5 trillion).[39] China's holdings of U.S. Treasury securities as of September 2011 were $1.27 trillion. The importance of China's holdings of U.S. debt securities (as of September 2011) can be measured as follows. They constituted: 25.9% of total foreign holdings of U.S. Treasury securities, 15.0% of U.S. privately-held Treasury securities, and 8.6% of the total level of U.S. federal debt (privately-held and intergovernmental).

The amount of interest payments the U.S. government makes to China each year is not precisely known since a breakdown of the types of Treasury securities, their maturity dates, and their yields, is not published.[40]

A rough estimate can be made by taking the Treasury Department's data on interest paid on the debt held by foreigners in FY2011($150.2 billion) and multiplying it by China's holdings of U.S. federal debt as percent of the total foreign debt . Based on these data, it is estimated that U.S. interest rate payments to China on its holdings of U.S. Treasury securities were $38.9 billion in FY2011, or about $107 million per day[41] China's holdings of U.S. Treasury debt in FY2011 was roughly equal to $4,073 for every American and $961 for every Chinese. According to one observer: "Never before has a country as poor as China provided so much financing to a country as rich as the United States."[42]

Some Chinese officials in the past have suggested that its holdings of U.S. debt could be used in regard to economic and political disputes with the United States. To illustrate, an August 7, 2007, article in the Telegraph (an online British newspaper) cited interviews with officials from two leading Chinese government think tanks who reportedly stated that China had the power to make the dollar collapse (if it chose to do so) by liquidating large portions of its U.S. Treasury securities holdings if the United States imposed trade sanctions to force an appreciation of the RMB, and that the threat to do so could be used as a "bargaining chip." Ding Gang, a senior editor with China's People's Daily wrote in an editorial in August 2011 that China should directly link the amount of U.S. Treasury holdings with U.S. arms sales to Taiwan, stating that "now is the time for China to use its 'financial weapon' to teach the United States a lesson if it moves forward with a plan to sale arms to Taiwan. In fact, China has never wanted to use its holdings of U.S. debt as a weapon. It is the United States that is forcing it to do so...to defend itself when facing threats to China's sovereignty." [43]

The likelihood that China would suddenly reduce its holdings of U.S. securities is questionable because doing so could have a significant negative impact on the Chinese economy. First, a large sell-off of China's U.S. holdings could diminish the value of these securities in international markets, which would lead to large losses on the sale, and would, in turn, decrease the value of China's remaining dollar-denominated assets.[44] This would also occur if the value of the dollar were greatly diminished in international currency markets due to China's sell-off.[45] Second, such a move would diminish U.S. demand for Chinese imports, either through a rise in the value of the RMB against the dollar or a reduction in U.S. economic growth (especially if other foreign investors sold their U.S. asset holdings, and the United States was forced to raise interest rates in response).[46] It is estimated that nearly one quarter of

Chinese exports went to the United States in 2010. A sharp reduction of U.S. imports from China could have a significant impact on China's economy, which heavily depends on exports for its economic growth (and is viewed by the government as a vital source of political stability).[47] Any major action by the Chinese government that destabilized (or further destabilized) the U.S. economy (whether deliberate or not) could provoke "protectionist" sentiment in the United States against China. One analyst described the financial interdependency between the United States and China as "a kind of balance of financial terror." According to Derek Scissors, a Research Fellow with the Heritage Foundation:

> One area of concern in the U.S. is Chinese financial influence. As noted, Chinese investment is largely involuntary, a function of having a great deal of money and no place else to put it. This refines the usual analogy of banker and customer to one where the banker has a choice of "lending" to one particular customer for the better part of her business, or crafting an exceptionally large mattress. The influence is mutual." Who needs the other more varies with American and international financial conditions. The more money the U.S. borrows, the more the American economy needs the PRC. The more desirable Treasury bonds are, the more China needs us. The U.S. is planning to run a federal deficit of over $1 trillion but there has been a flight to quality and American Treasury bonds are highly desired. There is balance on this score. The PRC can exercise little or no leverage over American policy by virtue of its purchase of our bonds.

However, Scissors goes on to state:

> There is future danger in the possibility that we will run sustained, gigantic deficits. The longer these last, the more likely it is that U.S. treasuries will become relatively less attractive, thereby tipping the balance of influence toward China. The U.S. could come to need Chinese purchases more than the PRC needs American bonds, yet another argument to control the federal budget.[48]

Many analysts contend that the U.S. debt securities market is the only global market that is big enough to absorb a big part of China's large and growing FX holdings. Economic problems in Japan and Europe do not leave China with many alternatives for investing its massive FX reserves. According to Andrew Peaple, a writer for the Wall Street Journal: "Some say China could switch holdings into gold—but that market's highly volatile, and not large enough to absorb more than a small proportion of China's reserves. It's not clear, meanwhile, that euro, or yen-denominated debt is any safer, more liquid, or profitable than U.S. debt—key criteria for China's leadership."[49] Legislation has been introduced in the 112th Congress that would seek to assess the implications for the United States of China's ownership of U.S. debt.

- H.R. 2166 (Sam Johnson) and S. 1028 (Cornyn), both titled "Foreign-Held Debt Transparency and Threat Assessment Act," would seek to increase the transparency of foreign ownership of U.S. debt instruments, especially in regard to China, in order to better assess the potential risks such holdings could pose for the United States. The bills state, for example, that under certain circumstances, China's holdings of U.S. debt could give it a tool with which it can try to manipulate U.S. domestic and foreign policymaking, including the U.S. relationship with Taiwan; and that China could attempt to destabilize the U.S. economy by rapidly divesting large portions of its holdings of U.S. debt instruments. The bills would require the President to issue a quarterly report on foreign holders of U.S. debt instruments, which would include a breakdown of foreign ownership by country of domicile and by the type of creditor (i.e., public, quasi-public, private); an analysis of the country's purpose and long-term intentions in regard to its U.S. debt holdings; an analysis of the current and foreseeable risks to U.S. national security and economic stability of each nation's U.S. debt holdings; and a determination whether such risks are "acceptable or unacceptable." If the President determined that a foreign country's holdings of U.S. debt instruments were an unacceptable risk, he would be required to formulate an action plan to reduce that risk.
- The conference report accompanying the National Defense Authorization Act of FY2012 (H.R. 1540, P.L. 112-81) included a provision requiring the Secretary of Defense to conduct a national security risk assessment of U.S. federal debt held by China. The Secretary of Defense issued a report in July 2012, stating that "attempting to use U.S. Treasury securities as a coercive tool would have limited effect and likely would do more harm to China than to the United States." As the threat is not credible and the effect would be limited even if carried out, it does not offer China deterrence options, whether in the diplomatic, military, or economic realms, and this would remain true both in peacetime and in scenarios of crisis or war.

WHAT IF CHINA REDUCES ITS HOLDINGS OF U.S. SECURITIES?[50]

As the previous data illustrate, China has accumulated large holdings of U.S. assets in recent years. These accumulations are the result of U.S. borrowing to finance its large trade deficit with China (the gap between U.S. exports and Chinese imports). All else equal, Chinese government purchases of U.S. assets increases the demand for U.S. assets, which reduces U.S. interest rates. What might happen if China no longer purchased U.S. securities and/or tried to sell a significant share of its dollar holdings?

If China stopped buying U.S. securities, the United States would need other investors (foreign and domestic) to fill in the gap. Such investors would presumably require higher interest rates than those prevailing today to be enticed to buy them. One economist in 2007 estimated that a Chinese move away from long-term U.S. securities could raise U.S. interest rates by as much as 50 basis points.[51] Higher interest rates would cause a decline in investment spending and other interest-sensitive spending. All else equal, the reduction in Chinese Treasury holdings would cause the overall foreign demand for U.S. assets to fall, and this would cause the dollar to depreciate. If the value of the dollar depreciated, the trade deficit would decline, as the price of U.S. exports fell abroad and the price of imports rose in the United States.[52] The magnitude of these effects would depend on how many U.S. securities China sold; modest reductions would have negligible effects on the economy given the large size of U.S. financial markets.

Since China held $1.7 trillion of U.S. private and public securities (largely U.S. Treasury securities) as of June 2011, any reduction in its U.S. holdings could potentially be large. If there were a large reduction in its holdings, the effect on the U.S. economy would still depend on whether the reduction were gradual or sudden. It should be emphasized that economic theory suggests that a *slow decline* in the trade deficit and dollar would not be troublesome for the overall economy. In fact, a slow decline could even have an expansionary effect on the economy, if the decrease in the trade deficit had a more stimulative effect on aggregate demand in the short run than the decrease in investment and other interest-sensitive spending resulting from higher interest rates. Historical experience seems to bear this out—the dollar declined by about 40% in real terms and the trade deficit declined continually in the late 1980s, from 2.8% of GDP in 1986 to nearly zero during the early 1990s. Yet economic growth was strong throughout the late 1980s.

A potentially serious short-term problem would emerge if China decided to *suddenly* reduce their liquid U.S. financial assets significantly. The effect could be compounded if this action triggered a more general financial reaction (or panic), in which all foreigners responded by reducing their holdings of U.S. assets. The initial effect could be a sudden and large depreciation in the value of the dollar, as the supply of dollars on the foreign exchange market increased, and a sudden and large increase in U.S. interest rates, as an important funding source for investment and the budget deficit was withdrawn from the financial markets. The dollar depreciation by itself would not cause a recession since it would ultimately lead to a trade surplus (or smaller deficit), which expands aggregate demand.[53] (Empirical evidence suggests that the full effects of a change in the exchange rate on traded goods takes time, so the dollar may have to "overshoot" its eventual depreciation level in order to achieve a significant adjustment in trade flows in the short run.)[54] However, a sudden increase in interest rates could swamp the trade effects and cause (or worsen) a recession. Large increases in interest rates could cause problems for the U.S. economy, as these increases reduce the market value of debt securities, cause prices on the stock market to fall, undermine efficient financial intermediation, and jeopardize the solvency of various debtors and creditors. Resources may not be able to shift quickly enough from interest-sensitive sectors to export sectors to make this transition fluid. The Federal Reserve could mitigate the interest rate spike by reducing short-term interest rates, although this reduction would influence long-term rates only indirectly, and could worsen the dollar depreciation and increase inflation. In March 2007, Federal Reserve Chairman Ben Bernanke reportedly stated in a letter to Senator Shelby that "because foreign holdings of U.S. Treasury securities represent only a small part of total U.S. credit market debt outstanding, U.S. credit markets should be able to absorb without great difficulty any shift of foreign allocations." [55]

U.S. financial markets experienced exceptional turmoil beginning in August 2007. Over the following year, the dollar declined by almost 8% in inflation-adjusted terms—a decline that was not, in itself, disruptive. But as the turmoil deepened and spread to the rest of the world in 2008, the value of the dollar began rising. Interest rates on U.S. Treasuries fell close to zero, implying excessive investor demand. Other interest rates also remained low, although access to credit was limited for some. Although comprehensive data will not be available for some time, a "sudden stop" in capital inflows does not appear to have been a feature of the downturn. Problems experienced in U.S. financial markets over the past few years have been widely viewed as "once in a lifetime" events. If these events failed to cause a sudden flight from U.S. assets and an unwinding of the current account deficit by China or other countries, it is hard to imagine what would.

CONCLUSION

Many economists argue that concerns over China's holdings of U.S. securities represent part of a broader problem for the U.S. economy, namely its dependence on foreign saving to finance its investment needs and federal budget deficits. The large U.S. current account deficit (the manifestation of the high U.S. saving/investment gap) cannot be sustained indefinitely because the U.S. net foreign debt cannot rise faster than GDP indefinitely.[56] Some economists argue that at some point foreign investors may view the growing level of U.S. foreign debt as unsustainable or more risky, or they may no longer view U.S. securities as offering the best return on their investment, and shift investment funds away from U.S. assets, thus forcing U.S. interest rates to rise to attract needed foreign capital. This would result in higher interest rates and lower investment rates, all else equal, which would reduce long-term growth.[57] A reliance on foreign governments such as China to finance the U.S. current account deficit (which includes the U.S. merchandise trade deficit) by increasing their foreign exchange reserves may prolong the necessary adjustment process. Thus, it is argued, the United States must boost its level of savings in the long run in order to reduce its vulnerability to a potential shift away from U.S. assets by foreign investors. It remains to be seen whether this adjustment process began in the United States in 2008, or whether the rise in private saving and decline in the current account deficit was only a temporary response to the recession. Some economists contend that, although the low U.S. savings rate is a problem, the U.S. current account deficit and high levels of foreign capital flows to the United States are also reflections of the strength of the U.S. economy and its attractiveness as a destination for foreign investment, and therefore discount the likelihood that foreign investors will suddenly shift their capital elsewhere.[58]

Some economists view China's purchases of U.S. securities as a type of subsidy that is transferred from Chinese savers to U.S. consumers in the form of lower-cost Chinese products and lower U.S. interest rates. That subsidy helps to boost U.S. consumption of Chinese products, which supports China's export industries. However, the subsidy is at the expense of Chinese consumers and non-export industries, largely because China's undervalued

RMB makes imports more expensive than they would be if the RMB was a floating currency. The lack of a social safety net forces Chinese workers to save a significant part of their income. That savings is used to finance the Chinese government's purchases of U.S. securities.

Chinese purchases and holdings of U.S. securities have reportedly been controversial in China according to some media reports, many of which cite complaints among some Chinese Internet bloggers over low return on Chinese investment of its FX reserves. Many analysts (including some in China) have questioned the wisdom of China's policy of investing a large level of FX reserves in U.S. government securities, which offer a relatively low rate of return, when China has such huge development needs at home. One Chinese blogger reportedly wrote: "Chinese people are working so hard, day in and day out, the economic environment is so good, but people's livelihoods are not so great — turns out it is because the government is tightening people's waist belts to lend money to the United States."[59] Some Chinese analysts have argued that the debt problems in Europe and the United States will decrease their demand for Chinese products, and that a depreciating dollar will lower the value of Chinese dollar assets. Thus, they argue, China will need to accelerate its economic reforms in order to boost domestic consumption (including increased imports), lower its dependency on exporting for economic growth, and slow or reduce China's FX reserves and holdings of U.S. securities. If China consumed more and saved less, it would have less capital to invest overseas, including in the United States. Thus, if the United States did not reduce its dependence on foreign savings for its investment needs, and China reduced its U.S. investments, the United States would need to obtain investment from other countries, and the overall U.S. current account balance would likely remain relatively unchanged but U.S. interest rates would be expected to rise.

End Notes

[1] IMF, *Global Financial Stability Report*, the Quest for Lasting Stability, April 2012, Statistical Appendix, p.3

[2] U.S. Department of the Treasury, *Treasury Bulletin*, September 2012.

[3] That level was 56.9% at the end of 2011. Foreign private holders of U.S. public debt include both private investors and government entities. The People's Bank of China, which is controlled by the Chinese government, is the biggest Chinese holder of U.S. public debt.

[4] China contends that its currency policy is intended to promote financial stability in China, while critics contend the main purpose is to keep the value of its currency low in order to benefit

Chinese exporters. See, CRS Report RS21625, *China's Currency Policy: An Analysis of the Economic Issues*, by Wayne M. Morrison and Marc Labonte

[5] China's investment in U.S. securities far exceed its foreign direct investment (FDI) in the United States. FDI data reflect ownership or investment in U.S. businesses (and are not covered by this report). For additional detail on China's FDI flows to the United States, see CRS Report RL33536, *China-U.S. Trade Issues*, by Wayne M. Morrison.

[6] For a discussion of the implications of a possible global sell-off of U.S. securities, see CRS Report RL34319, *Foreign Ownership of U.S. Financial Assets: Implications of a Withdrawal*, by James K. Jackson.

[7] These data are annual (end-June) changes in foreign holdings of U.S. public and private securities

[8] China states that it maintains a managed peg with a number of major currencies, but U.S. officials contend that, in fact, the RMB is pegged largely to the dollar.

[9] "Hot money" refers to inflows of capital from overseas investors who attempt to bypass Chinese government capital restrictions. Some attempt to purchase Chinese currency in the belief that the Chinese government will continue to appreciate the RMB in the near future, while others are seeking to invest in certain "high growth" sectors, such as real estate. The inflows of hot money force the government to intervene to buy the inflows of foreign currency, such as the dollar, to maintain its exchange rate targets.

[10] Some analysts contend that China's actual FX reserves are much higher than official Chinese data. For example, Brad Setser and Arpana Pandey contend that China's official data on FX reserves do not include holdings and assets held by China's main sovereign wealth fund, China Investment Corporation (CIC), and those held by state banks. They estimated that China's actual FX holdings were 18% higher than its official estimates. See Council on Foreign Relations, *China's $1.7 Trillion Bet: China's External Portfolio and Dollar Reserves*, by Brad Setser and Arpana Pandey, January 2009.

[11] The level of China's FX reserves peaked at $3,310 billion in February 2012.

[12] For additional information on foreign ownership of U.S. securities, see CRS Report RL32462, *Foreign Investment in U.S. Securities*, by James K. Jackson.

[13] See testimony of Brad Setser, Senior Economist, Roubini Global Economics and Research Associate, Global Economic Governance Programme, University College, Oxford, before the House Budget Committee, *Foreign Holdings of U.S. Debt: Is our Economy Vulnerable*?, June 26, 2007, p. 11. In addition, the *People's Daily Online* (August 28, 2006) estimated China's dollar holdings to total FX reserves at 70%.

[14] See CRS Report RL34582, *The Depreciating Dollar: Economic Effects and Policy Response*, by Craig K. Elwell.

[15] The global financial crisis, global economic slowdown, and public debt crisis in many countries have induced capital to flow to the United States, often referred to as a "flight to quality." This has pushed yields on U.S. Treasury securities to record lows. For November 30, 2012, the yields on one-year, five-year, and ten-year Treasury nominal constant maturities were 0.18%, 0.61%, and 1.62%, respectively. In comparison, the yields for the same securities on November 30, 2007, were 3.04%, 3.41%, and 4.40%. Source: Department of the Treasury, *Resource Center, Daily Treasury Yield Curve Rates*.

[16] See China's State Administration of Foreign Exchange (SAFE), *FAQs on Foreign Exchange Reserves*, July 20, 2010.

[17] Agency securities include both federal agencies and government-sponsored enterprises created by Congress (e.g., Fannie Mae and Freddie Mac) to provide credit to key sectors of the economy. Some of these securities are backed by assets (such as home mortgages).

[18] As of June 2011, 75% of U.S. short-term debt consisted on U.S. Treasury securities, followed by corporate debt (20.2%) and U.S. agency debt (4.9%).

[19] The report is prepared jointly by the Department of the Treasury, the Federal Reserve Bank of New York, and the Board of Governors of the Federal Reserve System.

[20] Department of the Treasury, Federal Reserve Bank of New York, and Board of Governors of the Federal Reserve System, *Report on Foreign Portfolio Holdings of U.S. Securities as of June 30, 2011, April 2012,* available at http://www.treasury.gov/resource-center/data-chart-center/tic/Documents/shla2011r.pdf.

[21] Data on China's holdings of U.S. securities exclude holdings by Hong Kong and Macao. These entities, though part of China, are reported separately by Treasury.

[22] In June 2008, China's holdings of LT U.S. Agency debt constituted 43.7% of its holding of U.S. securities, which were greater than its holdings of LT U.S. Treasury securities (43.3%). However, the bursting of the U.S. housing bubble and the subsequent federal takeover of Freddie Mac and Fannie Mae in 2008 led China to significantly reduce its holdings of U.S. Agency debt, while increasing its holdings of other securities, especially Treasury securities.

[23] China was the largest holder of Agency LT debt in 2010 at 33.2% of total).

[24] For a general discussion of foreign ownership of U.S. debt, see CRS Report RS22331, *Foreign Holdings of Federal Debt*, by Justin Murray and Marc Labonte. For a discussion on Treasury's debt management practices, see CRS Report R40767, *How Treasury Issues Debt*, by Mindy R. Levit.

[25] It was at $14.6 trillion as of August 8, 2011. See the Department of the Treasury, *The Debt to the Penny and Who Holds It*, available at http://www.treasurydirect.gov/NP/BPD Login?application=np.

[26] On the other hand, Japan's holdings of Treasury securities have grown sharply over the past year or so, rising from $765.7 billion in December 2009 to $1,130.7 billion in September 2012, a $365 billion increase (or 47.7%).

[27] See CRS Report RL34742, *The Global Financial Crisis: Analysis and Policy Implications*, coordinated by Dick K. Nanto.

[28] Low U.S. interest rates sharply contributed to U.S. demand for housing. Homeowners viewed growing home values as a source of income to draw from through home equities, which were used to buy consumer goods. The rise in U.S. domestic consumption boosted foreign imports, such as from China, which sharply increased the U.S. trade deficit.

[29] ABC News International, *Clinton Seeks to Reassure China on T-Bills*, February 21, 2009.

[30] China Daily, March 14, 2009, http://www.chinadaily.com.cn/china/2009-03/14/content_7578931.htm.

[31] Financial Times, *China Calls for New Reserve Currency*, March 24, 2009.

[32] Failure to extend the debt ceiling could have put the U.S. government in default of its debt obligations.

[33] The White House, Office of the Vice President, *Remarks by Vice President Biden at a Meeting with Chinese Premier Wen*, August 19, 2011, available at http://www.whitehouse.gov/the-press-office/2011/08/19/remarks-vice-presidentbiden-meeting-chinese-premier-wen.

[34] The White House, Office of the Vice President, *Remarks by Vice President Biden,* on *U.S.-China Relations followed by Q&A with Students, Sichuan University, Chengdu, China, August 21, 2011.*

[35] CRS Report R41540, *Quantitative Easing and the Growth in the Federal Reserve's Balance Sheet*, by Marc Labonte.

[36] China Daily, Dilemma of Yuan revaluation, August 25, 2011, available at http://www.chinadaily.com.cn/opinion/2011-08/25/content_13185617.htm.

[37] China has attempted to use the U.S. debt crisis to criticize U.S. economic policies and its political system, implying that Chinese economic and political policies are more stable.

[38] Congressional Quarterly, Congressional Transcripts, Senate Committee on Foreign Relations, *Hearing on the Nomination of Secretary of Commerce Gary Locke to Be Ambassador to People's Republic of China*, May 26, 2011.

[39] U.S. Treasury Department, Financial Management Service, *Ownership of Federal Securities*, available at http://www.fms.treas.gov/bulletin/index.html.

[40] For example, Treasury securities maturity dates range from one month to 30 years. Yields change on a daily basis.

[41] For an overview of the types of securities issue by Treasury and its management of U.S. debt, see CRS Report R40767, *How Treasury Issues Debt*, by Mindy R. Levit.

[42] Council on Foreign Relations, *China's $1.7 Trillion Bet: China's External Portfolio and Dollar Reserves*, by Brad Setser and Arpana Pandey, January 2009.

[43] People's Daily, *China must punish US for Taiwan arm sales with 'financial weapon'*, August 8, 2011, at http://english.people.com.cn/90780/91342/7562776.html.

[44] Since there are many other holders of U.S. assets, it is possible that if China believed a decline in asset values was imminent, it could minimize its losses by dumping its U.S. assets first.

[45] Selling off U.S. dollar assets could cause the RMB to appreciate against the dollar, which would lower the value of remaining U.S. assets since the assets are dollar-denominated.

[46] In addition, if a "dollar collapse" occurred, U.S. imports from other major trade partners would decline, which could slow their economies. This in turn could weaken their demand for Chinese products.

[47] Although a falling dollar may harm China's short-term growth via reduced Chinese exports (and export sector-related employment), it would also improve China's terms of trade with the United States, raising China's overall consumption since it could now spend less to acquire the same amount of American goods (which would also create jobs in other sectors of the economy because of increased consumer purchasing power).

[48] The Heritage Foundation, Testimony before the U.S.-China Economic and Security Review Commission on China's Role in the Origins of and Responses to the Global Recession, by Derek Scissors, Ph.D., March 3, 2009, available at http://www.heritage.org/Research/Testimony/Testimony-before-the-US-China-Economic-and-Security-ReviewCommission-on-Chinas-Role-in-the-Origins-of-and-Responses-to-the-Global-Recession.

[49] Wall Street Journal, *China's Limited Options on Treasurys*, March 16, 2009, available at http://online.wsj.com/article/SB123694305633018403.html?mod=googlenews_wsj.

[50] From the perspective of the macroeconomic effects on U.S. investment, interest rates, and so on, it does not matter what type of U.S. security is purchased when foreign capital flows to the United States. Thus, Chinese purchases of all types of U.S. securities (not just Treasury securities) should be considered when attempting to understand the impact China's investment decisions have on the U.S. economy.

[51] Testimony of Brad Setser before the House Budget Committee, *Foreign Holdings of U.S. Debt: Is our Economy Vulnerable?*, June 26, 2007. Brad Setser is Senior Economist, Roubini Global Economics, and Research Associate, Global Economic Governance Programme, University College, Oxford. Setser does not detail how much U.S. debt he assumes China would sell to reach his estimate.

[52] The extent that the dollar declined and U.S. interest rates rose would depend on how willing other foreigners were to supplant China's reduction in capital inflows. A greater willingness

would lead to less dollar depreciation and less of an increase in interest rates, and vice versa.

[53] A sharp decline in the value of the dollar would also reduce living standards, all else equal, because it would raise the price of imports to households. This effect, which is referred to as a decline in the terms of trade, would not be recorded directly in GDP, however.

[54] Since the decline in the dollar would raise import prices, this could temporarily increase inflationary pressures. The effect would likely be modest, however, since imports are small as a share of GDP and import prices would only gradually rise in response to the fall in the dollar.

[55] Reuters, *Bernanke-China Holdings of US Debt Not Problematic*, March 26, 2007.

[56] The U.S. current account deficit as a percent of GDP fell from a peak of 6.0% in 2006 to 2.7% in 2009; it rose to 3.0% in 2010 and to 3.1% in 2011. The IMF projects that his figure will be 3.1% in 2012 and will rise to 3.5% by 2017. (Source: IMF, *World Economic Database*, October 2012 edition.)

[57] See CRS Report RL33186, *Is the U.S. Current Account Deficit Sustainable?*, by Marc Labonte.

[58] See Council of Economic Advisors, Economic Report of the President, *The U.S. Capital Surplus*, February 2006, p. 144.

[59] NYTimes, *Chinese Fault Beijing Over Foreign Reserves*, August,9, 2011, available at http://www.nytimes.com/2011/08/09/business/global/chinese-fault-beijings-moves-on-foreign-reserves.html

INDEX

A

B

C

D

G

H

I

J

K

L

O

P

Q

R

S